Contents

Foreword... v

Executive Summary... vi

TIP Development Participants xiii

Publication Information xxiii

Chapter 1—A New Look at Motivation.. 1

    Motivation and Behavior Change 3

    Changing Perspectives on Addiction and Treatment.. 6

    TTM of the SOC 12

    Conclusion 15

Chapter 2—Motivational Counseling and Brief Intervention 17

    Elements of Effective Motivational Counseling Approaches 17

    Motivational Counseling and the SOC 24

    Special Applications of Motivational Interventions... 25

    Brief Motivational Interventions.. 30

    Screening, Brief Intervention, and Referral to Treatment.. 31

    Conclusion 32

Chapter 3—Motivational Interviewing as a Counseling Style 33

    Introduction to MI... 33

    What Is New in MI... 35

    Ambivalence.. 36

    Core Skills of MI: OARS.. 38

    Four Processes of MI... 45

    Benefits of MI in Treating SUDs 60

    Conclusion 61

Chapter 4—From Precontemplation to Contemplation: Building Readiness........................... 63

    Develop Rapport and Build Trust... 64

    Raise Doubts and Concerns About the Client's Substance Use 69

    Understand Special Motivational Counseling Considerations for Clients Mandated to Treatment 75

    Conclusion 78

Chapter 5—From Contemplation to Preparation: Increasing Commitment 79

    Normalize and Resolve Ambivalence... 80

Help Tip the Decisional Balance Toward Change...82

Conclusion...88

Chapter 6—From Preparation to Action: Initiating Change 89

Explore Client Change Goals 90

Develop a Change Plan 92

Support the Client's Action Steps 100

Evaluate the Change Plan 100

Conclusion...101

Chapter 7—From Action to Maintenance: Stabilizing Change 103

Stabilize Client Change...104

Support the Client's Lifestyle Changes..111

Help the Client Reenter the Change Cycle...113

Conclusion...118

Chapter 8—Integrating Motivational Approaches in SUD Treatment Settings....................121

Adaptations of Motivational Counseling Approaches 121

Workforce Development 127

Conclusion...131

Appendix A—Bibliography..133

Appendix B—Screening and Assessment Instruments 148

1. U.S. Alcohol Use Disorders Identification Test (AUDIT)..149

2. Drug Abuse Screening Test (DAST-10) 151

3. Drinker Inventory of Consequences (DrInC) (Lifetime)...153

4. What I Want From Treatment (2.0) 156

5. Readiness to Change Questionnaire (Treatment Version) (RCQ-TV) (Revised)..............159

6. Stages of Change Readiness and Treatment Eagerness Scale–Alcohol (SOCRATES 8A)...161

7. Stages of Change Readiness and Treatment Eagerness Scale–Drug (SOCRATES 8D)......162

8. University of Rhode Island Change Assessment (URICA) Scale 165

9. Alcohol and Drug Consequences Questionnaire (ADCQ)..168

10. Alcohol Decisional Balance Scale 170

11. Drug Use Decisional Balance Scale 172

12. Brief Situational Confidence Questionnaire (BSCQ) 174

13. Alcohol Abstinence Self-Efficacy Scale (AASES) 176

14. Motivational Interviewing Knowledge Test 178

Appendix C—Resources 182

   Motivational Interviewing and Motivational Enhancement Therapy 182

   Stages of Change 182

   Training and Supervision 182

   Substance Abuse and Mental Health Services Administration 183

Exhibits

Exhibit 1.1. Models of Addiction 6

Exhibit 1.2. Examples of Natural Changes 12

Exhibit 1.3. The Five Stages in the SOC in the TTM 13

Exhibit 2.1. The Drinker's Pyramid Feedback 19

Exhibit 2.2. Catalysts for Change 24

Exhibit 2.3. Counselor Focus in the SOC 25

Exhibit 2.4. RESPECT: A Mnemonic for Cultural Responsiveness 27

Exhibit 3.1. A Comparison of Original and Updated Versions of MI 35

Exhibit 3.2. Misconceptions and Clarifications About MI 36

Exhibit 3.3. Examples of Change Talk and Sustain Talk 37

Exhibit 3.4. Closed and Open Questions 39

Exhibit 3.5. Gordon's 12 Roadblocks to Active Listening 42

Exhibit 3.6. Types of Reflective Listening Responses 43

Exhibit 3.7. Components in a Sample Agenda Map 48

Exhibit 3.8. Examples of Open Questions to Evoke Change Talk Using DARN 50

Exhibit 3.9. The Importance Ruler 51

Exhibit 3.10. The Confidence Ruler 56

Exhibit 4.1. Counseling Strategies for Precontemplation 64

Exhibit 4.2. Styles of Expression in the Precontemplation Stage: The 5 Rs 67

Exhibit 4.3. An Opening Dialog With a Client Who Has Been
   Mandated to Treatment 76

Exhibit 5.1. Counseling Strategies for Contemplation 79

Exhibit 5.2. The Motivational Interviewing (MI) Hill of Ambivalence 80

Exhibit 5.3. Decisional Balance Sheet for Substance Use 83

Exhibit 5.4. Other Issues in Decisional Balance 84

Exhibit 5.5. Recapitulation Summary 87

Exhibit 6.1. Counseling Strategies for Preparation and Action 89

Exhibit 6.2. When Treatment Goals Differ 91

Exhibit 6.3. Change Plan Worksheet.. 93

Exhibit 6.4. Mapping a Path for Change When There Are Multiple Options............................... 96

Exhibit 7.1. Counseling Strategies for Action and Relapse 103

Exhibit 7.2. Options for Responding to a Missed Appointment 107

Exhibit 7.3. Triggers and Coping Strategies 110

Exhibit 7.4. A Menu of Coping Strategies 110

Exhibit 7.5. Susan's Story: A Client Lacking Social Support.. 113

Exhibit 7.6. Marlatt's RPC Process 115

Exhibit 8.1. Blending the Spirit of MI With CBT 125

Foreword

The Substance Abuse and Mental Health Services Administration (SAMHSA) is the U.S. Department of Health and Human Services agency that leads public health efforts to reduce the impact of substance abuse and mental illness on America's communities. An important component of SAMHSA's work is focused on dissemination of evidence-based practices and providing training and technical assistance to healthcare practitioners on implementation of these best practices.

The Treatment Improvement Protocol (TIP) series contributes to SAMHSA's mission by providing science-based, best-practice guidance to the behavioral health field. TIPs reflect careful consideration of all relevant clinical and health service research, demonstrated experience, and implementation requirements. Select nonfederal clinical researchers, service providers, program administrators, and patient advocates comprising each TIP's consensus panel discuss these factors, offering input on the TIP's specific topics in their areas of expertise to reach consensus on best practices. Field reviewers then assess draft content and the TIP is finalized.

The talent, dedication, and hard work that TIP panelists and reviewers bring to this highly participatory process have helped bridge the gap between the promise of research and the needs of practicing clinicians and administrators to serve, in the most scientifically sound and effective ways, people in need of care and treatment of mental and substance use disorders. My sincere thanks to all who have contributed their time and expertise to the development of this TIP. It is my hope that clinicians will find it useful and informative to their work.

Elinore F. McCance-Katz, M.D., Ph.D.
Assistant Secretary for Mental Health and Substance Use
U.S. Department of Health and Human Services
Substance Abuse and Mental Health Services Administration

Executive Summary

Motivation for change is a key component in addressing substance misuse. This Treatment Improvement Protocol (TIP) reflects a fundamental rethinking of the concept of motivation as a dynamic process, not a static client trait. Motivation relates to the probability that a person will enter into, continue, and adhere to a specific change strategy.

Although much progress has been made in identifying people who misuse substances and who have substance use disorders (SUDs) as well as in using science-informed interventions such as motivational counseling approaches to treat them, the United States still faces many SUD challenges. For example, the National Survey on Drug Use and Health (Substance Abuse and Mental Health Services Administration, 2018) reports that, in 2017, approximately:

- 140.6 million Americans ages 12 and older currently consumed alcohol, 66.6 million reported at least 1 episode of past-month binge drinking (defined as 5 or more drinks on the same occasion on at least 1 day in the past 30 days for men and 4 or more drinks on the same occasion on at least 1 day in the past 30 days for women), and 16.7 million drank heavily in the previous month (defined as binge drinking on 5 or more days in the past 30 days).

- 30.5 million people ages 12 and older had used illicit drugs in the past month.

- 11.4 million people ages 12 and older misused opioids (defined as prescription pain reliever misuse or heroin use) in the past year.

- 8.5 million adults ages 18 and older (3.4 percent of all adults) had both a mental disorder and at least 1 past-year SUD.

- 18.2 million people who needed SUD treatment did not receive specialty treatment.

- One in three people who perceived a need for substance use treatment did not receive it because they lacked healthcare coverage and could not afford treatment.

- Two in five people who perceived a need for addiction treatment did not receive it because they were not ready to stop using substances.

Millions of people in the United States with SUDs are not receiving treatment. Many are not seeking treatment because their motivation to change their substance use behaviors is low.

The motivation-enhancing approaches and strategies this TIP describes can increase participation and retention in SUD treatment and positive treatment outcomes, including:

- Reductions in alcohol and drug use.

- Higher abstinence rates.

- Successful referrals to treatment.

This TIP shows how SUD treatment counselors can influence positive behavior change by developing a therapeutic relationship that respects and builds on the client's autonomy. Through motivational enhancement, counselors become partners in the client's change process.

The TIP also describes different motivational interventions counselors can apply to all the stages in the Stages of Change (SOC) model related to substance misuse and recovery from addiction.

A consensus panel developed this TIP's content based on a review of the literature and on panel members' extensive experience in the field of addiction treatment. Other professionals also generously contributed their time and commitment to this project.

Intended Audience

The primary audiences for this TIP are:

- Drug and alcohol treatment service providers.
- Mental health service providers, such as psychologists, licensed clinical social workers, and psychiatric/mental health nurses.
- Peer recovery support specialists.
- Behavioral health program managers, directors, and administrators.
- Clinical supervisors.
- Healthcare providers, such as primary care physicians, nurse practitioners, general/family medicine practitioners, registered nurses, internal medicine specialists, and others who may need to enhance motivation to address substance misuse in their patients.

Secondary audiences include prevention specialists, educators, and policymakers for SUD treatment and related services.

Overall Key Messages

Motivation is key to substance use behavior change. Counselors can support clients' movement toward positive changes in their substance use by identifying and enhancing motivation that already exists.

Motivational approaches are based on the principles of person-centered counseling. Counselors' use of empathy, not authority and power, is key to enhancing clients' motivation to change. Clients are experts in their own recovery from SUDs. Counselors should engage them in collaborative partnerships.

Ambivalence about change is normal. Resistance to change is an expression of ambivalence about change, not a client trait or characteristic. Confrontational approaches increase client resistance and discord in the counseling relationship. Motivational approaches explore ambivalence in a nonjudgmental and compassionate way.

The Transtheoretical Model (TTM) of the SOC approach is an overarching framework that helps counselors tailor specific counseling strategies to different stages. Motivational counseling strategies should be tailored to clients' level of motivation to change their substance use behaviors at each of the five stages of the SOC:

- Precontemplation
- Contemplation
- Preparation
- Action
- Maintenance

Effective motivational counseling approaches can be brief. A growing body of evidence indicates that early and brief interventions demonstrate positive treatment outcomes in a wide variety of settings including specialty SUD treatment programs, primary care offices, and emergency departments. Brief interventions emphasize reducing the health-related risk of a person's substance use and decreasing consumption as an important treatment outcome.

Motivational interviewing (MI) and other motivational counseling approaches like motivational enhancement therapy are effective ways to enhance motivation throughout the SOC. Motivational counseling approaches are based on person-centered counseling principles that focus on helping clients resolve ambivalence about changing their substance use and other health-risk behaviors.

MI is the most widely researched and disseminated motivational counseling approach in SUD treatment. The spirit of MI (i.e., partnership, acceptance, compassion, and evocation) is the foundation of the core counseling skills required for enhancing clients' motivation to change. The core counseling skills of MI are described in the acronym OARS (**O**pen questions, **A**ffirmations, **R**eflective listening, and **S**ummarization).

Counselor empathy, as expressed through reflective listening, is fundamental to MI. Use of empathy, rather than power and authoritative approaches, is critical for helping clients achieve and maintain lasting behavior change.

Adaptations of MI enhance the implementation and integration of motivational interventions into standard treatment methods. Training, ongoing supervision, and coaching of counselors are essential for workforce development and integration of motivational counseling approaches into SUD treatment.

Content Overview

Chapter 1—A New Look at Motivation

This chapter lays the groundwork for understanding treatment concepts discussed later in the TIP. It is an overview of the nature of motivation and its link to changing substance use behaviors. The chapter describes changing perspectives on addiction and addiction treatment in the United States and uses the TTM of the SOC approach as an overarching framework to understand how people change their substance use behaviors.

In Chapter 1, readers will learn that:

- Motivation is essential to substance use behavior change. It is multidimensional, dynamic, and fluctuating; can be enhanced; and is influenced by the counselor's style.

- Benefits of using motivational counseling approaches include clients' enhancing motivation to change, preparing them to enter treatment, engaging and retaining clients in treatment, increasing their participation and involvement in treatment, improving their treatment outcomes, and encouraging a rapid return to treatment if they start misusing substances again.

- New perspectives on addiction treatment include focusing on clients' strengths instead of deficits, offering person-centered treatment, shifting away from labeling clients, using empathy, focusing on early and brief interventions, recognizing that there is a range of severity of substance misuse, accepting risk reduction as a legitimate treatment goal, and providing access to integrated care.

- People go through stages in the SOC approach; this concept is known as the TTM of change.

- The stages in the SOC model are:

  - Precontemplation, in which people are not considering change.

  - Contemplation, in which people are considering change but are unsure how to change.

  - Preparation, in which people have identified a change goal and are forming a plan to change.

  - Action, in which people are taking steps to change.

- Maintenance, in which people have met their change goal and the behavior change is stable.

Chapter 2—Motivational Counseling and Brief Intervention

This chapter is an overview of motivational counseling approaches, including screening, brief intervention, and referral to treatment (SBIRT). It describes elements of effective motivational counseling approaches, including FRAMES (**F**eedback, **R**esponsibility, **A**dvice, **M**enu of options, **E**mpathy, and **S**elf-efficacy), decisional balancing, discrepancy development, flexible pacing, and maintenance of contact with clients. The chapter describes counselors' focus in each stage of the SOC model. It addresses special applications of motivational counseling with clients from diverse cultures and with clients who have co-occurring substance use and mental disorders (CODs).

In Chapter 2, readers will learn that:

- Each stage in the SOC approach has predominant experiential and behavioral catalysts for client change on which counselors should focus.
- Counselors should adopt the principles of cultural responsiveness and adapt motivational interventions to those principles when treating clients from diverse backgrounds.
- Even mild substance misuse can impede functioning in people with CODs, including co-occurring severe mental illness. Counselors can adapt motivational interventions for these clients.
- Brief motivational interventions, including SBIRT, are effective in specialty SUD treatment facilities and opportunistic settings (e.g., primary care offices, emergency departments).
- Brief interventions emphasize risk reduction and referral to specialty addiction treatment if needed.

Chapter 3—Motivational Interviewing as a Counseling Style

This chapter provides an overview of the spirit of MI, the principles of person-centered counseling, the core counseling skills of MI (i.e. asking open questions, affirming, reflective listening, and summarizing), and the four processes of MI (i.e., engaging, focusing, evoking, and planning). It describes what's new in MI and dispels many misconceptions about MI. The chapter discusses the components that counselors use to help clients resolve ambivalence and move toward positive substance use behavior change.

In Chapter 3, readers will learn that:

- Ambivalence about substance use and change is normal and a motivational barrier to substance use behavior change, if not explored.
- The spirit of MI embodies the principles of person-centered counseling and is the basis of an empathetic, supportive counseling style.
- Sustain talk is essentially statements the client makes for not changing (i.e., maintaining the status quo), and change talk is statements the client makes in favor of change. The key to helping the client move in the direction toward changing substance use behaviors is to evoke change talk and soften or lessen the impact of sustain talk on the client's decision-making process.
- The acronym OARS describes the core skills of MI:
  - Asking **O**pen questions
  - **A**ffirming the client's strengths
  - Using **R**eflective listening
  - **S**ummarizing client statements
- Reflective listening is fundamental to person-centered counseling in general and MI in particular and

is essential for expressing empathy.

- The four processes in MI (i.e., engaging, focusing, evoking, and planning) provide an overarching framework for employing the core skills in conversations with a client.

- The benefits of MI include its broad applicability to diverse medical and behavioral health problems and its capacity to complement other counseling approaches and to mobilize client resources.

Chapter 4—From Precontemplation to Contemplation: Building Readiness

This chapter discusses strategies counselors can use to help clients raise doubt and concern about their substance use and move toward contemplating the possibility of change. It emphasizes the importance of assessing clients' readiness to change, providing personalized feedback to them about the effects and risks of substance misuse, involving their significant others in counseling to raise concern about clients' substance use behaviors, and addressing special considerations for treating clients who are mandated to treatment.

In Chapter 4, readers will learn that:

- A client in the Precontemplation stage is unconcerned about substance use or is not considering change.

- The counselor's focus in Precontemplation is to establish a strong counseling alliance and raise the client's doubts and concerns about substance use.

- Key strategies in this stage include eliciting the client's perception of the problem, exploring the events that led to entering treatment, and identifying the client's style of Precontemplation.

- Providing personalized feedback on assessment results and involving significant others in counseling sessions are key strategies for raising concern and moving the client toward contemplating change.

- Special considerations in motivational counseling approaches for clients mandated to treatment include acknowledging client ambivalence and emphasizing personal choice and responsibility.

Chapter 5—From Contemplation to Preparation: Increasing Commitment

This chapter describes strategies to increase clients' commitment to change by normalizing and resolving ambivalence and enhancing their decision-making capabilities. It emphasizes decisional balancing and exploring clients' self-efficacy as important to moving clients toward preparing to change substance use behaviors. Summarizing change talk and exploring the client's understanding of change prepare clients to take action.

In Chapter 5, readers will learn that:

- In the Contemplation stage, the client acknowledges concerns about substance use and is considering the possibility of change.

- The counselor's focus in Contemplation is to normalize and resolve client ambivalence and help the client tip the decisional balance toward changing substance use behaviors.

- Key motivational counseling strategies for resolving ambivalence include reassuring the client that ambivalence about change is normal; evoking DARN (**D**esire, **A**bility, **R**easons, and **N**eed) change talk; and summarizing the client's concerns.

- To reinforce movement toward change, the counselor reinforces the client's understanding of the change process, reintroduces personalized feedback, explores client self-efficacy, and summarizes client change talk.

- The counselor encourages the client to strengthen his or her commitment to change by taking small steps, going public, and envisioning life after changing substance use behaviors.

Chapter 6—From Preparation to Action: Initiating Change

This chapter describes the process of helping clients identify and clarify change goals. It also focuses on how and when to develop change plans with clients and suggests ways to ensure that plans are accessible, acceptable, and appropriate for clients.

In Chapter 6, readers will learn that:

- In the Preparation stage, the client is committed and planning to make a change but is unsure of what to do next. In the Action stage, the client is actively taking steps to change but has not reached stable recovery.
- In Preparation, the counselor focuses on helping the client explore change goals and develop a change plan. In Action, the counselor focuses on supporting client action steps and helping the client evaluate what is working and not working in the change plan.
- The client who is committed to change and who believes change is possible is prepared for the Action stage.
- Sobriety sampling, tapering down, and trial moderation are goal-sampling strategies that may be helpful to the client who is not committed to abstinence as a change goal.
- Creating a change plan is an interactive process between the counselor and client. The client should determine and drive change goals.
- Identifying and helping the client reduce barriers to the Action stage are important to the change-planning process.
- Counselors can support client action by reinforcing client commitment and continuing to evoke and reflect CAT (i.e., Commitment, Activation, and Taking steps) change talk in ongoing conversations.

Chapter 7—From Action to Maintenance: Stabilizing Change

This chapter addresses ways in which motivational strategies can be used effectively to help clients maintain the gains they have made by stabilizing change, supporting lifestyle changes, managing setbacks during the Maintenance stage, and helping them reenter the cycle of change if they relapse or return to substance misuse. It emphasizes creating a coping plan to reduce the risk of recurrence in high-risk situations, identifying new behaviors that reinforce change, and establishing relapse prevention strategies.

In Chapter 7, readers will learn that:

- During the Maintenance stage, the client has achieved the initial change goals and is working toward maintaining those changes.
- In Maintenance, the counselor focuses on helping the client stabilize change and supports the client's lifestyle changes.
- During a relapse, the client returns to substance misuse and temporarily exits the change cycle. The counselor focuses on helping the client reenter the cycle of change and providing relapse prevention counseling in accordance with the principles of person-centered counseling.
- Maintenance of substance use behavior change in the SOC model must address the issue of relapse. Relapse should be reconceptualized as a return to or recurrence of substance use behaviors and viewed as a common occurrence.
- Relapse prevention counseling is a cognitive–behavioral therapy (CBT) method, but the counselor

can use motivational counseling strategies to engage the client in the process and help the client resolve ambivalence about learning and practicing new coping skills.

- Strategies to help a client reenter the change cycle after a recurrence include affirming the client's willingness to reconsider positive change, exploring reoccurrence as a learning opportunity, helping the client find alternative coping strategies, and maintaining supportive contact with the client.

Chapter 8—Integrating Motivational Approaches in SUD Treatment Settings

This chapter discusses some of the adaptations of motivational counseling approaches applicable to SUD treatment programs and workforce development issues that treatment programs should address to fully integrate and sustain motivational counseling approaches. It emphasizes blending MI with other counseling approaches. It also explores ways in which ongoing training, supervision, and coaching are essential to successful workforce development and integration.

In Chapter 8, readers will learn that:

- Integrating motivational counseling approaches into a treatment program requires a broad integration of the philosophy and underlying spirit of MI throughout the organization.
- Adapted motivational interventions may be more cost effective, accessible to clients, and easily integrated into existing treatment approaches than expected and may ease some workload demands on counselors.
- Technology adaptations, including motivational counseling and brief interventions over the phone or via text messaging, are effective, cost effective, and adaptable to different client populations.
- MI is effective when blended with other counseling approaches including group counseling, the motivational interviewing assessment, CBT, and recovery management checkups.
- The key to workforce development is to train all clinical and support staffs in the spirit of MI so that the entire program's philosophy is aligned with person-centered principles, like emphasizing client autonomy and choice.
- Program administrators should assess the organization's philosophy and where it is in the SOC model before implementing a training program.
- Training counseling staff in MI takes more than a 1- or 2-day workshop. Maintenance of skills requires ongoing training and supervision.
- Supervision and coaching in MI should be competency based. These activities require directly observing the counselor's skill level and using coding instruments to assess counselor fidelity. Supervision should be performed in the spirit of MI.
- Administrators need to balance training, supervision, and strategies to enhance counselor fidelity to MI with costs, while partnering with counseling staff to integrate a motivational counseling approach throughout the organization.

TIP Development Participants[1]

Consensus Panel

Each Treatment Improvement Protocol's (TIP) consensus panel is a group of primarily nonfederal addiction-focused clinical, research, administrative, and recovery support experts with deep knowledge of the TIP's topic. With the Substance Abuse and Mental Health Services Administration's Knowledge Application Program team, members of the consensus panel develop each TIP via a consensus-driven, collaborative process that blends evidence-based, best, and promising practices with the panel members' expertise and combined wealth of experience.

Chair

William R. Miller, Ph.D.
Regents Professor of Psychology and Psychiatry
Director of Research
Center on Alcoholism, Substance Abuse, and Addictions
Department of Psychology
University of New Mexico
Albuquerque, New Mexico

Workgroup Leaders

Edward Bernstein, M.D., F.A.C.E.P.
Associate Professor and Academic Affairs
Vice Chairman
Boston University School of Medicine
Boston, Massachusetts

Suzanne M. Colby, Ph.D.
Assistant Professor of Psychiatry and Human Behavior
Center for Alcohol and Addiction Studies
Brown University
Providence, Rhode Island

Carlo C. DiClemente, Ph.D.
Department of Psychology
University of Maryland, Baltimore County
Baltimore, Maryland

Robert J. Meyers, M.A.
Center on Alcoholism, Substance Abuse, and Addictions
University of New Mexico
Albuquerque, New Mexico

Maxine L. Stitzer, Ph.D.

---

[1] The information given indicates participants' affiliations at the time of their participation in this TIP's original development and may no longer reflect their current affiliations.

Professor of Psychiatry and Behavioral Biology
Johns Hopkins University School of Medicine
Baltimore, Maryland

Allen Zweben, D.S.W.
Director and Associate Professor of Social Work
Center for Addiction and Behavioral Health Research
University of Wisconsin at Milwaukee
Milwaukee, Wisconsin

Panelists

Ray Daw
Executive Director
Northwest New Mexico Fighting Back, Inc.
Gallup, New Mexico

Jeffrey M. Georgi, M.Div., C.S.A.C., C.G.P.
Program Coordinator
Duke Alcoholism and Addictions Program
Clinical Associate
Department of Psychiatry and Behavioral Science
Duke University Medical Center
Durham, North Carolina

Cheryl Grills, Ph.D.
Department of Psychology
Loyola Marymount University
Los Angeles, California

Rosalyn Harris-Offutt, C.R.N.A., L.P.C., A.D.S.
UNA Psychological Associates
Greensboro, North Carolina

Don M. Hashimoto, Psy.D.
Clinical Director
Ohana Counseling Services, Inc.
Hilo, Hawaii

Dwight McCall, Ph.D.
Evaluation Manager
Substance Abuse Services
Virginia Department of Mental Health, Mental Retardation and Substance Abuse Services
Richmond, Virginia

Jeanne Obert, M.F.C.C., M.S.M.
Director of Clinical Services
Matrix Center
Los Angeles, California

Carole Janis Otero, M.A., L.P.C.C.
Director

Albuquerque Metropolitan Central Intake
Albuquerque, New Mexico

Roger A. Roffman, D.S.W.
Innovative Programs Research Group
School of Social Work
Seattle, Washington

Linda C. Sobell, Ph.D.
Professor
NOVA Southeastern University
Fort Lauderdale, Florida

Field Reviewers, Resource Panel, and Editorial Advisory Board

Field reviewers represent each TIP's intended target audiences. They work in addiction, mental health, primary care, and adjacent fields. Their direct front-line experience related to the TIP's topic allows them to provide valuable input on a TIP's relevance, utility, accuracy, and accessibility. Additional advisors to this TIP include members of a resource panel and an editorial advisory board.

Field Reviewers

Noel Brankenhoff, L.M.F.T., L.C.D.P.
Child and Family Services
Middletown, Rhode Island

Rodolfo Briseno, L.C.D.C.
Coordinator for Cultural/Special Populations and Youth Treatment Program Services
Program Initiatives Texas Commission on Alcohol and Drug Abuse
Austin, Texas

Richard L. Brown, M.D., M.P.H.
Associate Professor
Department of Family Medicine
University of Wisconsin School of Medicine
Madison, Wisconsin

Michael Burke
Senior Substance Abuse Specialist
Student Health
Rutgers University
New Brunswick, New Jersey

Kate Carey, Ph.D.
Associate Professor
Department of Psychology
Syracuse University
Syracuse, New York

Anthony J. Cellucci, Ph.D.
Director of Idaho State University Clinic

Associate Professor of Psychology
Idaho State University
Pocatello, Idaho

Gerard Connors, Ph.D.
Research Institute on Alcoholism
Buffalo, New York

John Cunningham, Ph.D.
Scientist
Addiction Research Foundation Division
Centre for Addiction and Mental Health
Toronto, Ontario

Janie Dargan, M.S.W.
Senior Policy Analyst
Office of National Drug Control Policy/Executive Office of the President
Washington, D.C.

George De Leon, Ph.D.
Center for Therapeutic Community Research
New York, New York

Nereida Diaz-Rodriguez, L.L.M., J.D.
Project Director
Director to the Master in Health Science in Substance Abuse
Centro de Entudion on Adiccion (Altos Salud Mental)
Edif. Hosp. Regional de Bayamon
Santa Juanita, Bayamon, Puerto Rico

Thomas Diklich
Portsmouth CSR
Portsmouth, Virginia

Chris Dunn, Ph.D., M.A.C., C.D.C.
Psychologist
Psychiatry and Behavioral Science
University of Washington
Seattle, Washington

Madeline Dupree, L.P.C.
Harrisonburg-Rockingham CSB
Harrisonburg, Virginia

Gary L. Fisher, Ph.D.
Nevada Addiction Technology Transfer Center
College of Education
University of Nevada at Reno
Reno, Nevada

Cynthia Flackus, M.S.W., L.I.C.S.W.
Therapist

Camp Share Renewal Center
Walker, Minnesota

Stephen T. Higgins, Ph.D.
Professor
Departments of Psychiatry and Psychology
University of Vermont
Burlington, Vermont

Col. Kenneth J. Hoffman, M.D., M.P.H., M.C.F.S.
Preventive Medicine Consultant
HHC 18th Medical Command
Seoul, South Korea

James Robert Holden, M.A.
Program Director
Partners in Drug Abuse Rehabilitation Counseling
Washington, D.C.

Ron Jackson, M.S.W.
Executive Director
Evergreen Treatment Services
Seattle, Washington

Linda Kaplan
Executive Director
National Association of Alcoholism and Drug Abuse Counselors
Arlington, Virginia

Matthew Kelly, Ph.D.
Clinical Director
Robert Wood Johnson Foundation
Northwest Mexico Fighting Back, Inc.
Gallup, New Mexico

Karen Kelly-Woodall, M.S., M.A.C., N.C.A.C. II
Criminal Justice Coordinator
Cork Institute
Morehouse School of Medicine
Atlanta, Georgia

Richard Laban, Ph.D.
Laban's Training
Harrisburg, Pennsylvania

Lauren Lawendowski, Ph.D.
Acting Project Director
Center on Alcoholism, Substance Abuse, and Addiction
University of New Mexico
Albuquerque, New Mexico

Bruce R. Lorenz, N.C.A.C. II

Director
Thresholds, Inc.
Dover, Delaware

Russell P. MacPherson, Ph.D., C.A.P., C.A.P.P., C.C.P., D.A.C., D.V.C.
President
RPM Addiction Prevention Training
Deland, Florida

George Medzerian, Ph.D.
Pensacola, Florida

Lisa A. Melchior, Ph.D.
Vice President
The Measurement Group
Culver City, California

Paul Nagy, M.S., C.S.A.C.
Director
Duke Alcoholism and Addictions Program
Duke University Medical Center
Durham, North Carolina

Tracy A. O'Leary, Ph.D.
Clinical Supervisor
Assistant Project Coordinator
Center for Alcohol and Addiction Studies
Brown University
Providence, Rhode Island

Gwen M. Olitsky, M.S.
CEO
The Self-Help Institute for Training and Therapy
Lansdale, Pennsylvania

Michele A. Packard, Ph.D.
Executive Director
SAGE Institute Training and Consulting
Boulder, California

Michael Pantalon, Ph.D.
Yale School of Medicine
New Haven, Connecticut

Joe Pereira, L.I.C.S.W., C.A.S.
Recovery Strategies
Medford, Massachusetts

Harold Perl, Ph.D.
Public Health Analyst
Division of Clinical and Prevention Research
National Institute on Alcohol Abuse and Alcoholism

Bethesda, Maryland

Raul G. Rodriguez, M.D.
Medical Director
La Hacienda Treatment Center
Hunt, Texas

Richard T. Suchinsky, M.D.
Associate Director for Addictive Disorders and Psychiatric Rehabilitation
Mental Health and Behavioral Sciences Services
Department of Veterans Affairs
Washington, D.C.

Suzan Swanton, M.S.W.
Clinical Director
R.E.A.C.H. Mobile Home Services
Baltimore, Maryland

Michael J. Taleff, Ph.D., C.A.C., M.A.C., N.C.A.C.II
Assistant Professor and Coordinator
Graduate Programs in Chemical Dependency
Department of Counselor Education
Counseling Psychology and Rehabilitation Services
Pennsylvania State University
University Park, Pennsylvania

Nola C. Veazie, Ph.D., L.P.C., C.A.D.A.C.
Superintendent
Medical Services Department
United States Air Force
Family Therapist/Drug and Alcohol Counselor
Veazie Family Therapy
Santa Maria, California

Mary Velasquez, Ph.D.
Psychology Department
University of Houston
Houston, Texas

Christopher Wagner, Ph.D.
Division of Substance Abuse Medicine
Virginia Commonwealth University
Richmond, Virginia

Resource Panel

Peter J. Cohen, M.D., J.D.
Adjunct Professor of Law
Georgetown University Law Center
Washington, D.C.

Frances Cotter, M.A., M.P.H.

Senior Public Health Advisor
Office of Managed Care
Center for Substance Abuse Treatment
Substance Abuse and Mental Health Services Administration
Rockville, Maryland

Dorynne Czechowicz, M.D.
Associate Director
Division of Clinical and Services Research Treatment Research Branch
National Institute on Drug Abuse
Bethesda, Maryland

James G. (Gil) Hill
Director
Office of Substance Abuse
American Psychological Association
Washington, D.C.

Linda Kaplan
Executive Director
National Association of Alcoholism and Drug Abuse Counselors
Arlington, Virginia

Pedro Morales, J.D.
Director
Equal Employment Civil Rights
Substance Abuse and Mental Health Services Administration
Rockville, Maryland

Harold I. Perl, Ph.D.
Public Health Analyst
Division of Clinical and Prevention Research
National Institute on Alcohol Abuse and Alcoholism
Bethesda, Maryland

Barbara J. Silver, Ph.D.
Center for Mental Health Services
Substance Abuse and Mental Health Services Administration
Rockville, Maryland

Lucretia Vigil
Policy Advisor
National Coalition of Hispanic Health and Human Services Organization
Washington, D.C.

Editorial Advisory Board

Karen Allen, Ph.D., R.N., C.A.R.N.
Professor and Chair
Department of Nursing
Andrews University

Berrien Springs, Michigan

Richard L. Brown, M.D., M.P.H.
Associate Professor
Department of Family Medicine
University of Wisconsin School of Medicine
Madison, Wisconsin

Dorynne Czechowicz, M.D.
Associate Director
Medical/Professional Affairs
Treatment Research Branch
Division of Clinical and Services Research
National Institute on Drug Abuse
Rockville, Maryland

Linda S. Foley, M.A.
Former Director
Project for Addiction Counselor Training
National Association of State Alcohol and Drug Abuse Directors
Washington, D.C.

Wayde A. Glover, M.I.S., N.C.A.C. II
Director
Commonwealth Addictions Consultants and Trainers
Richmond, Virginia

Pedro J. Greer, M.D.
Assistant Dean for Homeless Education
University of Miami School of Medicine
Miami, Florida

Thomas W. Hester, M.D.
Former State Director
Substance Abuse Services
Division of Mental Health, Mental Retardation and Substance Abuse
Georgia Department of Human Resources
Atlanta, Georgia

James G. (Gil) Hill, Ph.D.
Director
Office of Substance Abuse
American Psychological Association
Washington, D.C.

Douglas B. Kamerow, M.D., M.P.H.
Director
Office of the Forum for Quality and Effectiveness in Health Care
Agency for Healthcare Research and Quality
Rockville, Maryland

Stephen W. Long
Director
Office of Policy Analysis
National Institute on Alcohol Abuse and Alcoholism
Rockville, Maryland

Richard A. Rawson, Ph.D.
Executive Director
Matrix Center and Matrix Institute on Addiction
Deputy Director
UCLA Addiction Medicine Services
Los Angeles, California

Ellen A. Renz, Ph.D.
Former Vice President of Clinical Systems
MEDCO Behavioral Care Corporation
Kamuela, Hawaii

Richard K. Ries, M.D.
Director and Associate Professor
Outpatient Mental Health Services and Dual Disorder Programs
Harborview Medical Center
Seattle, Washington

Sidney H. Schnoll, M.D., Ph.D.
Chairman
Division of Substance Abuse Medicine
Medical College of Virginia
Richmond, Virginia

Publication Information

Acknowledgements

This publication was prepared under contract numbers 270-95-0013, 270-14-0445, 270-19-0538, and 283-17-4901 by the Knowledge Application Program (KAP) for the Center for Substance Abuse Treatment, Substance Abuse and Mental Health Services Administration (SAMHSA), U.S. Department of Health and Human Services (HHS). Sandra Clunies, M.S., I.C.A.D.C., served as the Contracting Officer's Representative (COR) for initial Treatment Improvement Protocol (TIP) development. Suzanne Wise served as the COR; Candi Byrne as the Alternate COR; and Reed Forman, M.S.W., as the Project Champion for the TIP update.

Disclaimer

The views, opinions, and content expressed herein are the views of the consensus panel members and do not necessarily reflect the official position of SAMHSA. No official support of or endorsement by SAMHSA for these opinions or for the instruments or resources described is intended or should be inferred. The guidelines presented should not be considered substitutes for individualized client care and treatment decisions.

Public Domain Notice

All materials appearing in this publication except those taken directly from copyrighted sources are in the public domain and may be reproduced or copied without permission from SAMHSA or the authors. Citation of the source is appreciated. However, this publication may not be reproduced or distributed for a fee without the specific, written authorization of the Office of Communications, SAMHSA.

Electronic Access and Copies of Publication

This publication may be ordered or downloaded from SAMHSA's Publications and Digital Products webpage at https://store.samhsa.gov. Or, please call SAMHSA at 1-877-SAMHSA-7 (1-877-726-4727) (English and Español).

Recommended Citation

Substance Abuse and Mental Health Services Administration. *Enhancing Motivation for Change in Substance Use Disorder Treatment.* Treatment Improvement Protocol (TIP) Series No. 35. SAMHSA Publication No. PEP19-02-01-003. Rockville, MD: Substance Abuse and Mental Health Services Administration, 2019.

Originating Office

Quality Improvement and Workforce Development Branch, Division of Services Improvement, Center for Substance Abuse Treatment, Substance Abuse and Mental Health Services Administration, 5600 Fishers Lane, Rockville, MD 20857.

Nondiscrimination Notice

SAMHSA complies with applicable federal civil rights laws and does not discriminate on the basis of race, color, national origin, age, disability, or sex. SAMHSA cumple con las leyes federales de derechos civiles aplicables y no discrimina por motivos de raza, color, nacionalidad, edad, discapacidad, o sexo.

SAMHSA Publication No. PEP19-02-01-003
First printed 1999
Updated 2019

Chapter 1—A New Look at Motivation

"Motivation to initiate and persist in change fluctuates over time regardless of the person's stage of readiness. From the client's perspective, a decision is just the beginning of change."

Miller & Rollnick, 2013, p. 293

Key Messages

- Motivation is the key to substance use behavior change.
- Counselor use of empathy, not authority and power, is essential to enhancing client motivation to change.
- The Transtheoretical Model (TTM) of the Stages of Change (SOC) approach is a useful overarching framework that can help you tailor specific counseling strategies to the different stages.

Why do people change? How is motivation linked to substance use behavior change? How can you help clients enhance their motivation to engage in substance use disorder (SUD) treatment and initiate recovery? This Treatment Improvement Protocol (TIP) will answer these and other important questions. Using the TTM of behavioral change as a foundation, Chapter 1 lays the groundwork for answering such questions. It offers an overview of the nature of motivation and its link to changing substance use behaviors. It also addresses the shift away from abstinence-only addiction treatment perspectives toward client-centered approaches that enhance motivation and reduce risk.

In the past three decades, the addiction treatment field has focused on discovering and applying science-informed practices that help people with SUDs enhance their motivation to stop or reduce alcohol, drug, and nicotine use. Research and clinical literature have explored how to help clients sustain behavior change in ongoing recovery. Such recovery support helps prevent or lessen the social, mental, and health problems that result from a recurrence of substance use or a relapse to previous levels of substance misuse.

This TIP examines motivational enhancement and substance use behavior change using two science-informed approaches (DiClemente, Corno, Graydon, Wiprovnick, & Knobloch, 2017):

1. Motivational interviewing (MI), which is a respectful counseling style that focuses on helping clients resolve ambivalence about and enhance motivation to change health-risk behaviors, including substance misuse

2. The TTM of the SOC, which provides an overarching framework for motivational counseling approaches throughout all phases of addiction treatment

---

Key Terms

Addiction*: The most severe form of SUD, associated with compulsive or uncontrolled use of one or more substances. Addiction is a chronic brain disease that has the potential for both recurrence (relapse) and recovery.

Alcohol misuse: The use of alcohol in any harmful way, including use that constitutes alcohol use disorder (AUD).

Alcohol use disorder: Per the American Psychiatric Association's (APA) *Diagnostic and Statistical Manual of Mental Disorders*, Fifth Edition (DSM-5; APA, 2013), a diagnosis applicable to a person who uses alcohol and experiences at least 2 of the 11 symptoms in a 12-month period. Key aspects of AUD include loss of control, continued use despite adverse consequences, tolerance, and withdrawal. AUD covers a range of severity and replaces what DSM-IV, termed "alcohol abuse" and "alcohol dependence" (APA, 1994).

Health-risk behavior: Any behavior (e.g., tobacco or alcohol use, unsafe sexual practices, nonadherence to prescribed medication regimens) that increases the risk of disease or injury.

Recovery*: A process of change through which individuals improve their health and wellness, live a self-directed life, and strive to reach their full potential. Even individuals with severe and chronic SUDs can, with help, overcome their disorder and regain health and social function. This is called remission. When those positive changes and values become part of a voluntarily adopted lifestyle, that is called "being in recovery." Although abstinence from all substance misuse is a cardinal feature of a recovery lifestyle, it is not the only healthy, pro-social feature.

Recurrence: An instance of substance use that occurs after a period of abstinence. Where possible, this TIP uses the terms "recurrence" or "return to substance use" instead of "relapse," which can have negative connotations (see entry below).

Relapse*: A return to substance use after a significant period of abstinence.

Substance*: A psychoactive compound with the potential to cause health and social problems, including SUDs (and their most severe manifestation, addiction). The table at the end of this exhibit lists common examples of such substances.

Substance misuse*: The use of any substance in a manner, situation, amount, or frequency that can cause harm to users or to those around them. For some substances or individuals, any use would constitute misuse (e.g., underage drinking, injection drug use).

Substance use*: The use—even one time—of any of the substances listed in the table at the end of this exhibit.

Substance use disorder*: A medical illness caused by repeated misuse of a substance or substances. According to DSM-5 (APA, 2013), SUDs are characterized by clinically significant impairments in health, social function, and impaired control over substance use and are diagnosed through assessing cognitive, behavioral, and psychological symptoms. SUDs range from mild to severe and from temporary to chronic. They typically develop gradually over time with repeated misuse, leading to changes in brain circuits governing incentive salience (the ability of substance-associated cues to trigger substance seeking), reward, stress, and executive functions like decision making and self-control. Multiple factors influence whether and how rapidly a person will develop an SUD. These factors include the substance itself; the genetic vulnerability of the user; and the amount, frequency, and duration of the misuse. A severe SUD is commonly called an addiction.

Substance Category	Representative Examples
Alcohol	• Beer • Wine • Malt liquor • Distilled spirits

Illicit Drugs	• Cocaine, including crack
	• Heroin
	• Hallucinogens, including LSD, PCP, ecstasy, peyote, mescaline, psilocybin
	• Methamphetamines, including crystal meth
	• Marijuana, including hashish*
	• Synthetic drugs, including K2, Spice, and "bath salts"**
	• Prescription-type medications that are used for nonmedical purposes
	   ○ Pain Relievers - Synthetic, semi-synthetic, and non-synthetic opioid medications, including fentanyl, codeine, oxycodone, hydrocodone, and tramadol products
	   ○ Tranquilizers, including benzodiazepines, meprobamate products, and muscle relaxants
	   ○ Stimulants and Methamphetamine, including amphetamine, dextroamphetamine, and phentermine products; mazindol products; and methylphenidate or dexmethylphenidate products
	   ○ Sedatives, including temazepam, flurazepam, or triazolam and any barbiturates

Over-the-Counter Drugs and Other Substances	• Cough and cold medicines** • Inhalants, including amyl nitrite, cleaning fluids, gasoline and lighter gases, anesthetics, solvents, spray paint, nitrous oxide

* As of June 2016, 25 states and the District of Columbia have legalized medical marijuana use, four states have legalized retail marijuana sales, and the District of Columbia has legalized personal use and home cultivation (both medical and recreational). It should be noted that none of the permitted uses under state laws alter the status of marijuana and its constituent compounds as illicit drugs under Schedule I of the federal Controlled Substances Act. See the section on Marijuana: A Changing Legal and

*The definitions of all terms marked with an asterisk correspond closely to those given in Facing Addiction in America: The Surgeon General's Report on Alcohol, Drugs, and Health (Office of the Surgeon General, 2016). This resource provides a great deal of useful information about substance misuse and its impact on U.S. public health. The report is available online (*https://addiction.surgeongeneral.gov/sites/default/files/surgeon-generals-report.pdf*).

Motivation and Behavior Change

Motivation is a critical element of behavior change (Flannery, 2017) that predicts client abstinence and reductions in substance use (DiClemente et al., 2017). You cannot give clients motivation, but you can help them identify their reasons and need for change and facilitate planning for change. Successful SUD treatment approaches **acknowledge motivation as a multidimensional, fluid state during which people make difficult changes to health-risk behaviors, like substance misuse.**

The Nature of Motivation

The following factors define motivation and its ability to help people change health-risk behaviors.

- **Motivation is a key to substance use behavior change.** Change, like motivation, is a complex construct with evolving meanings. One framework for understanding motivation and how it relates to behavior changes is the self-determination theory (SDT). SDT suggests that people inherently want to engage in activities that meet their need for autonomy, competency (i.e., self-efficacy), and relatedness (i.e., having close personal relationships) (Deci & Ryan, 2012; Flannery, 2017). SDT describes two kinds of motivation:
    - Intrinsic motivation (e.g., desires, needs, values, goals)
    - Extrinsic motivation (e.g., social influences, external rewards, consequences)

- **MI is a counseling approach that is consistent with SDT and emphasizes enhancing internal motivation to change.** In the SDT framework, providing a supportive relational context that promotes client autonomy and competence enhances intrinsic motivation, helps clients internalize extrinsic motivational rewards, and supports behavior change (Flannery, 2017; Kwasnicka, Dombrowski, White, & Sniehotta, 2016; Moyers, 2014).

- **Contingency management is a counseling strategy that can reinforce extrinsic motivation.** It uses external motivators or reinforcers (e.g., expectation of a reward or negative consequence) to enhance behavior change (Sayegh, Huey, Zara, & Jhaveri, 2017).

- **Motivation helps people resolve their ambivalence about making difficult lifestyle changes.** Helping clients strengthen their own motivation increases the likelihood that they will commit to a specific behavioral change plan (Miller & Rollnick, 2013). Research supports the importance of SDT-based client motivation in positive addiction treatment outcomes (Wild, Yuan, Rush, & Urbanoski, 2016). Motivation and readiness to change are consistently associated with increased help seeking, treatment adherence and completion, and positive SUD treatment outcomes (Miller & Moyers, 2015).

- **Motivation is multidimensional.** Motivation includes clients' internal desires, needs, and values. It also includes external pressures, demands, and reinforcers (positive and negative) that influence clients and their perceptions about the risks and benefits of engaging in substance use behaviors. Two components of motivation predict good treatment outcomes (Miller & Moyers, 2015):
  - The importance clients associate with changes
  - Their confidence in their ability to make changes

- **Motivation is dynamic and fluctuates.** Motivation is a dynamic process that responds to interpersonal influences, including feedback and an awareness of different available choices (Miller & Rollnick, 2013). Motivation is a strong predictor of addiction treatment outcomes (Miller & Moyers, 2015). Motivation can fluctuate over different stages of the SOC and varies in intensity. It can decrease when the client feels doubt or ambivalence about change and increase when reasons for change and specific goals become clear. In this sense, motivation can be an ambivalent state or a resolute commitment to act—or not to act.

- **Motivation is influenced by social interactions.** An individual's motivation to change can be positively influenced by supportive family and friends as well as community support and negatively influenced by lack of social support, negative social support (e.g., a social network of friends and associates who misuse alcohol), and negative public perception of SUDs.

- **Motivation can be enhanced.** Motivation is a part of the human experience. No one is totally unmotivated (Miller & Rollnick, 2013). Motivation is accessible and can be enhanced at many points in the change process. Historically, in addiction treatment it was thought that clients had to "hit bottom" or experience terrible, irreparable consequences of their substance misuse to become ready to change. Research now shows that counselors can help clients identify and explore their desire, ability, reasons, and need to change substance use behaviors; this effort enhances motivation and facilitates movement toward change (Miller & Rollnick, 2013).

- **Motivation is influenced by the counselor's style.** The way you interact with clients impacts how they respond and whether treatment is successful. Counselor interpersonal skills are associated with better treatment outcomes. In particular, an empathetic counselor style predicts increased retention in treatment and reduced substance use across a wide range of clinical settings and types of clients (Moyers & Miller, 2013). The most desirable attributes for the counselor mirror those recommended in the general psychology literature and include nonpossessive warmth, genuineness, respect, affirmation, and empathy. In contrast, an argumentative or confrontational style of counselor interaction with clients, such as challenging client defenses and arguing, tends to be counterproductive and is associated with poorer outcomes for clients, particularly when counselors are less skilled (Polcin, Mulia, & Jones, 2012; Roman & Peters, 2016).

- **Your task is to elicit and enhance motivation.** Although change is the responsibility of clients and many people change substance use behaviors on their own without formal treatment (Kelly, Bergman, Hoeppner, Vilsaint, & White, 2017), you can enhance clients' motivation for positive change at each stage of the SOC process. Your task is not to teach, instruct, or give unsolicited advice. Your role is to help clients recognize when a substance use behavior is inconsistent with their values or stated goals, regard positive change to be in their best interest, feel competent to change, develop a plan for change, begin taking action, and continue using strategies that lessen the risk of a return to substance misuse (Miller & Rollnick, 2013). Finally, you should be sensitive and responsive to cultural factors that may influence client motivation. For more information about enhancing cultural awareness and responsiveness, see TIP 59: *Improving Cultural Competence* (Substance Abuse and Mental Health Services Administration [SAMHSA], 2014a).

Counselor Note: Are You Ready, Willing, and Able?

Motivation is captured, in part, in the popular phrase that a person is ready, willing, and able to change:

- "Ability" refers to the extent to which a person has the necessary skills, resources, and confidence to make a change.
- "Willingness" is linked to the importance a person places on changing—how much a change is wanted or desired. However, even willingness and ability are not always enough.
- "Ready" represents a final step in which a person finally decides to change a particular behavior.

Your task is to help the client become ready, willing, and able to change.

Why Enhance Motivation?

Although much progress has been made in identifying people who misuse substances and who have SUD and in using science-informed interventions such as motivational counseling approaches to treat them, the United States is still facing many SUD challenges. For example, the National Survey on Drug Use and Health (SAMHSA, 2018) reports that, in 2017, approximately:

- 140.6 million Americans ages 12 and older currently consumed alcohol, 66.6 million engaged in past-month binge drinking (defined as 5 or more drinks on the same occasion on at least 1 day in the past 30 days for men and 4 or more drinks on the same occasion on at least 1 day in the past 30 days for women), and 16.7 million drank heavily in the past month (defined as binge drinking on 5 or more days in the past 30 days).
- 30.5 million people ages 12 and older had past-month illicit drug use.
- 11.4 million people misused opioids (defined as prescription pain reliever misuse or heroin use) in the past year.
- 8.5 million adults ages 18 and older (3.4 percent of all adults) had both a mental disorder and at least one past-year SUD.
- 18.2 million people who needed SUD treatment did not receive specialty treatment.
- One-third of people who perceived a need for addiction treatment did not receive it because they lacked health insurance and could not pay for services.

Enhancing motivation can improve addiction treatment outcomes. In the United States, millions of people with SUDs are not receiving treatment. Many do not seek treatment because their motivation to change their substance use behaviors is low. Motivational counseling approaches are associated with greater participation in treatment and positive treatment outcomes. Such outcomes include increased motivation to change; reductions in consumption of alcohol, tobacco, cannabis, and other substances; increased abstinence rates; higher client confidence in ability to change behaviors; and greater treatment engagement (Copeland, McNamara, Kelson, & Simpson, 2015; DiClemente et al., 2017; Lundahl et al., 2013; Smedslund et al., 2011).

The benefits of motivational enhancement approaches include:

- Enhancing motivation to change.
- Preparing clients to enter treatment.
- Engaging and retaining clients in treatment.
- Increasing participation and involvement.
- Improving treatment outcomes.
- Encouraging rapid return to treatment if clients return to substance misuse.

Changing Perspectives on Addiction and Treatment

Historically, in the United States, different views about the nature of addiction and its causes have influenced the development of treatment approaches. For example, after the passage of the Harrison Narcotics Act in 1914, it was illegal for physicians to treat people with drug addiction. The only options for people with alcohol or drug use disorders were inebriate homes and asylums. The underlying assumption pervading these early treatment approaches was that alcohol and drug addiction was either a moral failing or a pernicious disease (White, 2014).

By the 1920s, compassionate treatment of opioid addiction was available in medical clinics. At the same time, equally passionate support for the temperance movement, with its focus on drunkenness as a moral failing and abstinence as the only cure, was gaining momentum.

The development of the modern SUD treatment system dates only from the late 1950s. Even "modern" addiction treatment has not always acknowledged counselors' capacity to support client motivation. Historically, motivation was considered a static client trait; the client either had it or did not have it, and there was nothing a counselor could do to influence it.

This view of motivation as static led to blaming clients for tension or discord in therapeutic relationships. Clients who disagreed with diagnoses, did not adhere to treatment plans, or refused to accept labels like "alcoholic" or "drug addict" were seen as difficult or resistant (Miller & Rollnick, 2013).

SUD treatment has since evolved in response to new technologies, research, and theories of addiction with associated counseling approaches. Exhibit 1.1 summarizes some models of addiction that have influenced treatment methods in the United States (DiClemente, 2018).

Exhibit 1.1. Models of Addiction		
Model	Underlying Assumptions	Treatment Approaches
Moral/legal	Addiction is a set of behaviors that violates religious, moral, or legal codes.	Abstinence and use of willpower External control through hospitalization or incarceration

Psychological	Addiction results from deficits in learning, emotional dysfunction, or psychopathology.	Cognitive, behavioral, psychoanalytic, or psychodynamic psychotherapies
Sociocultural	Addiction results from socialization and sociocultural factors. Contributing factors include socioeconomic status, cultural and ethnic beliefs, availability of substances, laws and penalties regulating substance use, norms and rules of families and other social groups, parental and peer expectations, modeling of acceptable behaviors, and the presence or absence of reinforcers.	Focus on building new social and family relationships, developing social competency and skills, and working within a client's culture
Spiritual	Addiction is a spiritual disease. Recovery is predicated on a recognition of the limitations of the self and a desire to achieve health through a connection with that which transcends the individual.	Integrating 12-Step recovery principles or other culturally based spiritual practices (e.g., American Indian Wellbriety principles) into addiction treatment Linking clients to 12-Step, faith- and spiritual-based recovery, and other support groups
Medical	Addiction is a chronic, progressive, disease. Genetic predisposition and neurochemical brain changes are primary etiological factors.	Medical and behavioral interventions including pharmacotherapy, education, and behavioral change advice and monitoring
Integrated treatment	Addiction is a chronic disease that is best treated by collaborative and comprehensive approaches that address biopsychosocial and spiritual components.	Integrated treatment with a recovery focus across treatment settings

Earlier Perspectives

Although the field is evolving toward a more comprehensive understanding of SUD, **earlier views of addiction still persist in parts of the U.S. addiction treatment system.** For example, the psychological model of addiction treatment gave rise, in part, to the idea of an "addictive personality" and that psychological defenses (e.g., denial) need to be confronted. Remnants of earlier perspectives of addiction and their associated treatment approaches, which are not supported by research, include:

- **An addictive personality leads to SUDs.** Although it is commonly believed that people with SUDs possess similar personality traits that make treatment difficult, no distinctive personality traits have been found to predict that an individual will develop an SUD (Amodeo, 2015). The tendencies of an addictive personality most often cited are denial, projection, poor insight, and poor self-esteem. This idea is a deficit-based concept that can lead to counselors and clients viewing addiction as a fixed part of an underlying personality disorder and therefore difficult to treat (Amodeo, 2015).

- **Rationalization and denial are characteristics of addiction.** Another leftover from earlier psychological perspectives on addiction is that people with SUDs have strong psychological defenses, such as denial and rationalization, which lead to challenging behaviors like evasiveness, manipulation, and resistance (Connors, DiClemente, Velasquez, & Donovan, 2013). The clinical and research literature does not support the belief that people with SUDs have more or stronger defenses than other clients (Connors et al., 2013).

- **Resistance is a characteristic of "unmotivated" clients in addiction treatment** (Connors et al., 2013). When clients are labeled as manipulative or resistant, given no voice in selecting treatment goals, or directed authoritatively to do or not to do something, the result is a predictable response of resistance or reactivity to the counselor's directives (Beutler, Harwood, Michelson, Song, & Holman, 2011). Viewing resistance—along with rationalization and denial—as characteristic of addiction and making efforts to weaken these defenses actually strengthens them. This paradox seemed to confirm the idea that resistance and denial were essential components of addiction and traits of clients.

- **Confrontation of psychological defenses and substance misuse behaviors is an effective counseling approach.** Historically, the idea that resistance and denial are characteristic of addiction led to the use of confrontation as a way to aggressively break down these defenses (White & Miller, 2007). However, adversarial confrontation is one of the least effective methods for helping clients change substance use behaviors, can paradoxically reduce motivation for beneficial change, and often contributes to poor outcomes (Bertholet, Palfai, Gaume, Daeppen, & Saitz, 2013; Moos, 2012; Moyers & Miller, 2013; Romano & Peters, 2016). Yet there is a constructive type of confrontation. This kind of confrontation must be done within the context of a trusting and respectful relationship and is delivered it in a supportive way that also elicits hope for change (Polcin et al., 2012).

Expert Comment: A Brief History of Confrontation in Addiction Treatment

For many reasons, the U.S. treatment field fell into some rather aggressive, argumentative, "denial-busting" methods for confronting people with alcohol and drug problems. This perspective was guided, in part, by the belief that substance misuse links to a particular personality pattern characterized by such rigid defense mechanisms as denial and rationalization. In this perspective, the counselor must take responsibility for impressing reality on clients, who cannot see it on their own. Such confrontation found its way into the popular Minnesota model of treatment and into Synanon (a drug treatment community known for group sessions in which participants verbally attacked each other) and other similar therapeutic community programs.

After the 1970s, the treatment field began to move away from such methods. The Hazelden Foundation officially renounced the "tear them down to build them up" approach in 1985, expressing regret that such confrontational approaches had become associated with the Minnesota model. Psychological studies have found no consistent pattern of personality or defense mechanisms associated with SUDs. Clinical studies have linked worse outcomes to more confrontational counselors, groups, and programs (Miller & Wilbourne, 2002; Moos, 2012; Romano & Peters, 2016). Instead, successful outcomes (Moyers, Houck, Rice, Longabaugh, & Miller, 2016) generally have been associated with counselors showing high levels of empathy as defined by Carl Rogers (1980). The Johnson Institute now emphasizes a supportive, compassionate style for conducting family interventions.

I was at first surprised when counselors attending my MI workshops and watching me demonstrate the style observed, "In a different way, you're very confrontational." This comes up in almost every training now. Some call it "gentle confrontation." This got me thinking about what confrontation really means.

The linguistic roots of the verb "to confront" mean "to come face-to-face." When you think about it that way, confrontation is precisely what we are trying to accomplish: to allow our clients to come face-to-face with a difficult and often threatening reality, to "let it in" rather than "block it out," and to allow this reality to change them. That makes confrontation a **goal** of counseling rather than a particular **style** or **technique**.

Once you see this—namely, that opening to new information, face-to-face, is a **goal** of counseling—then the question becomes, "What is the best way to achieve that goal?" Strong evidence suggests that direct, forceful, aggressive approaches are perhaps the **least** effective way to help people consider new information and change their perceptions. Such confrontation increases the very phenomenon it is supposed to overcome— defensiveness—and decreases clients' likelihood of change (Miller, Benefield, & Tonigan, 1993; Miller & Wilbourne, 2002; Moos, 2012; Romano & Peters, 2016). It is also inappropriate in many cultures. Getting in a

> client's face may work for some, but for most, it is exactly the opposite of what is needed—to come face-to-face with painful reality and to change.
>
> William R. Miller, Ph.D., Consensus Panel Chair

A New Perspective

As the addiction treatment field has matured, it has tried to integrate conflicting theories and approaches and to incorporate research findings into a comprehensive model. The following sections address recent changes in addiction treatment with important implications for applying motivational methods.

Focus on client strengths

Historically the treatment field has focused on the deficits and limitations of clients. Today, greater emphasis is placed on **identifying, enhancing, and using clients' strengths, abilities, and competencies.** This trend parallels the principles of motivational counseling, which affirm clients, emphasize personal autonomy, support and strengthen self-efficacy, and reinforce that change is possible (see Chapter 4). The responsibility for recovery rests with clients, and the judgmental tone, which is a remnant of the moral model of addiction, is eliminated.

Individualized and person-centered treatment

In the past, clients frequently received standardized treatment, no matter what their problems or SUD severity. Today, **treatment is increasingly based on clients' individual needs, which are carefully and comprehensively assessed at intake.** Positive outcomes such as higher levels of engagement in psychosocial treatments, decreased alcohol use, and improved quality of life are associated with person-centered care and a focus on individualized treatment (Barrio & Gual, 2016; Bray et al., 2017; Jackson et al., 2014). In this perspective, clients have choices about desirable, suitable treatment options—they are not prescribed treatment. Motivational approaches emphasize choice by eliciting personal goals from clients and involving them in selecting the type of treatment needed or desired from a menu of options.

A shift away from labeling

Historically, a diagnosis or disease defined the client and became a dehumanizing attribute of the individual. Today, individuals with asthma or a psychosis are seldom referred to as "the asthmatic" or "the psychotic." Similarly, in the addiction treatment arena, there is a trend to avoid labeling clients with SUDs as "addicts" or "alcoholics." **Using a motivational style will help you avoid labeling clients,** especially those who may not agree with the diagnosis or do not see a particular behavior as problematic. Person-first language (e.g., a person with an SUD) is the new standard; it reduces stigma, helps clients disentangle addiction from identity, and eliminates the judgmental tone left over from the moral model of addiction (SAMHSA, Center for the Application of Prevention Technologies, 2017).

Therapeutic partnerships for change

In the past, especially in the medical model, the client passively **received** treatment. Today, treatment usually entails **a partnership in which you and the client agree on treatment goals and together develop strategies to meet those goals.** The client is seen as an active participant in treatment planning. Using motivational strategies fosters a therapeutic alliance with the client and elicits goals and change strategies from the client. The client has ultimate responsibility for making changes.

Use of empathy, not authority and power

Historically, addiction treatment providers were placed in the position of an authority with the power to recommend client termination for rule infractions, penalties for positive urine drug screens, or promotion to a higher phase of treatment for successfully following direction. Research now demonstrates that **counselors who operate from a more authority-driven way of relating to clients, such as confronting or being overly directive, are less effective than counselors who employ empathy, understanding, and support** with clients (Martin & Rehm, 2012). This style of counseling is a particularly poor match for clients who are angry or reactive to counselor direction (Beutler et al., 2011). Positive treatment outcomes, including decreased substance use, abstinence, and increased treatment retention, are associated with high levels of counselor empathy, good interpersonal skills, and a strong therapeutic alliance (Miller & Moyers, 2015; Moyers & Miller, 2013).

Focus on early and brief interventions

In the past, addiction treatment consisted of detoxification, inpatient rehabilitation, long-term rehabilitation in residential settings, and aftercare. When care was standardized, most programs had not only a routine protocol of services but also a fixed length of stay. Twenty-eight days was considered the proper length of time for successful inpatient (usually hospital-based) care in the popular Minnesota model of SUD treatment. Residential facilities and outpatient clinics also had standard courses of treatment. These services were geared to clients with chronic, severe SUDs. Addiction treatment was viewed as a discrete event instead of a range of services over a continuum of care as the treatment provided for other chronic diseases like heart disease (Miller, Forehimes, & Zweben, 2011).

Recently, with the shift to a continuum of care model, **a variety of treatment programs have been established to intervene earlier** with those whose drinking or drug use is causing social, financial, or legal problems or increases their risk of health-related harms. These early intervention efforts range from educational programs (e.g., sentencing review or reduction for people apprehended for driving while intoxicated who participate in such programs) to brief interventions in opportunistic settings such as general hospital units, emergency departments (EDs), clinics, and doctors' offices that use motivational strategies to offer personalized feedback, point out the risks of substance use and misuse, suggest behavior change, and make referrals to formal treatment programs when necessary.

Early and brief interventions demonstrate positive outcomes such as reductions in alcohol consumption and drug use, reductions in alcohol misuse, decreases in tobacco and cannabis use, lower mortality rates, reductions in alcohol-related injuries, and decreases in ED return visits (Barata et al., 2017; Blow et al., 2017; DiClemente et al., 2017; McQueen, Howe, Allan, Mains, & Hardy, 2011).

Recognition of a continuum of substance misuse

Formerly, substance misuse was viewed as a progressive condition that, if left untreated, would inevitably lead to full-blown dependence and, likely, early death. Today, the addiction treatment field recognizes that **substance misuse exists along a continuum** from misuse to an SUD that meets the diagnostic criteria in DSM-5 (APA, 2013). Not all SUDs increase in severity. Many individuals never progress beyond substance use that poses a health risk, and others cycle back and forth through periods of abstinence, substance misuse, and meeting criteria for SUD.

Recovery from SUDs is seen as a multidimensional process along a continuum (Office of the Surgeon General, 2016) that differs among people and changes over time within the individual. Motivational strategies can be effectively applied to a person throughout the addiction process. The crucial variable is not the severity of the substance use pattern but the client's readiness for change.

Recognition of multiple SUDs

Counselors have come to recognize not only that SUDs vary in intensity but also that **most involve more than one substance.** Formerly, alcohol and drug treatment programs were completely separated by ideology and policy, even though most individuals with SUDs also drink heavily and many people who misuse alcohol also experiment with other substances, including prescribed medications that can be substituted for alcohol or that alleviate withdrawal symptoms. Although many treatment programs specialize in serving particular types of clients for whom their treatment approaches are appropriate (e.g., methadone maintenance programs for clients with opioid use disorder [OUD]), most now also treat other SUDs, substance use, and psychological problems or at least identify these and make referrals as necessary. Some evidence shows that motivational counseling approaches (including individual and group MI and brief interventions) demonstrate positive outcomes for clients who misuse alcohol and other substances (Klimas et al., 2014). Motivational counseling approaches with this client population should involve engaging clients and prioritizing their change goals.

Acceptance of new treatment goals

In the past, addiction treatment, at least for clients having trouble with alcohol, was considered successful only if the client became abstinent and never returned to substance use following discharge. The focus of treatment was almost entirely to have the client stop using and to start understanding the nature of addiction. Today, **treatment goals include a broad range of biopsychosocial measures,** such as improved health and psychosocial functioning, improved employment stability, and reduction in crime. In addition, recent efforts have focused on trauma-informed care and treating co-occurring disorders in an integrated treatment setting, where client concerns are addressed simultaneously with SUDs. For more information on treating clients with trauma and co-occurring disorders, see TIP 57: *Trauma-Informed Care in Behavioral Health Services* (SAMHSA, 2014b) and TIP 42: *Substance Abuse Treatment for Persons With Co-Occurring Disorders* (SAMHSA, 2013), respectively.

Focus on risk reduction

The field has **expanded the definition of positive treatment outcomes to include intermediate goals of risk reduction.** The goal of risk reduction is to decrease clients' risks for alcohol- and drug-related health risks, legal involvement, sexual behavior that can lead to sexually transmitted diseases, social and financial problems, ED visits, hospitalization and rehospitalization, and relapse of substance use and mental disorders. Risk-reduction interventions include medication-assisted treatment for AUD and OUD and reduction in substance use as an intermediate step toward abstinence for clients who are not ready or willing to commit to full abstinence. Risk-reduction strategies can be an important goal in early treatment and have demonstrated effectiveness in reducing substance-use–related consequences (Office of the Surgeon General, 2016).

Integration of addiction, behavioral health, and healthcare services

Historically, the SUD treatment system was isolated from mainstream health care by different funding streams, health insurance restrictions, and lack of awareness and training among healthcare providers on recognizing, screening, assessing, and treating addiction as a chronic illness. Today, a concerted effort is under way to **integrate addiction treatment with other behavioral health and primary care services** to build a comprehensive healthcare delivery system. Key findings of *Facing Addiction in America: The Surgeon General's Report on Alcohol, Drugs, and Health* (Office of the Surgeon General, 2016) include the following:

- The separation of SUD treatment from mainstream healthcare services has created obstacles to successful treatment and care coordination.

- SUDs are medical conditions. Integration helps address health disparities, reduces healthcare costs, and improves general health outcomes.

- Many people with SUDs do not seek specialty addiction treatment but often enter the healthcare system through general medical settings. This is an important but neglected opportunity to screen for substance misuse and provide brief interventions or referrals to specialty care.

Motivational enhancement strategies delivered in all settings can support client engagement in treatment and improve substance use outcomes, whether in EDs, primary care offices, office-based opioid treatment programs, criminal justice settings, social service programs, or specialized addiction treatment programs. Screening, brief intervention, and referral to treatment (SBIRT), which includes motivational enhancement strategies, is an early intervention approach that can be a bridge from medical settings to specialty SUD treatment in an integrated healthcare system (McCance-Katz & Satterfeld, 2012). Chapter 2 provides detailed information on SBIRT.

TTM of the SOC

In developing a new understanding of motivation, substantial addiction research has focused on the determinants and mechanisms of change. By understanding better how people change without professional assistance, researchers and counselors have become better able to develop and apply interventions to facilitate changes in clients' substance use behaviors.

Natural Change

Many adults in the United States resolve an alcohol or drug use problem without assistance (Kelly et al., 2017). This is called "natural recovery." Recovery from SUDs can happen with limited treatment or participation in mutual-aid support groups such as Alcoholics Anonymous and Narcotics Anonymous. As many as 45 percent of participants in the National Prevalence Survey resolved their substance use problems through participation in mutual-aid support programs (Kelly et al., 2017).

Behavior change is a process that occurs over time; it is not an outcome of any one treatment episode (Miller et al., 2011). Everyone must make decisions about important life changes, such as marriage or divorce or buying a house. Sometimes, individuals consult a counselor or other specialist to help with these ordinary decisions, but usually people decide on such changes without professional assistance. Natural change related to substance use also entails decisions to increase, decrease, or stop substance use. Some decisions are responses to critical life events, others reflect different kinds of external pressures, and still others are motivated by personal values.

Exhibit 1.2 illustrates two kinds of natural change. Natural changes related to substance use can go in either direction. In response to an impending divorce, for example, one individual may begin to drink heavily whereas another may reduce or stop using alcohol. Recognizing the processes involved in natural recovery and self-directed change illustrates how changes related to substance use behaviors can be precipitated and stimulated by enhancing motivation.

Exhibit 1.2. Examples of Natural Changes	
Common Natural Changes	Natural Changes in Substance Use
• Going to college • Getting married • Getting divorced	• Stopping drinking after an automobile accident • Reducing alcohol use after college • Stopping substance use before pregnancy

• Changing jobs • Joining the Army • Taking a vacation • Moving • Buying a home • Having a baby • Retiring	• Increasing alcohol use during stressful periods • Decreasing cigarette use after a price increase • Quitting cannabis use before looking for employment • Refraining from drinking with some friends • Reducing consumption following a physician's advice

SOC

Prochaska and DiClemente (1984) theorized that the change process is a journey through stages in which people typically think about behavior change, initiate behavior change, and maintain new behaviors. This model emerged from an examination of 18 psychological and behavioral theories about how change occurs, including components that compose a biopsychosocial framework for understanding addiction. In this sense, the model is "transtheoretical" (Prochaska & DiClemente, 1984). This model has come to be known as the TTM of the SOC. TTM is not the only SOC model, but it is the most widely researched (Connors et al., 2013).

SOC is not a specific counseling method but a framework that can help you tailor specific counseling strategies to clients in different stages. Although results are mixed regarding its usefulness, in the past 30 years, TTM has demonstrated effectiveness in predicting positive addiction treatment outcomes and has shown value as an overarching theoretical framework for counseling (Harrell, Trenz, Scherer, Martins, & Latimer, 2013; Norcross, Krebs, & Prochaska, 2011). Exhibit 1.3 displays the relationship among the five stages (i.e., Precontemplation, Contemplation, Preparation, Action, and Maintenance) in the SOC approach in the original TTM.

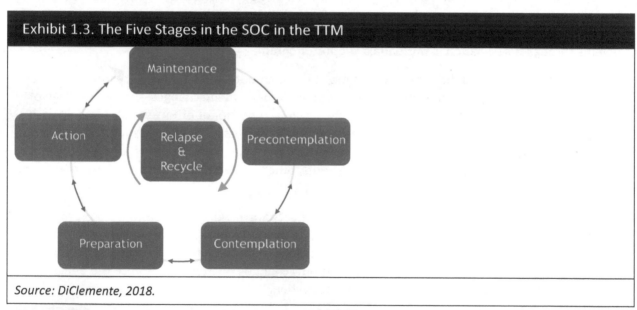

Exhibit 1.3. The Five Stages in the SOC in the TTM

Source: DiClemente, 2018.

The associated features of the SOC approach are (Connors et al., 2013):

• **Precontemplation:** People who use substances are not considering change and do not intend to change in the foreseeable future. They may be partly or completely unaware that a problem exists, that they have to make changes, and that they may need help to change. Alternatively, they may be unwilling or too discouraged to change their behavior. Individuals in this stage often are not convinced that their pattern of use is problematic.

- **Contemplation:** As these individuals become aware that a problem exists, they begin to perceive that there may be cause for concern and reasons to change. Typically, they are ambivalent, simultaneously seeing reasons to change and reasons not to change. Individuals in this stage are still using substances, but they are considering the possibility of stopping or cutting back in the near future. At this point, they may seek relevant information, reevaluate their substance use behavior, or seek help to support the possibility of changing. They typically weigh the positive and negative aspects of making a change. It is not uncommon for individuals to remain in this stage for extended periods, often for years, vacillating between wanting and not wanting to change.

- **Preparation:** When individuals perceive that the envisioned advantages of change and adverse consequences of substance use outweigh the benefits of maintaining the status quo, the decisional balance tips in favor of change. Once initiation of change occurs, individuals enter the Preparation stage and strengthen their commitment. Preparation entails more specific planning for change, such as making choices about whether treatment is needed and, if so, what kind. Preparation also entails examining clients' self-efficacy or confidence in their ability to change. Individuals in the Preparation stage are still using substances, but typically they intend to stop using very soon. They may already be making small changes, like cutting down on their substance use. They begin to set goals for themselves and make commitments to stop using, even telling close associates or significant others about their plans.

- **Action:** Here, individuals choose a strategy for change and begin to pursue it. Clients are actively engaged in changing substance use behaviors. They are making lifestyle changes and may face challenging situations (e.g., temptations to use, physiological effects of withdrawal). Clients may begin to reevaluate their self-image as they move from substance misuse to nonuse or safe use. Clients are committed to the change process and are willing to follow suggested change strategies.

- **Maintenance:** This stage entails efforts to sustain gains made during the Action stage and to prevent recurrence. Extra precautions may be necessary to keep from reverting to health-risk behaviors. Individuals learn to identify situations that may trigger a return to substance use and develop coping skills to manage such situations. During Maintenance, clients are building a new lifestyle that no longer includes the old substance use behaviors.

Most people who misuse substances progress through the stages in a circular or spiral pattern, not a linear one. Individuals typically move back and forth between the stages and cycle through the stages at different rates, as shown in the bidirectional arrows in Exhibit 1.3. As clients progress through the stages, they often have setbacks. However, most people do not typically return to the Precontemplation stage to start over again (Connors et al., 2013) and are unlikely to move from Precontemplation back to Maintenance. This movement through the stages can vary in relation to different behaviors or treatment goals. For example, a client might be in the Action stage with regard to quitting drinking but be in Precontemplation regarding his or her use of cannabis.

Relapse or recurrence of substance misuse is a common part of the process as people cycle through the different stages (note the circular movement of Relapse & Recycle in Exhibit 1.3). Although clients might return to substance misuse during any of the stages, relapse is most often discussed as a setback during the Maintenance stage (Connors et al., 2013). In this model, recurrence is viewed as a normal (not pathological) event because many clients cycle through different stages several times before achieving stable change. Recurrence is not considered a failure but rather a learning opportunity. Remember that each time clients have a setback, they are learning from the experience and applying whatever skills or knowledge they have gained to move forward in the process with greater understanding and awareness.

Counselor Note: Making Decisions

People make decisions about important life changes by weighing potential gains and losses associated with making a choice (Janis & Mann, 1977). Weighing the pros and cons of continuing to use substances or changing substance use behaviors is a key counseling strategy in the SOC model. During Contemplation, pros and cons tend to balance or cancel each other out. In Preparation, pros for changing substance use behavior outweigh cons. When the decisional balance tips toward commitment to change, clients are ready to take action.

Conclusion

Recent understanding of the key role motivation plays in addiction treatment has led to the development of clinical interventions to increase client motivation to change their substance use behaviors (DiClemente et al., 2017). Linking this new view of motivation, the strategies found to enhance it, and the SOC model, along with an understanding of what causes change, creates an effective motivational approach to helping clients with substance misuse and SUDs. This approach encourages clients to progress at their own pace toward deciding about, planning, making, and sustaining positive behavioral change.

In this treatment approach, motivation for change is seen as a dynamic state that you can help the client enhance. Motivational enhancement has evolved, and various myths about clients and what constitutes effective counseling have been dispelled. The notion of the addictive personality has lost credence, and a confrontational style has been discarded or significantly modified. Other factors in contemporary counseling practices have encouraged the development and implementation of motivational interventions, which are client centered and focus on client strengths. Counseling relationships are more likely to rely on empathy rather than authority and involve the client in all aspects of the treatment process. Less-intensive treatments have also become increasingly common.

Motivation is what propels people with SUDs to make changes in their lives. It guides clients through several stages of the SOC that are typical of people thinking about, initiating, and maintaining new behaviors. The remainder of this TIP examines how motivational interventions, when applied to SUD treatment, can help clients move from not even considering changing their behavior to being ready, willing, and able to do so.

This page intentionally left blank.

Chapter 2—Motivational Counseling and Brief Intervention

"The prevalent clinical focus on denial and motivation as client traits was misguided. Indeed, client motivation clearly was a dynamic process responding to a variety of interpersonal influences including advice, feedback, goal setting, contingencies, and perceived choice among alternatives."

Miller & Rollnick, 2013, p. 374

Key Messages

- Personalized feedback about a client's use of substances relative to others and level of health-related risk can enhance client motivation to change substance use behaviors.
- Counselor focus and motivational counseling strategies should be tailored to the client's stage in the Stage of Change (SOC) model.
- Effective motivational counseling approaches can be brief and include a brief intervention (BI) and brief treatment (BT) or comprehensive and include screening, brief intervention, and referral to treatment (SBIRT).

Chapter 2 examines science-informed elements of motivational approaches that are effective in treating substance use disorders (SUDs). Any clinical strategy that enhances client motivation for change is a motivational intervention. Such interventions can include counseling, assessment, and feedback. They can occur over multiple sessions or during one BI, and they can be used in specialty SUD treatment settings or in other healthcare settings. Chapter 2 also highlights what you should focus on in each stage of the SOC approach and discusses how to adapt motivational interventions to be culturally responsive and suitable for clients with co-occurring substance use and mental disorders (CODs).

Elements of Effective Motivational Counseling Approaches

Motivational counseling strategies have been used in a wide variety of settings and with diverse client populations to increase motivation to change substance use behaviors. The following elements are important parts of motivational counseling:

- FRAMES approach
- Decisional balancing
- Developing discrepancy between personal goals and current behavior
- Flexible pacing
- Maintaining contact with clients

FRAMES Approach

Miller and Sanchez (1994) identified six common elements of effective motivational counseling, which are summarized by the acronym FRAMES:

- **F**eedback on personal risk relative to population norms is given to clients after substance use assessment.
- **R**esponsibility for change is placed with the client.
- **A**dvice about changing the client's substance use is given by the counselor nonjudgmentally.

- **M**enu of options and treatment alternatives is offered to the client.

- **E**mpathetic counseling style (i.e., warmth, respect, an understanding) is demonstrated and emphasized by the counselor.

- **S**elf-efficacy is supported by the counselor to encourage client change.

Since FRAMES was developed, research and clinical experience have expanded and refined elements of this motivational counseling approach. FRAMES is often incorporated into SBIRT interventions. It has also been combined with other interventions and tested in diverse settings and cultural contexts (Aldridge, Linford, & Bray, 2017; Manuel et al., 2015; Satre, Manuel, Larios, Steiger, & Satterfield, 2015).

Feedback

Give personalized feedback to clients about their substance use; feedback presented in this way is effective in reducing substance misuse and other health-risk behaviors (Davis, Houck, Rowell, Benson, & Smith, 2015; DiClemente, Corno, Graydon, Wiprovnick, & Knoblach, 2017; Field et al., 2014; Kahler et al., 2018; McDevitt-Murphy et al., 2014; Walker et al., 2017). This type of feedback usually compares a client's scores or ratings on standard screening or assessment instruments with normative data from a general population or treatment groups. Feedback should address cultural differences and norms related to substance misuse. For example, a review of the research on adaptations of BI found that providing feedback specifically related to cultural and social aspects of drinking to Latino clients reduced drinking among these clients to a greater degree than standard feedback (Manuel et al., 2015; Satre et al., 2015).

Counselor Note: Motivational Enhancement Therapy

Motivational enhancement therapy (MET) is an early offshoot of the "drinker's check-up," which gave feedback nonjudgmentally to clients about their drinking. MET is a brief motivational counseling approach that provides personalized, neutral, motivational interviewing (MI)-style feedback to clients. Counselors elicit clients' understanding of feedback, followed by reflections and listening for signs that clients are considering behavioral changes based on the feedback (Miller & Rollnick, 2013). Research on MET shows moderate to strong support for reductions in substance use versus no intervention (DiClemente et al., 2017; Lenz, Rosenbaum, & Sheperis, 2016).

Presenting and discussing assessment results can enhance client motivation to change health-risk behaviors. Providing personalized feedback is sometimes enough to move clients from the Precontemplation stage to Contemplation without additional counseling and guidance.

Structure a feedback session thoughtfully. Establish rapport before giving a client his or her score. Strategies to focus the conversation before offering feedback include the following:

- **Express appreciation** for the client's efforts in providing the information.

- **Ask whether the client had any difficulties** with answering questions or filling out forms. Explore specific questions that might need clarification.

- **Make clear that you may need the client's help** to interpret the findings accurately.

- **Encourage questions:** "I'll be giving you lots of information. Please stop me if you have a question or don't understand something. We have plenty of time today or in the next session, if needed."

- **Stress that the instruments provides objective data.** Give some background, if appropriate, about how the tests are standardized for all populations and how widely they are used.

When you provide feedback, show the client his or her score on any screening or assessment instrument and explain what the score means. Exhibit 2.1 is a sample feedback handout to share with a client after

TIP 35: *Enhancing Motivation for Change in Substance Use Disorder Treatment*
Chapter 3—Motivational Interviewing as a Counseling Style

October 2019

completing the Alcohol Use Disorders Identification Test (AUDIT). Appendix B presents the U.S AUDIT questionnaire and scoring instructions.

Exhibit 2.1. The Drinker's Pyramid Feedback

The AUDIT questionnaire was developed by the World Health Organization to assess alcohol consumption, drinking behaviors, and alcohol-related problems. Your AUDIT score shows the level of health-related risks and other problems associated with your drinking. Higher scores can reflect more serious alcohol-related problems. AUD refers to an alcohol use disorder as defined by the American Psychiatric Association (2013).

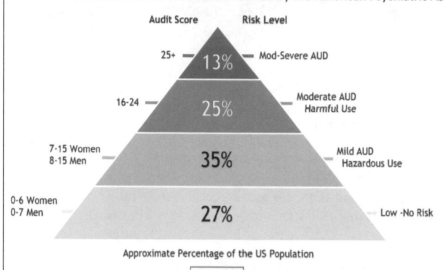

Your score indicates _____

Check here if applicable _____	Check here if applicable _____
Your response to AUDIT Question 3 indicates that you have experienced episodes of binge drinking (e.g., 5 drinks for men and 4 drinks for women consumed within 2 hours on a single occasion). The immediate risks of intoxication or binge drinking include:	Your responses to AUDIT Questions 1 (frequency) and 2 (number of drinks consumed) indicate that you are drinking more than the recommended limits (no more than 3 drinks on a single day and 7 drinks per week for all women and for men older than 65; no more than 4 drinks on a single day and 14 drinks per week for men ages 65 and younger). Long-term risks of alcohol misuse use include:
• Motor crashes or other serious accidents. • Falls and other physical injuries. • Intimate partner violence. • Depressed mood. • Suicidal or homicidal thoughts or behavior. • Unintended firearm injuries. • Alcohol poisoning. • Assaults and sexual assaults. • Unprotected sex (leading to sexually transmitted diseases and unintended pregnancy). • Child abuse and neglect. • Property and other crime. • Fires.	• Gastric distress. • Hypertension. • Cardiovascular disease. • Permanent liver damage. • Cancer. • Pancreatitis. • Diabetes. • Chronic depression. • Neurologic damage. • Fetal alcohol spectrum disorders in newborns (which include physical, behavioral, and learning disabilities).

Sources: Babor, Higgins-Biddle, & Robaina, 2016; Venner, Sánchez, Garcia, Williams, & Sussman, 2018.

Use a motivational style to present the information. Do not pressure clients to accept a diagnosis or offer unsolicited opinions about the meaning of results. Instead, preface explanations with statements like, "I don't know whether this will concern you, but …" or "I don't know what you'll make of this result, but…." Let clients form their own conclusions, but help them by asking, "What do you make of this?" or "What do you think about this?" Focus the conversation on clients' understanding of the feedback.

Strategies for presenting personalized feedback to clients include:

- Asking about the client's initial reaction to the tests (e.g., "Sometimes people learn surprising things when they complete an assessment. What were your reactions to the questionnaire?").

- Providing a handout or using visual aids that show the client's scores on screening instruments, normative data, and risks and consequences of his or her level of substance use (see Exhibit 2.1 above). Written materials should be provided in the client's first language.

- Offering information in a neutral, nonjudgmental, and respectful way.

- Using easy-to-understand and culturally appropriate language.

- Providing small chunks of information.

- Using open questions to explore the client's understanding of the information.

- Using reflective listening and an empathetic counseling style that emphasizes the client's perspective on feedback and how it may have affected the client's readiness to change.

- Summarizing results, including risks and problems that have emerged, the client's reactions, and any change talk the feedback has prompted, then asking the client to add to or correct the summary.

- Providing a written summary to the client.

Clients' responses to feedback differ. One may be alarmed to find that she drinks much more in a given week than comparable peers but be unconcerned about potential health risks of drinking. Another may be concerned about his potential health risks at this level of drinking. The key to using feedback to enhance motivation is to **continue to explore the client's understanding of the information and what it may suggest about possible behavior change.** Personalized feedback is applicable to other health-risk behaviors issues, such as tobacco use (Steinberg, Williams, Stahl, Budsock, & Cooperman, 2015).

Responsibility

Use a motivational approach to encourage clients to actively participate in the change process by reinforcing personal autonomy. Individuals have the choice of continuing their behavior or changing it. Remind clients that it is up to them to make choices about whether they will change their substance use behaviors or enter treatment. Reinforcing personal autonomy is aligned with the self-determination theory discussed in Chapter 1 (Deci & Ryan, 2012; Flannery, 2017).

Strategies for emphasizing client responsibility include the following:

- Ask clients' permission to talk about their substance use; invite them to consider the information you are presenting. If clients have choices, they feel less need to oppose or dismiss your ideas.

- State clearly that you will not ask clients to do anything they are unwilling to do. Let them know that it is up to them to make choices about behavior change.

- Determine a common agenda for each session.

- Agree on treatment goals that are acceptable to clients.

When clients realize they are responsible for the change process, they feel empowered and more invested in it. This results in better treatment outcomes (Deci & Ryan, 2012).

TIP 35: *Enhancing Motivation for Change in Substance Use Disorder Treatment*
Chapter 3—Motivational Interviewing as a Counseling Style

October 2019

Advice

Practice the act of giving advice; this simple act can promote positive behavioral change. BI that includes advice delivered in the MET/MI counseling style can be effective in changing substance use behaviors such as drinking, drug use, and tobacco use (DiClemente et al., 2017; Steinberg et al., 2015). As with feedback, the manner in which you advise clients influences how or whether the client will use your advice. It is better **not to tell** people what to do; **suggestions** yield better results. A motivational approach to offering advice may be either directive (making a suggestion) or educational (providing information). Educational advice should be based on credible scientific evidence, such as safe drinking limits recommended by the National Institute on Alcohol Abuse and Alcoholism or facts that relate to the client's conditions (e.g., blood alcohol concentration levels at the time of an automobile crash).

Expert Comment: A Realistic Model of Change—Advice to Clients

Throughout the treatment process, clients should have permission to talk about their problems with substance use. During these dialogs, I often point out some of the realities of the recovery process:

- Most change does not occur overnight.
- Change is best viewed as a gradual process with occasional setbacks, much like hiking up a bumpy hill.
- Difficulties and setbacks can be reframed as learning experiences, not failures.

Linda C. Sobell, Ph.D., Consensus Panel Member

Strategies for offering advice include the following:

- **Ask permission** to offer suggestions or provide information. For example, "Would you like to hear about safe drinking limits?" or "Can I tell you what tolerance to alcohol is?" Such questions provide a nondirective opportunity to share your knowledge about substance use in a respectful manner.
- **Ask what the client thinks** about your suggestions or information.
- **Ask for clarification** if the client makes a specific request, rather than give advice immediately.
- **Offer simple suggestions** that match the client's level of understanding and readiness, the urgency of the situation, and his or her culture. In some cultures, a directive approach is required to convey the importance of advice or situations; in others, a directive style is considered rude and intrusive.

This style of giving advice requires patience. The timing of any advice is important, relying on your ability to hear what clients are requesting and willing to receive. Chapter 3 provides more information about the structured format used in MI for offering clients feedback or giving advice.

Expert Comment: The PIES Approach

In World War I, military psychiatrists first realized that motivational interventions, done at the right time, could return many stressed soldiers to duty. To remember this method, they used the acronym PIES:

- **P**roximity: Provide treatment near the place of duty; don't evacuate to a hospital.
- **I**mmediacy: Intervene and treat at the first sign of the problem.
- **E**xpectancy: Expect the intervention to be successful and return the person to duty.
- **S**implicity: Listen, offer empathy, and show understanding; this simple approach works best.

Highlight that the person's reactions are normal; it is the situation that is abnormal. The person will recover with rest and nourishment. No prolonged or complex therapy is needed for most cases. In the context of World War I, evacuation to higher levels of care was reserved for the low percentage of individuals who did not respond to this straightforward approach.

Kenneth J. Hoffman, M.D., Field Reviewer

Menu of options

Offer choices to facilitate treatment initiation and engagement. These choices have been shown to enhance the therapeutic alliance, decrease dropout rates, and improve outcomes (Van Horn et al., 2015). Clients are more likely to adhere to a specific change strategy if they can choose from a menu of options. Giving clients choices for treatment goals and types of available service increases their motivation to participate in treatment.

Strategies for offering a menu of options include the following:

- Provide accurate information on each option and potential implications for choosing that option.
- Elicit from clients which options they think would work or what has worked for them in the past.
- Brainstorm alternative options if none offered are acceptable to clients.

Providing a menu of options is consistent with the motivational principle of supporting client autonomy and responsibility. Clients feel more empowered when they take responsibility for their choices. Your role is to enhance their ability to make informed choices. When clients make independent decisions, they are likely to be more committed to them. This concept is examined more fully in Chapter 6.

Empathic counseling style

Use an empathic counseling style by showing active interest in understanding clients' perspectives (Miller & Rollnick, 2013). Counselors who show high levels of empathy are curious, spend time exploring clients' ideas about their substance use, show an active interest in what clients are saying, and often encourage clients to elaborate on more than just the content of their story (Miller & Rollnick, 2013). Counselor empathy is a moderately strong predictor of client treatment outcomes (Elliot, Bohart, Watson, & Murphy, 2018).

As explained in Chapter 3, reflective listening effectively communicates empathy. The client does most of the talking when a counselor uses an empathic style. It is your responsibility to create a safe environment that encourages a free flow of communication with the client. An empathic style appears easy to adopt, but it requires training and significant effort on your part. This counseling style can be particularly effective with clients in the Precontemplation stage.

Self-efficacy

Help clients build self-efficacy by being supportive, identifying their strengths, reviewing past successes, and expressing optimism and confidence in their ability to change (Kaden & Litt, 2011). To succeed in changing, clients must believe they can undertake specific tasks in a specific situation (Bandura, 1977). In addiction treatment, self-efficacy usually refers to clients' ability to identify high-risk situations that trigger their urge to drink or use drugs and to develop coping skills to manage that urge and not return to substance use. Considerable evidence points to self-efficacy as an important factor in addiction treatment outcomes (Kadden & Litt, 2011; Kuerbis, Armeli, Muench, & Morgenstern, 2013; Litt & Kadden, 2015; Morgenstern et al., 2016).

Ask clients to identify how they have successfully coped with problems in the past: "How did you get from where you were to where you are now?" or "How have you resisted the urge to use in stressful situations?" Once you identify strengths, you can help clients build on past successes. Affirm small steps and reinforce any positive changes. Self-efficacy is discussed again in Chapters 3, 5, and 7.

TIP 35: *Enhancing Motivation for Change in Substance Use Disorder Treatment*
Chapter 3—Motivational Interviewing as a Counseling Style

October 2019

Decisional Balancing

Explore with the client the benefits and drawbacks of change (Janis & Mann, 1977). Individuals naturally explore the pros and cons of any major life choice, such as changing jobs or getting married. In SUD recovery, the client weighs the pros and cons of changing versus not changing substance use behaviors. You assist this process by asking the client to articulate the positive and negative aspects of using substances. This process is usually called decisional balancing and is further described in Chapter 5.

Exploring the pros and cons of substance use behaviors can tip the scales toward a decision for positive change. The actual number of reasons a client lists on each side of a decisional balance sheet is not as important as the weight—or personal value—of each. For example, a 20-year-old who smokes cigarettes may put less weight on getting lung cancer than an older adult, but he may be very concerned that his diminished lung capacity interferes with playing basketball.

Developing Discrepancy

To enhance motivation for change, **help clients recognize any discrepancy or gap between their future goals and their current behavior.** You might clarify this discrepancy by asking, "How does drinking fit or not fit with your goal of improving your family relationships?" When individuals see that present actions conflict with important personal goals, such as good health, job success, or close personal relationships, change is more likely to occur (Miller & Rollnick, 2013). This concept is expanded in Chapter 3.

Flexible Pacing

Assess the client's readiness for change; resist your urges to go faster than the client's pace. Every client moves through the SOC at his or her own pace. Some will cycle back and forth numerous times between stages. Others need time to resolve their ambivalence about current substance use before making a change. A few are ready to get started and take action immediately. Knowing where a client has been and is now in the SOC helps you facilitate the change process at the right pace. Be aware of any discrepancies between where you want the client to be and where he or she actually is in the SOC. For example, if a client is still in the Contemplation stage, your suggestion to take steps that are in the Action stage can create discord.

Flexible pacing requires you to meet clients at their level and allow them as much or as little time as they need to address the essential tasks of each stage in the SOC. For example, with some clients, you may have to schedule frequent sessions at the beginning of treatment and fewer later. In other cases, clients might need a break from the intensity of treatment to focus on specific aspect of recovery. If you push clients at a faster pace than they are ready to take, the treatment alliance may break down.

Maintaining Contact With Clients

Employ simple activities to enhance continuity of contact between you and the client. Such activities may include personal handwritten letters, telephone calls, texts, or emails. Use these simple motivation-enhancing interventions to encourage clients to return for another counseling session, return to treatment following a missed appointment, and stay involved in treatment.

Activities that foster consistent, ongoing contact with clients strengthen the therapeutic alliance. The treatment alliance is widely recognized as a significant factor in treatment outcomes in most treatment methods including addiction counseling (Brorson, Arnevik, Rand-Hendriksen, & Duckert, 2013). Low alliance predicts higher risk of clients dropping out of treatment (Brorson et al., 2013).

Make sure you and your clients follow all agency policies and ethical guidelines for making contact

TIP 35: *Enhancing Motivation for Change in Substance Use Disorder Treatment*
Chapter 3—Motivational Interviewing as a Counseling Style

October 2019

outside of sessions or after discharge. For more information on using technology to maintain contact with clients, see Treatment Improvement Protocol (TIP) 60: *Using Technology-Based Therapeutic Tools in Behavioral Health Services* (Substance Abuse and Mental Health Services Administration [SAMHSA], 2015b).

Motivational Counseling and the SOC

People considering major changes in their lives, such as adopting an alcohol- or drug-free lifestyle, go through different change processes. Your job as a counselor is to match your treatment focus and counseling strategies with these processes throughout the SOC.

Catalysts for Change

Understand how catalysts for change operate. This will help you use motivational counseling strategies that support and enhance changes clients are contemplating. Prochaska (1979) identified common personal growth processes linked to different behavioral counseling approaches. These processes or catalysts for change have been further developed and applied to the SOC model (Connors, DiClemente, Velasquez, & Donovan, 2013). Catalysts are experiential or behavioral (Exhibit 2.2). Experiential catalysts are linked more frequently with early SOC phases and behavioral catalysts with later SOC phases.

Exhibit 2.2. Catalysts for Change

Type	Specific Client Change Processes	SOC
Experiential	**Consciousness raising:** Gains new awareness and understanding of substance use behavior.	Precontemplation/Contemplation
	Emotional arousal: Is motivated to contemplate change after an important emotional reaction to current substance use behavior or the need to change.	Precontemplation/Contemplation
	Environmental reevaluation: Evaluates pros and cons of current substance use behavior and its effects on others and the community.	Precontemplation/Contemplation
	Self-reevaluation: Explores the current substance use behavior and the possibility of change in relation to own values.	Contemplation
	Social liberation: Recognizes and increases available positive social supports.	Contemplation/Preparation
Behavioral	**Counterconditioning:** Begins to recognize the links between internal and external cues to use substances and experiments with substituting more healthful behaviors and activities in response to those cues.	Preparation/Action
	Helping relationships: Seeks and cultivates relationships that offer support, acceptance, and reinforcement for positive behavioral change.	Preparation/Action/Maintenance
	Self-liberation: Begins to believe in ability to make choices/to change. Develops enhanced self-efficacy and commits to changing substance use behaviors.	Preparation/Action/Maintenance
	Stimulus control: Avoids stimuli and cues that could trigger substance use.	Action
	Reinforcement management: Begins to self-reward positive behavioral changes and eliminates reinforcements for substance use.	Action/Maintenance

TIP 35: *Enhancing Motivation for Change in Substance Use Disorder Treatment*
Chapter 3—Motivational Interviewing as a Counseling Style

October 2019

Counselor Focus in the SOC

Use motivational supports that match the client's SOC. If you try to use strategies appropriate to a stage other than the one the client is in, the client might drop out or not follow through on treatment goals. For example, if a client in Contemplation is ambivalent about changing substance use behaviors and you argue for change or jump into the Preparation stage, the client is likely to become reactive.

Examples of how to tailor motivation support to the client's stage in the SOC include helping the client:

- In Precontemplation consider change by increasing awareness of behavior change.
- In Contemplation resolve ambivalence by helping him or her choose positive change over the current situation.
- In Preparation identify potential change strategies and choose the most appropriate one for the circumstances.
- In Action carry out and follow through with the change strategies.
- In Maintenance develop new skills to maintain recovery and a lifestyle without substance misuse. If misuse resumes, help the client recover as fast as possible; support reentering the change cycle.

Exhibit 2.3 depicts the overarching counseling focus in each stage. Chapters 4 through 7 examine specific counseling strategies for each stage.

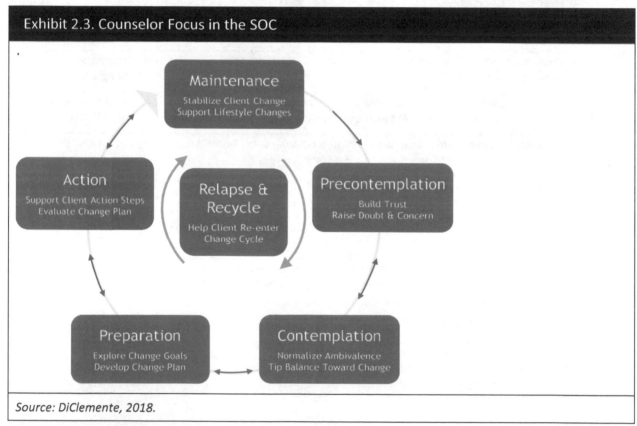

Exhibit 2.3. Counselor Focus in the SOC

Source: DiClemente, 2018.

Special Applications of Motivational Interventions

The principles underlying motivational counseling approaches have been applied across cultures, to different types of problems, in various treatment settings, and with many different populations (Miller & Rollnick, 2013). The research literature suggests that motivational interventions (i.e., MI, MET, and BI)

TIP 35: *Enhancing Motivation for Change in Substance Use Disorder Treatment*
Chapter 3—Motivational Interviewing as a Counseling Style

October 2019

are associated with successful outcomes including adherence to and retention in SUD treatment; reduction in or abstinence from alcohol, cannabis, illicit drugs, and tobacco use; and reductions in substance misuse consequences and related problems (DiClemente et al., 2017). Motivational interventions have demonstrated efficacy across ages (i.e., adolescents, young adults, and older adults), genders, and racial and ethnic groups (Lenz et al., 2016).

Special applications of motivational approaches have been successfully employed as stand-alone or add-on interventions for people with diabetes, chronic pain, cardiovascular disease, HIV, CODs, eating disorders, and opioid use disorder, as well as for pregnant women who drink or use illicit drugs (Alperstein & Sharpe, 2016; Barnes & Ivezaj, 2015; Dillard, Zuniga, & Holstad, 2017; Ekong & Kavookjian, 2016; Hunt, Siegfried, Morley, Sitharthan, & Cleary, 2013,: Ingersoll, Ceperich, Hettema, Farrell-Carnahan, & Penberthy, 2013; Lee, Choi, Yum, Yu, & Chair, 2016; Moore, Flamez, & Szirony, 2017; Mumba, Findlay, & Snow, 2018; Osterman, Lewis, & Winhusen, 2017; Soderlund, 2017; Vella-Zarb, Mills, Westra, Carter, & Keating, 2014). The universality of motivational intervention concepts permits broad application and offers great potential to reach diverse clients with many types of problems and in many settings.

Cultural Responsiveness

Clients in treatment for SUDs differ in ethnic, racial, and cultural backgrounds. Research and experience suggest that the change process is similar across different populations. The principles and mechanisms of enhancing motivation to change seem to be broadly applicable. For example, one study found that MI was one of two evidence-based treatments endorsed as culturally appropriate by a majority of surveyed SUD treatment programs serving American Indian and Alaska Native (AI/AN) clients (Novins, Croy, Moore, & Rieckmann, 2016).

"Processes for engaging do differ across cultures, but listening lies at the heart of nearly all of them. Good listening crosses cultures as well. It stretches the imagination to think of people who don't appreciate being welcomed, heard, understood, affirmed, and recognized as autonomous human beings. In our experience these are universally valued."–Miller & Rollnick, 2013, p. 349

There may be important differences among populations and cultural contexts regarding expression of motivation for change and the importance of critical life events. Get familiar with the populations with whom you expect to establish treatment relationships, be open to listening to and learning from clients about their cultures and their own theories of change, and adapt motivational counseling approaches in consideration of specific cultural norms (Ewing, Wray, Mead, & Adams, 2012). For example, a manual for adapting MI for use in treating AI/AN populations includes a spiritual component that uses a prayer to describe MI and several spiritual ceremonies to explain MI (Venner, Feldstein, & Tafoya, 2006).

MI's core elements, including its emphasis on collaboration, evoking clients' perspectives, and honoring clients' autonomy, align well culturally with African Americans (Harley, 2017; Montgomery, Robinson, Seaman, & Haeny, 2017). However, some African American women may be less comfortable with a purely client-centered approach (Ewing et al., 2012). Viable approaches to adapting MI for African Americans include training peers to deliver MI, incorporating moderate amounts of advice, and implementing MI approaches in community settings such as a local church (Harley, 2017).

Because motivational strategies emphasize the client's responsibility to voice personal goals and values as well as to select among options for change, you should respond in a nonjudgmental way to cultural differences. Cultural differences might be reflected in the value of health, the meaning of time, the meaning of alcohol or drug use, or responsibilities to community and family. Try to understand the

TIP 35: *Enhancing Motivation for Change in Substance Use Disorder Treatment*
Chapter 3—Motivational Interviewing as a Counseling Style

October 2019

client's perspective rather than impose mainstream values or make quick judgments. This requires knowledge of the influences that promote or sustain substance use and enhance motivation to change among different populations. Motivation-enhancing strategies should be congruent with a client's cultural and social principles, standards, and expectations. Exhibit 2.4 provides a mnemonic to help you remember the basic principles of cultural responsiveness.

Exhibit 2.4. RESPECT: A Mnemonic for Cultural Responsiveness	
Respect	Understand how respect is shown in different cultures and demonstrate it through verbal and nonverbal communication.
Explanatory model	Explore the client's understanding about his or her substance use and any cultural beliefs or attitudes about substance misuse and how people change.
Sociocultural context	Recognize how class, gender, race, ethnicity, sexual or gender identity, age, socioeconomic status, and other personal characteristics that might affect treatment.
Power	Acknowledge the power differential between the counselor and the client.
Empathy	Express empathy in ways that communicate that you are genuinely interested in the client's perspective and concerns.
Concerns and fears	Elicit client concerns about seeking help and entering treatment.
Trust/therapeutic alliance	Recognize that trust must be earned, and demonstrate actions that enhance the therapeutic relationship.

Source: SAMHSA, 2014a.

Expert Comment: Cultural Responsiveness

In my practice with persons who have different worldviews, I've made a number of observations on the ways in which culture influences the change process. I try to pay attention to cultural effects on a person's style of receiving and processing information, making decisions, pacing, and being ready to act. The more clients are assimilated into the surrounding culture, the more likely they are to process information, respond, and make choices that are congruent with mainstream beliefs and styles. The responsibility for being aware of different cultural value systems lies with the provider, not the client being treated.

More specifically, the manner in which a person communicates, verbally and nonverbally, is often directly related to culture. One young American Indian stated on initial contact that he "might not be able to come back because his shoes were too tight." This was his way of saying he had no money.

However, ethnicity doesn't always determine the culture or values one chooses to live by. For example, White Americans may adopt Eastern worldviews and value systems. Furthermore, an advanced education doesn't necessarily indicate one's degree of assimilation or acculturation. Asian Americans or African Americans who are well educated may choose to live according to their traditional cultural value system and process information for change accordingly.

Culture is a powerful contributor to defining one's identity. Not having a healthy ethnic sense of self affects all stages of the change process. To have a strong sense of self, you have to be powerful in the areas of being, knowing, doing, and having. Racially and ethnically diverse individuals who have been raised in environments that isolate them from their own cultures may not have accurate information about their ethnicity and may not develop a healthy ethnic sense of self.

TIP 35: *Enhancing Motivation for Change in Substance Use Disorder Treatment*
Chapter 3—Motivational Interviewing as a Counseling Style

October 2019

> I believe counselors who use MET need to know different cultural value systems and be culturally sensitive. If in doubt of the client's beliefs, explore them with the client. Acknowledging and honoring differing cultural worldviews greatly influence both motivational style and therapeutic outcome.
>
> *Rosalyn Harris-Offutt, Consensus Panel Member*

Understand not just how a client's cultural values encourage change, but how they may present barriers to change. Some clients identify strongly with cultural or religious traditions and work hard to gain respect from elders or group leaders. Others find membership or participation in such groups unhelpful. Some cultures support involvement of family members in counseling; others find this disrespectful.

Know what personal and material resources are available to clients, and be sensitive to issues of poverty, social isolation, historical trauma, and recent losses. Recognize that access to financial and social resources is an important part of the motivation for and process of change. Poverty and lack of resources make change more difficult. It is hard to affirm self-efficacy and stimulate hope and optimism in clients who lack material resources and have experienced discrimination. You can firmly acknowledge the facts of the situation yet still enhance hope and motivation to change by affirming clients' strengths and capacity for endurance and growth despite difficult circumstances. For more information on cultural issues in treatment, see TIP 59: *Improving Cultural Competence* (SAMHSA, 2014a).

Adults With COD

Substance use and mental disorders often co-occur. According to 2017 data from the National Survey on Drug Use and Health (SAMHSA, 2018), 46.6 million adults ages 18 and older (19 percent of all U.S. adults) had any mental illness during the previous year, including 11.2 million (4.5 percent of all adults) with serious mental illness (SMI). Of this 46.6 million, 18 percent also had an SUD versus only 5 percent of adults without any mental illness in the past year. Of the 11.2 million adults with an SMI in the previous year, almost 28 percent also had a co-occurring SUD.

Even low levels of substance misuse can have a serious impact on the functioning of people with SMI (Hunt et al., 2013). For example, AUD often co-occurs with major depressive disorder (MDD), which results in greater disease burdens than either disorder separately (Riper et al., 2014). MI and MI combined with cognitive–behavioral therapy produce positive treatment outcomes, such as reductions in alcohol consumption, cannabis use, alcohol misuse, and depression and other psychiatric symptoms like anxiety (Baker et al., 2014; Baker, Thornton, Hiles, Hides, & Lubman, 2012; Riper et al., 2014; Satre, Delucchi, Lichtmacher, Sterling, & Weisner, 2013; Satre, Leibowitz, et al., 2016).

Having any mental disorder increases the risk of substance misuse. As indicated in TIP 42: *Substance Abuse Treatment for Persons With Co-Occurring Disorders* (SAMHSA, 2013), clients with mental illness or COD may find it harder to engage and remain in treatment. **Motivational interventions that engage and retain clients in treatment, increase motivation to adhere to treatment interventions, and reduce substance use are a good fit for these clients.** A meta-analysis of randomized controlled treatment studies of people with SMI and substance misuse found that, although MI was not any more effective, in general, than other psychosocial treatments, clients who participated in an MI group reported to their first aftercare appointment significantly more often than clients in other treatment interventions and these clients had greater alcohol abstinence rates (Hunt et al., 2013). Another meta-analysis found that MI-based interventions emphasizing adherence to treatment significantly improved adherence and psychiatric symptoms (Wong-Anuchit, Chantamit-O-Pas, Schneider, & Mills, 2018). Dual Diagnosis MI (DDMI), a modified version of MI for adults with CODs, can effectively increase task-specific motivation and adherence to cognitive training interventions (Fiszdon, Kurtz, Choi, Bell, & Martino, 2015).

TIP 35: *Enhancing Motivation for Change in Substance Use Disorder Treatment*
Chapter 3—Motivational Interviewing as a Counseling Style

October 2019

Counselor Note: Dual Diagnosis Motivational Interviewing

DDMI is a two-session intervention for substance misuse in clients with psychotic disorders (Fiszdon et al., 2015). It includes accommodations for cognitive impairments such as:

- Asking questions and reflecting in simple terms.
- Repeating information and summarizing session content frequently.
- Providing more structure to sessions.
- Being sensitive to emotional material.
- Using simple, concrete examples.
- Presenting information using visual aids and written materials.
- Restating information frequently.
- Going at a slower pace.
- Allowing pauses so clients can process questions, reflections, and information.

Motivational interventions for SMI and co-occurring SUDs should be modified to take into account potential cognitive impairment and focused on specific tasks that lead to the accomplishment of treatment goals, as defined by each client. For more information, see TIP 42: *Substance Abuse Treatment for Persons With Co-Occurring Disorders* (SAMHSA, 2013).

Expert Comment: MI for Adults With COD

I became interested in MI when my team and I were trying to improve the rate of attendance at aftercare appointments for clients with COD discharged from our psychiatric units. So, my team and I decided to investigate MI's effectiveness with clients with COD. We randomly assigned half of our clients to standard treatment, in which they received standard inpatient psychiatric care, including standard discharge planning where the team would encourage and explain the importance of aftercare. The other half were assigned to standard treatment but also received a motivational assessment, feedback on the results at admission, and a 1-hour MI just before discharge.

We found that clients in the MI group attended their first outpatient appointment at a rate that was two and a half times greater than the standard treatment group. MI with virtually no modification, was effective, particularly for clients with very low motivation. This could have been because these clients were more verbal about their ambivalence than others and because we viewed MI as a perfect way to resolve ambivalence. Another thing we learned was that asking clients about why they would **not attend** aftercare had surprise value and greatly enhanced the rapport between therapist and client. It appeared to let clients know that we were not only going to tell them about the importance of aftercare, but that we were actually willing to discuss their ambivalence about it.

Clients were also surprised when we did not directly counter their reasons for not going to aftercare. For example, if a client said, "I'm better now, I don't need aftercare," we would not say, "But to stay well, you need to continue your treatment." Instead, we used **open end questions** (e.g., "What do you think helped you get better?" or "Tell me more about that") or **amplified reflection** (e.g., "So, you're saying you probably won't need any other treatment ever again" or, for more fragile clients, "It's hard for you to imagine a reason why you might continue to need treatment"). When clients offered specific disadvantages of pursuing aftercare, such as loss of time from work or negative reactions from family, we similarly responded with open end questions and reflective listening (e.g., "It sounds like your job is very important to you and that you wouldn't want anything to get in the way of that"). Frequently such questions and reflections would lead a client to counter his or her own statements. It turned out that client could sell themselves on the idea of aftercare better than we ever could, and MI gave us the perfect method for facilitating this process. What was most important, however, was what we did **not** do—namely, argue with the client or even attempt to therapeutically dispute his or her (sometimes) illogical ideas about aftercare. Instead, we waited for kernels of motivation and simply shaped them along until the client finally heard himself or herself arguing in favor of seeking further services.

Michael V. Pantalon, Ph.D., Field Reviewer

Brief Motivational Interventions

A growing trend worldwide is to view substance misuse in a much broader context than diagnosable SUDs. The recognition that people who misuse substances make up a much larger group—and pose a serious and costly public health threat—than the smaller number of people needing specialized addiction treatment is not always reflected in the organization and availability of treatment services. As part of a movement toward early identification of alcohol misuse and the development of effective and low-cost methods to ameliorate this widespread problem, BI strategies, which include motivational components, are widely disseminated in the United States and other countries (Joseph & Basu, 2016).

The impetus to expand the use of BI is a response to:

- The need for a broader base of treatment and prevention components to serve all segments of the population that have minimal to severe use and misuse patterns.

- The need for cost-effective interventions that satisfy cost-containment policies in an era of managed health care (Babor, Del Boca, & Bray, 2017).

- A growing body of research findings that consistently demonstrate the efficacy of BI relative to no intervention (DiClemente et al., 2017).

BI is a structured, person-centered counseling approach that can be delivered by trained health and behavioral health professionals in one to four sessions and typically lasts from 5 to 30 minutes (Mattoo, Prasad, & Gosh, 2018). Even single-session interventions incorporating MET/MI modalities have demonstrated effectiveness in reducing substance use behaviors (Samson & Tanner-Smith, 2015). BI for individuals who use substances are applied most often outside specialty addiction treatment settings (in what are often referred to as **opportunistic** settings), where clients are not seeking help for an SUD but have come, for example, to seek medical attention or treatment for a mental disorder (Mattoo et al., 2018). In these situations, people seeking services are routinely screened for substance misuse or asked about their substance use patterns. Those found to be misusing substances or who have related problems receive a specific BI.

Expert Comment: BI in the Emergency Department

When I apply an MI style in my practice of emergency medicine, I experience considerable professional satisfaction. Honestly, it's a struggle to let go of the need to be the expert in charge. It helps to recognize that the person I'm talking with in these medical encounters is also an expert—an expert in her own lifestyle, needs, and choices.

After learning about the FRAMES principles in 1987, I tried them once or twice, and they worked, so I tried them again and again. This is not to say that I don't fall back to old ways and sometimes ask someone, "Do you want to go to detox?" But more often than not, I try to ask permission to discuss each individual's substance use. I ask clients to help me understand what they enjoy about using substances and then what they enjoy less about it. Clients often tell me they like to get high because it helps them relax and forget their problems and it's a part of their social life. But they say they don't like getting sick from drugs. They don't like their family avoiding them or having car crashes. I listen attentively and reflect back what I understood each person to have said, summarize, and ask, "Where does this leave you?" I also inquire about how ready they are to change their substance use on a scale of 1 to 10. If someone is low on the scale, I inquire about what it will take to move forward. If someone is high on the scale, indicating readiness to change, I ask what this person thinks would work to change his or her substance use.

TIP 35: *Enhancing Motivation for Change in Substance Use Disorder Treatment*
Chapter 3—Motivational Interviewing as a Counseling Style

October 2019

> If a client expresses interest in treatment, I explore pros and cons of different choices. An emergency department (ED) specialist in SUDs then works with the person to find placement in a program and, if needed, provides a transportation voucher. This systematic approach, which incorporates MI principles, is helpful to me in our hectic practice setting. It's not only ethically sound, based as it is on respect for the individual's autonomy, but it's less time consuming and frustrating. Each person does the work for himself or herself by naming the problem and identifying possible solutions. My role is to facilitate that process.
>
> *Ed Bernstein, M.D., Consensus Panel Member*

The purpose of a BI is usually to counsel individuals, using a motivational approach, about substance misuse patterns; increase awareness about the negative effects of substance misuse; and advise them to limit or stop their use altogether, depending on the circumstances (Nunes, Richmond, Marzano, Swenson, & Lockhart, 2017). If the initial intervention does not result in substantial improvement, the provider can make a referral for specialized SUD treatment. A BI also can explore the pros and cons of entering treatment and present a menu of options for treatment, as well as facilitate contact with the treatment system. There are several BI models, but FRAMES is the dominant BI method for substance misuse (Mattoo et al., 2018).

BI strategies have been used effectively in SUD treatment settings where people seek assistance but are placed on waiting lists, as a motivational prelude to engagement and participation in more intensive treatment, and as a first attempt to facilitate behavior change. A series of BI can constitute BT, an approach that applies motivational and other treatment methods (e.g., cognitive–behavioral therapy) for a limited timeframe, making the modality particularly effective for clients who want to abstain from, instead of reduce, alcohol or drug use (Barbosa et al., 2017). Research has found that BT may be more effective than BI in reducing illicit drug use patterns (Aldridge, Dowd, & Bray, 2017).

Screening, Brief Intervention, and Referral to Treatment

A specific BI called SBIRT, which adds screening and referral components, has been implemented widely in the United States in diverse settings, including EDs, primary care offices, and community-based health clinics, through a SAMHSA multisite initiative (Babor et al., 2017). It is the largest SBIRT dissemination effort in the United States (Aldridge, Linford, & Bray, 2017). SBIRT was specifically developed for nonspecialized treatment settings. It has demonstrated effectiveness in primary care offices, EDs, and general inpatient medical units in reducing substance use and misuse among adolescents, young adults, and adults, as well as in increasing participation in follow-up care (Barata et al., 2017; DiClemente et al., 2017; Kohler & Hoffman, 2015; McQueen, Howe, Allan, Mains, & Hardy, 2015; Merchant, Romanoff, Zhang, Liu, & Baird, 2017; Timko, Kong, Vittorio, & Cucciare, 2016; Woolard et al., 2013).

People often seek treatment for medical concerns that may be related to or impacted by substance misuse but are not specifically seeking help for substance use problems. Screening has become an integral component of BI in these opportunistic settings (Mattoo et al., 2018). The results of the screening determine whether the person seeking services is offered a BI such as FRAMES or is referred to specialized addiction treatment when the person meets the criteria for moderate or severe SUD. From a public health perspective, SBIRT is seen as both a prevention and a treatment strategy. Although, research results about the effectiveness of SBIRT for illicit drug use are mixed (Hingson & Compton, 2014), recent outcome data from a SAMHSA initiative demonstrate its effectiveness to lower alcohol consumption, alcohol misuse, and illicit drug use (Aldridge, Linford, & Bray, 2017). Other studies found that initiation of buprenorphine treatment in the ED significantly increased clients' engagement in specialty addiction treatment and decreased illicit drug use (Bernstein & D'Onofrio, 2017) and that motivational interventions in ED and public health settings reduced overdose risk behaviors and

TIP 35: *Enhancing Motivation for Change in Substance Use Disorder Treatment*
Chapter 3—Motivational Interviewing as a Counseling Style

October 2019

nonmedical use of opioids (Bohnert et al., 2016; Coffin et al., 2017).

In addition, a growing body of evidence supports the use of SBIRT with adolescents, young adults, adults, and older adults, as well as ethnically and culturally diverse populations, particularly with careful selection of screening tools and tailoring the BI and referrals to each client's needs (Appiah-Brempong, Okyere, Owusu-Addo, & Cross, 2014; Gelberg et al., 2017; Manuel et al., 2015; Satre et al., 2015; Schonfeld et al., 2010; Tanner-Smith & Lipsey, 2015). For information about an SBIRT initiative for older adults (the BRITE Project), see the upcoming TIP on *Treating Addiction in Older Adults* (SAMHSA, planned).

Conclusion

Motivational interventions can be used in BI, in BT, and throughout the SOC process. Some strategies, like screening and FRAMES, are more applicable to BI methods whereas others, like developing discrepancy and decisional balancing, are more useful in specialized addiction counseling settings where clients receive longer and more intensive treatment. What is common in all motivational interventions, no matter the treatment setting or the client population, is the focus on engaging clients, building trust through empathetic listening, and demonstrating respect for clients' autonomy and cultural customs and perspectives.

TIP 35: *Enhancing Motivation for Change in Substance Use Disorder Treatment*
Chapter 3—Motivational Interviewing as a Counseling Style

October 2019

Chapter 3—Motivational Interviewing as a Counseling Style

"Motivational interviewing is a person-centered counseling style for addressing the common problem of ambivalence about change."

Miller & Rollnick, 2013, p. 21

Key Messages

- The spirit of motivational interviewing (MI) is the foundation of the counseling skills required for enhancing clients' motivation to change.
- Ambivalence about change is normal; resolving clients' ambivalence about substance use is a key MI focus.
- Resistance to change is an expression of ambivalence about change, not a client trait or characteristic.
- Reflective listening is fundamental to the four MI process (i.e., engaging, focusing, evoking, and planning) and core counseling strategies.

Chapter 3 explores specific MI strategies you can use to help clients who misuse substances or who have substance use disorders (SUDs) strengthen their motivation and commitment to change their substance use behaviors. This chapter examines what's new in MI, the spirit of MI, the concept of ambivalence, core counseling skills, and the four processes of MI, as well as the effectiveness of MI in treating SUDs.

Introduction to MI

MI is a counseling style based on the following assumptions:

- Ambivalence about substance use and change is normal and is an important motivational barrier to substance use behavior change.
- Ambivalence can be resolved by exploring the client's intrinsic motivations and values.
- Your alliance with the client is a collaborative partnership to which you each bring important expertise.
- An empathic, supportive counseling style provides conditions under which change can occur.

You can use MI to effectively reduce or eliminate client substance use and other health-risk behaviors in many settings and across genders, ages, races, and ethnicities (DiClemente, Corno, Graydon, Wiprovnick, & Knoblach, 2017; Dillard, Zuniga, & Holstad, 2017; Lundahl et al., 2013). Analysis of more than 200 randomized clinical trials found significant efficacy of MI in the treatment of SUDs (Miller & Rollnick, 2014).

The MI counseling style helps clients resolve ambivalence that keeps them from reaching personal goals. MI builds on Carl Rogers' (1965) humanistic theories about people's capacity for exercising free choice and self-determination. Rogers identified the sufficient conditions for client change, which are now called "common factors" of therapy, including counselor empathy (Miller & Moyers, 2017).

As a counselor, your main goals in MI are to express empathy and elicit clients' reasons for and commitment to changing substance use behaviors (Miller & Rollnick, 2013). MI is particularly helpful when clients are in the Precontemplation and Contemplation stages of the Stages of Change (SOC), when readiness to change is low, but it can also be useful throughout the change cycle.

The Spirit of MI

Use an MI counseling style to support partnership with clients. Collaborative counselor–client relationships are the essence of MI, without which MI counseling techniques are ineffective. Counselor MI spirit is associated with positive client engagement behaviors (e.g., self-disclosure, cooperation) (Romano & Peters, 2016) and positive client outcomes in health-related behaviors (e.g., exercise, medication adherence) similar to those in addiction treatment (Copeland, McNamara, Kelson, & Simpson, 2015).

The spirit of MI (Miller & Rollnick, 2013) comprises the following elements:

- **Partnership** refers to an active collaboration between you and the client. A client is more willing to express concerns when you are empathetic and show genuine curiosity about the client's perspective. In this partnership, you are influential, but the client drives the conversation.

- **Acceptance** refers to your respect for and approval of the client. This doesn't mean agreeing with everything the client says but is a demonstration of your intention to understand the client's point of view and concerns. In the context of MI, there are four components of acceptance:
  - *Absolute worth:* Prizing the inherent worth and potential of the client
  - *Accurate empathy:* An active interest in, and an effort to understand, the client's internal perspective reflected by your genuine curiosity and reflective listening
  - *Autonomy support:* Honoring and respecting a client's right to and capacity for self-direction
  - *Affirmation:* Acknowledging the client's values and strengths

- **Compassion** refers to your active promotion of the client's welfare and prioritization of client needs.

- **Evocation** elicits and explores motivations, values, strengths, and resources the client already has.

To remember the four elements, use the acronym PACE (Stinson & Clark, 2017). The specific counseling strategies you use in your counseling approach should emphasize one or more of these elements.

Principles of Person-Centered Counseling

MI reflects a longstanding tradition of humanistic counseling and the person-centered approach of Carl Rogers. It is theoretically linked to his theory of the "critical conditions for change," which states that clients change when they are engaged in a therapeutic relationship in which the counselor is genuine and warm, expresses unconditional positive regard, and displays accurate empathy (Rogers, 1965).

MI adds another dimension in your efforts to provide person-centered counseling. In MI, the counselor follows the principles of person-centered counseling but also guides the conversation toward a specific, client-driven change goal. MI is more directive than purely person-centered counseling; it is guided by the following broad person-centered counseling principles (Miller & Rollnick, 2013):

- SUD treatment services exist to help recipients. The needs of the client take precedence over the counselor's or organization's needs or goals.

- The client engages in a process of self-change. You facilitate the client's natural process of change.

- The client is the expert in his or her own life and has knowledge of what works and what doesn't.

- As the counselor, you **do not** make change happen.

- People have their own motivation, strengths, and resources. Counselors help activate those resources.

- You are not responsible for coming up with all the good ideas about change, and you probably don't have the best ideas for any particular client.

TIP 35: *Enhancing Motivation for Change in Substance Use Disorder Treatment*
Chapter 3—Motivational Interviewing as a Counseling Style

October 2019

- Change requires a partnership and "collaboration of expertise."

- You must understand the client's perspectives on his or her problems and need to change.

- The counseling relationship is not a power struggle. Conversations about change should not become debates. Avoid arguing with or trying to persuade the client that your position is correct.

- Motivation for change is evoked from, not given to, the client.

- People make their own decisions about taking action. It is not a change goal until the client says so.

- The spirit of MI and client-centered counseling principles foster a sound therapeutic alliance.

Research on person-centered counseling approaches consistent with MI in treating alcohol use disorder (AUD) found that several sessions improved client outcomes, including readiness to change and reductions in alcohol use (Barrio & Gual, 2016).

What Is New in MI

Much has changed in MI since Miller and Rollnick's original (1991) and updated (2002) work. Exhibit 3.1 summarizes important changes to MI based on decades of research and clinical experience.

Exhibit 3.1. A Comparison of Original and Updated Versions of MI	
Original Version	Updated Version
Four principles as the basis for the MI approach: 1. **Express empathy:** Demonstrate empathy through reflective listening. 2. **Develop discrepancy:** Guide conversations to highlight the difference between clients' goals or values and their current behavior. 3. **Roll with resistance:** Avoid arguing against the status quo or arguing for change. 4. **Support self-efficacy:** Support clients' beliefs that change is possible. Although these general principles are still helpful, the new emphasis in MI is on **evoking change talk** and **commitment to change** as primary principles.	Four processes as the basis for the MI approach: 1. **Engaging** is the relational foundation. 2. **Focusing** identifies agenda and change goals. 3. **Evoking** uses MI core skills and strategies for moving toward a specific change goal. 4. **Planning** is the bridge to behavior change. The four processes replace Phase I and II stages in the original version of MI. Core skills and strategies of MI include asking open questions, affirming, using reflective listening, and summarizing; all are integrated into the four processes. The original four principles have been folded into the four processes as reflective listening or strategic responses to move conversations along.
Resistance is a characteristic of the client.	Resistance is an expression of sustain talk and the status quo side of ambivalence, arising out of counselor–client discord.
Rolling with resistance	Strategies to lessen sustain talk and counselor–client discord
Self-motivating statements	Change talk
Decisional balancing is a strategy to help clients move in one direction toward changing a behavior.	Decisional balancing is used to help clients make a decision without favoring a specific direction of change. It may be useful as a way to assess client readiness to change but also may increase ambivalence for clients who are contemplating change.
Source: Miller & Rollnick, 1991, 2002, 2013; Miller & Rose, 2013.	

Exhibit 3.2 presents common misconceptions about MI and provides clarification of MI's underlying theoretical assumptions and counseling approach, which are described in the rest of this chapter.

Exhibit 3.2. Misconceptions and Clarifications About MI	
Misconception	Clarification
MI is a form of nondirective, Rogerian therapy.	MI shares many principles of the humanistic, person-centered approach pioneered by Rogers, but it is not Rogerian therapy. Characteristics that differentiate MI from Rogerian therapy include clearly identified target behaviors and change goals and differential evoking and strengthening of clients' motivation for changing target behavior. Unlike Rogerian therapy, MI has a strategic component that emphasizes helping clients move toward a specific behavioral change goal.
MI is a counseling technique.	Although there are specific MI counseling strategies, MI is not a counseling technique. It is a style of being with people that uses specific clinical skills to foster motivation to change.
MI is a "school" of counseling or psychotherapy.	Some psychological theories underlie the spirit and style of MI, but it was not meant to be a theory of change with a comprehensive set of associated clinical skills.
MI and the SOC approach are the same.	MI and the SOC were developed around the same time, and people confuse the two approaches. MI is not the SOC. MI is not an essential part of the SOC and vice versa. They are compatible and complementary. MI is also compatible with counseling approaches like cognitive–behavioral therapy (CBT).
MI always uses assessment feedback.	Assessment feedback delivered in the MI style was an adaptation of MI that became motivational enhancement therapy (MET). Although personalized feedback may be helpful to enhance motivation with clients who are on the lower end of the readiness to change spectrum, it is not a necessary part of MI.
Counselors can motivate clients to change.	You cannot manufacture motivation that is not already in clients. MI does not motive clients to change or to move toward a predetermined treatment goal. It is a collaborative partnership between you and clients to discover their motivation to change. It respects client autonomy and self-determination about goals for behavior change.
Sources: Miller & Rollnick, 2013, 2014; Moyers, 2014.	

Ambivalence

A key concept in MI is ambivalence. It is normal for people to feels two ways about making an important change in their lives. **Frequently, client ambivalence is a roadblock to change, not a lack of knowledge or skills about how to change** (Forman & Moyers, 2019). Individuals with SUDs are often aware of the risks associated with their substance use but continue to use substances anyway. They may need to stop using substances, but they continue to use. The tension between these feelings is ambivalence.

Ambivalence about changing substance use behaviors is natural. As clients move from Precontemplation to Contemplation, their feelings of conflict about change increase. This tension may help move people toward change, but often the tension of ambivalence leads people to avoid thinking about the problem. They may tell themselves things aren't so bad (Miller & Rollnick, 2013). **View ambivalence not as denial or resistance, but as a normal experience in the change process.** If you interpret ambivalence as denial or resistance, you are likely to evoke discord between you and clients, which is counterproductive.

Sustain Talk and Change Talk

Recognizing sustain talk and change talk in clients will help you better explore and address their ambivalence. Sustain talk consists of client statements that support not changing a health-risk behavior, like substance misuse. Change talk consists of client statements that favor change (Miller & Rollnick, 2013). Sustain talk and change talk are expressions of both sides of ambivalence about change. Over time, MI has evolved in its understanding of what keeps clients stuck in ambivalence about change and what supports clients to move in the direction of changing substance use behaviors. Client stuck in ambivalence will engage in a lot of sustain talk, whereas clients who are more ready to change will engage in more change talk with stronger statements supporting change.

Greater frequency of client sustain talk in sessions is linked to poorer substance use treatment outcomes (Lindqvist, Forsberg, Enebrink, Andersson, & Rosendahl, 2017; Magill et al., 2014; Rodriguez, Walters, Houck, Ortiz, & Taxman, 2017). Conversely, MI-consistent counselor behavior focused on eliciting and reflecting change talk, more client change talk compared with sustain talk, and stronger commitment change talk are linked to better substance use outcomes (Barnett, Moyers, et al., 2014; Borsari et al., 2018; Houck, Manuel, & Moyers, 2018; Magill et al., 2014, 2018; Romano & Peters, 2016). Counselor empathy is also linked to eliciting client change talk (Pace et al., 2017).

> In MI, your main goal is to evoke change talk and minimize evoking or reinforcing sustain talk in counseling sessions.

Another development in MI is the delineation of different kinds of change talk. The acronym for change talk in MI is DARN-CAT (Miller & Rollnick, 2013):

- **D**esire to change: This is expressed in statements about wanting something different—"I want to find an Alcoholics Anonymous (AA) meeting" or "I hope to start going to AA."

- **A**bility to change: This is expressed in statements about self-perception of capability—"I could start going to AA."

- **R**easons to change: This is expressed as arguments for change—"I'd probably learn more about recovery if I went to AA" or "Going to AA would help me feel more supported."

- **N**eed to change: This is expressed in client statements about importance or urgency—"I have to stop drinking" or "I need to find a way to get my drinking under control."

- **C**ommitment: This is expressed as a promise to change—"I swear I will go to an AA meeting this year" or "I guarantee that I will start AA by next month."

- **A**ctivation: This is expressed in statements showing movement toward action—"I'm ready to go to my first AA meeting."

- **T**aking steps: This is expressed in statements indicating that the client has already done something to change—"I went to an AA meeting" or "I avoided a party where friends would be doing drugs."

Exhibit 3.3 depicts examples of change talk and sustain talk that correspond to DARN-CAT.

Exhibit 3.3. Examples of Change Talk and Sustain Talk

Type of Statement	Examples of Change Talk	Examples of Sustain Talk
Desire	"I want to cut down on my drinking."	"I love how cocaine makes me feel."
Ability	"I could cut back to 1 drink with dinner on weekends."	"I can manage my life just fine without giving up the drug."
Reasons	"I'll miss less time at work if I cut down."	"Getting high helps me feel energized."

TIP 35: *Enhancing Motivation for Change in Substance Use Disorder Treatment*
Chapter 3—Motivational Interviewing as a Counseling Style

October 2019

Need	"I have to cut down. My doctor told me that the amount I am drinking puts my health at risk."	"I need to get high to keep me going every day."
Commitment	"I promise to cut back this weekend."	"I am going to keep snorting cocaine."
Activation	"I am ready to do something about the drinking."	"I am not ready to give up the cocaine."
Taking steps	"I only had one drink with dinner on Saturday."	"I am still snorting cocaine every day."
Source: Miller & Rollnick, 2013.		

To make the best use of clients' change talk and sustain talk that arise in sessions, remember to:

- Recognize client expressions of change talk but don't worry about differentiating various kinds of change talk during a counseling session.
- Use reflective listening to reinforce and help clients elaborate on change talk.
- Use DARN-CAT in conversations with clients.
- Recognize sustain talk and use MI strategies to lessen the impact of sustain talk on clients' readiness to change (see discussion of responding to change talk and sustain talk in the next section).
- Be aware that both sides of ambivalence (change talk and sustain talk) will be present in your conversations with clients.

A New Look at Resistance

Understanding the role of resistance and how to respond to it can help you maintain good counselor–client rapport. Resistance in SUD treatment has historically been considered a problem centered in the client. As MI has developed over the years, its understanding of resistance has changed. Instead of emphasizing resistance as a pathological defense mechanism, MI views resistance as a normal part of ambivalence and a client's reaction to the counselor's approach in the moment (Miller & Rollnick, 2013).

A client may express resistance in sustain talk that favors the "no change" side of ambivalence. The way you respond to sustain talk can contribute to the client becoming firmly planted in the status quo or help the client move toward contemplating change. For example, the client's show of ambivalence about change and your arguments for change can create discord in your therapeutic relationship.

Client sustain talk is often evoked by discord in the counseling relationship (Miller & Rollnick, 2013). **Resistance is a two-way street. If discord arises in conversation, change direction or listen more carefully.** This is an opportunity to respond in a new, perhaps surprising, way and to take advantage of the situation without being confrontational. This new way of looking at resistance is consistent with the principles of person-centered counseling described at the beginning of the chapter.

Core Skills of MI: OARS

To remember the core counseling skills of MI, use the acronym OARS (Miller & Rollnick, 2013):

- Asking **O**pen questions
- **A**ffirming
- **R**eflective listening
- **S**ummarizing

TIP 35: *Enhancing Motivation for Change in Substance Use Disorder Treatment*
Chapter 3—Motivational Interviewing as a Counseling Style

October 2019

These core skills are consistent with the principles of person-centered counseling and can be used throughout your work with clients. If you use these skills, you will more likely have greater success in engaging clients and less incidence of discord within the counselor–client relationship. These core skills are described below.

Asking Open Questions

Use open questions to invite clients to tell their story rather than closed questions, which merely elicit brief information. Open questions are questions that invite clients to reflect before answering and encourage them to elaborate. Asking open questions helps you understand their point of view. Open questions facilitate a dialog and do not require any particular response from you. They encourage clients to do most of the talking and keep the conversation moving forward. Closed questions evoke yes/no or short answers and sometimes make clients feel as if they have to come up with the right answer. One type of open question is actually a statement that begins with "Tell me about" or "Tell me more about." The "Tell me about" statement invites clients to tell a story and serves as an open question.

Exhibit 3.4 provides examples of closed and open questions. As you read these examples, imagine you are a client and notice the difference in how you might receive and respond to each kind of question.

Exhibit 3.4. Closed and Open Questions

Closed Questions	Open Questions
"So you are here because you are concerned about your use of alcohol, correct?"	"What is it that brings you here today?"
"How many children do you have?"	"Tell me about your family."
"Do you agree that it would be a good idea for you to go through detoxification?"	"What do you think about the possibility of going through detoxification?"
"On a typical day, how much marijuana do you smoke?"	"Tell me about your marijuana use on a typical day."
"Did your doctor tell you to quit smoke?"	"What did your doctor tell you about the health risks of smoking?"
"How has your drug use been this week compared with last week: more, less, or about the same?"	"What has your drug use been like during the past week?"
"Do you think you use amphetamines too often?"	"In what ways are you concerned about your use of amphetamines?"
"How long ago did you have your last drink?"	"Tell me about the last time you drank."
"Are you sure that your probation officer told you that it's only cocaine he is concerned about in your urine screens?"	"Tell me more about the conditions of your probation."
"When do you plan to quit drinking?"	"What do you think you want to do about your drinking?"

There may be times when you must ask closed questions, for example, to gather information for a screening or assessment. However, if you use open questions—"Tell me about the last time you used methamphetamines"—you will often get the information you need and enhance the process of engagement. **During assessment, avoid the question-and-answer trap, which can decrease rapport, become an obstacle to counselor–client engagement, and stall conversations.**

MI involves maintaining a balance between asking questions and reflective listening (Miller & Rollnick, 2013). Ask one open question, and follow it with two or more reflective listening responses.

Affirming

Affirming is a way to express your genuine appreciation and positive regard for clients (Miller & Rollnick, 2013). Affirming clients supports and promotes self-efficacy. By affirming, you are saying, "I see you, what you say matters, and I want to understand what you think and feel" (Miller & Rollnick, 2013). **Affirming can boost clients' confidence about taking action.** Using affirmations in conversations with clients consistently predicts positive client outcomes (Romano & Peters, 2016).

When affirming:

- Emphasize client strengths, past successes, and efforts to take steps, however small, to accomplish change goals.

- Do not confuse this type of feedback with praise, which can sometimes be a roadblock to effective listening (Gordon, 1970; see Exhibit 3.5 below in the section "Reflective Listening").

- Frame your affirming statements with "you" instead of "I." For example, instead of saying "I am proud of you," which focuses more on you than on the client, try "You have worked really hard to get to where you are now in your life," which demonstrates your appreciation, but keeps the focus on the client (Miller & Rollnick, 2013).

- Use statements such as (Miller & Rollnick, 2013):
  - "You took a big step in coming here today."
  - "You got discouraged last week but kept going to your AA meetings. You are persistent."
  - "Although things didn't turn out the way you hoped, you tried really hard, and that means a lot."
  - "That's a good idea for how you can avoid situations where you might be tempted to drink."

There may be ethnic, cultural, and even personal differences in how people respond to affirming statements. Be aware of verbal and nonverbal cues about how the client is reacting and be open to checking out the client's reaction with an open question—"How was that for you to hear?" Strategies for forming affirmations that account for cultural and personal differences include (Rosengren, 2018):

- Focusing on specific behaviors to affirm.

- Avoiding using "I."

- Emphasizing descriptions instead of evaluations.

- Emphasizing positive developments instead of continuing problems.

- Affirming interesting qualities and strengths of clients.

- Holding an awareness of client strengths instead of deficits as you formulate affirmations.

Reflective Listening

Reflective listening is the key component of expressing empathy. Reflective listening is fundamental to person-centered counseling in general and MI in particular (Miller & Rollnick, 2013). Reflective listening (Miller & Rollnick, 2013):

- Communicates respect for and acceptance of clients.

- Establishes trust and invites clients to explore their own perceptions, values, and feelings.

TIP 35: *Enhancing Motivation for Change in Substance Use Disorder Treatment*
Chapter 3—Motivational Interviewing as a Counseling Style

October 2019

- Encourages a nonjudgmental, collaborative relationship.
- Allows you to be a supportive without agreeing with specific client statements.

Reflective listening builds collaboration and a safe and open environment that is conducive to examining issues and eliciting the client's reasons for change. It is both an expression of empathy and a way to selectively reinforce change talk (Romano & Peters, 2016). Reflective listening demonstrates that you are genuinely interested in understanding the client's unique perspective, feelings, and values. Expressions of counselor empathy predict better substance use outcomes (Moyers, Houck, Rice, Longabaugh, & Miller, 2016). Your attitude should be one of acceptance but not necessarily approval or agreement, recognizing that ambivalence about change is normal.

Consider ethnic and cultural differences when expressing empathy through reflective listening. These differences influence how both you and the client interpret verbal and nonverbal communications.

Expert Comment: Expressing Empathy With American Indian/Native American Clients

For many traditional American Indian groups, expressing empathy begins with the introduction. Native Americans generally expect the counselor to be aware of and practice the culturally accepted norms for introducing oneself and showing respect. For example, during the first meeting, the person often is expected to say his or her name, clan relationship or ethnic origin, and place of origin. Physical contact is kept to a minimum, except for a brief handshake, which may be no more than a soft touch of the palms.

Ray Daw, Consensus Panel Member

Expert Comment: Expressing Empathy With African American Clients

One way I empathize with African American clients is, first and foremost, to be a genuine person (not just a counselor). Clients may begin the relationship asking questions about you the person, not the professional, in an attempt to locate you in the world. It's as if clients' internal dialog says, "As you try to understand me, by what pathways, perspectives, life experiences, and values are you coming to that understanding of me?"

Typical questions my African American clients have asked me are:

- "Are you Christian?"
- "Where are you from?"
- "What part of town do you live in?"
- "Who are your folks?"
- "Are you married?"

All of these are reasonable questions that work to establish a real, not contrived, relationship with the counselor. As part of a democratic partnership, clients have a right and, in some instances, a cultural expectation to know about the helper.

On another level, many African Americans are very spiritual people. This spirituality is expressed and practiced in ways that supersede religious affiliations. Young people pat their chests and say, "I feel you," as a way to describe this sense of empathy. Understanding and working with this can enhance the counselor's expression of empathy. In other words, the therapeutic counselor–client alliance can be deepened, permitting another level of empathic connection that some might call an intuitive understanding and others might call a spiritual connection to each client. What emerges is a therapeutic alliance—a spiritual connection—that goes beyond what mere words can say. The more counselors express that side of themselves, whether they call it intuition or spirituality, the more intense the empathic connection the African American client will feel.

Cheryl Grills, Ph.D., Consensus Panel Member

TIP 35: *Enhancing Motivation for Change in Substance Use Disorder Treatment*
Chapter 3—Motivational Interviewing as a Counseling Style

October 2019

Reflective listening is not as easy as it sounds. It is not simply a matter of being quiet while the client is speaking. **Reflective listening requires you to make a mental hypothesis about the underlying meaning or feeling of client statements and then reflect that back to the client with your best guess about his or her meaning or feeling** (Miller & Rollnick, 2013). Gordon (1970) called this "active listening" and identified 12 kinds of responses that people often give to others that are not active listening and can actually derail a conversation. Exhibit 3.5 describes these roadblocks to listening.

Exhibit 3.5. Gordon's 12 Roadblocks to Active Listening	
1. Ordering, directing, or commanding	Direction is given with a voice of authority. The speaker may be in a position of power (e.g., parent, employer, counselor) or the words may simply be phrased and spoken in a way that communicates that the speaker is the expert.
2. Warning, cautioning, or threatening	These statements carry an overt or covert threat of negative consequences. For example, "If you don't stop drinking, you are going to die."
3. Giving advice, making suggestions, or providing solutions prematurely or when unsolicited	The message recommends a course of action based on your knowledge and personal experience. These recommendations often begin with phrases like "What I would do is."
4. Persuading with logic, arguing, or lecturing	The underlying assumption of these messages is that the client has not reasoned through the problem adequately and needs help to do so. Trying to persuade the client that your position is correct will most likely evoke a reaction and the client taking the opposite position.
5. Moralizing, preaching, or telling people what they should do	These statements contain such words as "should" or "ought," which imply or directly convey negative judgment.
6. Judging, criticizing, disagreeing, or blaming	These messages imply that something is wrong with the client or with what the client has said. Even simple disagreement may be interpreted as critical.
7. Agreeing, approving, or praising	Praise or approval can be an obstacle if the message sanctions or implies agreement with whatever the client has said or if the praise is given too often or in general terms, like "great job." This can lessen the impact on the person or simply disrupt the flow of the conversation
8. Shaming, ridiculing, or labeling	These statements express disapproval and intent to correct a specific behavior or attitude. They can damage self-esteem and cause major disruptions in the counseling alliance.
9. Interpreting or analyzing	You may be tempted to impose your own interpretations on a client's statement and to find some hidden, analytical meaning. Interpretive statements might imply you know what the client's "real" problem is and puts you in a one-up position.
10. Reassuring, sympathizing, or consoling	Counselors often want to console the client. It is human nature to want to reassure someone who is in pain; however, sympathy is not the same as empathy. Such reassurance can interrupt the flow of communication and interfere with careful listening.
11. Questioning or probing	Do not mistake questioning for good listening. Although you may ask questions to learn more about the client, the underlying message is that you might find the right answer to all the client's problems if enough questions are asked. In

TIP 35: *Enhancing Motivation for Change in Substance Use Disorder Treatment*
Chapter 3—Motivational Interviewing as a Counseling Style

October 2019

	fact, intensive questioning can disrupt communication, and sometimes the client feels as if he or she is being interrogated
12. **Withdrawing, distracting, humoring, or changing the subject**	Although shifting the focus or using humor may be helpful at times, it can also be a distraction and disrupt the communication.
Source: Gordon, 1970.	

If you engage in any of these 12 activities, you are talking and not listening. However well intentioned, these roadblocks to listening shift the focus of the conversation from the client to the counselor. They are not consistent with the principles of person-centered counseling.

Types of reflective listening

In MI, there are several kinds of reflective listening responses that range from simple (i.e., repeating or rephrasing a client statement) to complex (i.e., using different words to reflect the underlying meaning or feeling of a client statement). **Simple reflections engage clients and let them know that you're genuinely interested in understanding their perspective. Complex reflections invite clients to deepen their self-exploration** (Miller & Rollnick, 2013). In MI, there are special complex reflections that you can use in specific counseling situations, like using a double-sided reflection when clients are expressing ambivalence about changing a substance use behavior. Exhibit 3.6 provides examples of simple and complex reflective listening responses to client statements about substance use.

Exhibit 3.6. Types of Reflective Listening Responses				
Type	Client Statement	Counselor Response	Purpose	Special Considerations
Simple				
Repeat	"My wife is nagging me about my drinking."	"Your wife is nagging you about your drinking."	Builds rapport. Expresses empathy.	Avoid mimicking.
Rephrase	"My wife is nagging me about my drinking."	"Your wife is pressuring you about your drinking."	Expresses empathy. Highlights selected meaning or feeling.	Move the conversation along, but more slowly than complex reflections.
Complex				
Feeling	"I'd like to quit smoking marijuana so that the second-hand pot smoke won't worsen my daughter's asthma."	"You're afraid that your daughter's asthma will get worse if you continue smoking marijuana."	Highlights selected feeling. Highlights discrepancy between values and current behavior.	Selectively reinforce change talk. Avoid reinforcing sustain talk.
Meaning	"I'd like to quit smoking marijuana because I read that second-hand pot smoke can make asthma	"You want to protect your daughter from the possibility that her asthma will get worse	Highlights selected meaning. Highlights discrepancy between	Selectively reinforce change talk.

	worse and I don't want that to happen to my daughter."	if you continue smoking marijuana."	values and current behavior.	Avoid reinforcing sustain talk.
Double-sided	"I know I should give up drinking, but I can't imagine life without it."	"Giving up drinking would be hard, **and** you recognize that it's time to stop."	Resolves ambivalence. Acknowledges sustain talk **and** emphasizes change talk.	Use "and" to join two reflections. Start with sustain talk reflection and end with change talk reflection.
Amplified	"I think my cocaine use is just not a problem for me."	"There are absolutely no negative consequences of using cocaine."	Intensifies sustain talk to evoke change talk.	Use sparingly. Avoid getting stuck in sustain talk.

Source: *Miller & Rollnick, 2013.*

Forming complex reflections

Simple reflections are fairly straightforward. You simply repeat or paraphrase what the client said. Complex reflections are more challenging. A statement could have many meanings. The first step in making a complex reflection of meaning or feelings is to make a hypothesis in your mind about what the client is trying to say (Miller & Rollnick, 2013).

Use these steps to form a mental hypothesis about meaning or feelings:

1. If the client says, "I drink because I am lonely," think about the possible meanings of "lonely." Perhaps the client is saying, "I lost my spouse" or "It is hard for me to make friends" or "I can't think of anything to say when I am with my family."

2. Consider the larger conversational context. Has the client noted not having much of a social life?

3. Make your best guess about the meaning of the client's statement.

4. Offer a reflective listening response—"You drink because it is hard for you to make friends."

5. Wait for the client's response. The client will tell you either verbally or nonverbally if your guess is correct. If the client continues to talk and expands on the initial statement, you are on target.

6. Be open to being wrong. If you are, use client feedback to make another hypothesis about the client's meaning.

Remember that reflective listening is about refraining from making assumptions about the underlying message of client statements, making a hypothesis about the meaning or feeling of the statement, and then checking out your hypothesis by offering a reflective statement and listening carefully to the client's response (Miller & Rollnick, 2013). Reflective listening is basic to all of four MI processes. **Follow open questions with at least one reflective listening response—but preferably two or three responses—before asking another question.** A higher ratio of reflections to questions consistently predicts positive client outcomes (Romano & Peters, 2016). It takes practice to become skillful, but the effort is worth it because careful reflective listening builds a strong therapeutic alliance and facilitates the client's self-exploration—two essential components of person-centered counseling (Miller & Rollnick, 2013). The key to expressing accurate empathy through reflective listening is your ability to shift gears from being an expert who gives advice to being an individual supporting the client's autonomy and expertise in making decisions about changing substance use behaviors (Moyers, 2014).

Summarizing

Summarizing is a form of reflective listening that distills the essence of several client statements and reflects them back to him or her. It is not simply a collection of statements. You intentionally select statements that may have particular meaning for the client and present them in a summary that paints a fuller picture of the client's experience than simply using reflections (Miller & Rollnick, 2013).

There are several types of summarization in MI (Miller & Rollnick, 2013):

- **Collecting summary:** Recalls a series of related client statements, creating a narrative to reflect on.
- **Linking summary:** Reflects a client statement; links it to an earlier statement.
- **Transitional summary:** Wraps up a conversation or task; moves the client along the change process.
- **Ambivalence summary:** Gathers client statements of sustain talk and change talk during a session. This summary should acknowledge sustain talk but reinforce and highlight change talk.
- **Recapitulation summary:** Gathers all of the change talk of many conversations. It is useful during the transition from one stage to the next when making a change plan.

At the end of a summary, ask the client whether you left anything out. This opportunity lets the client correct or add more to the summary and often leads to further discussion. Summarizing encourages client self-reflection.

Summaries reinforce key statements of movement toward change. Clients hear change talk once when they make a statement, twice when the counselor reflects it, and again when the counselor summarizes the discussion.

Four Processes of MI

MI has moved away from the idea of phases of change to overlapping processes that more accurately describe how MI works in clinical practice. This change is a shift away from a linear, rigid model of change to a circular, fluid model of change within the context of the counseling relationship. This section reviews these MI processes, summarizes counseling strategies appropriate for each process, and integrates the four principles of MI from previous versions.

Engaging

Engaging clients is the first step in all counseling approaches. Specific counseling strategies or techniques will not be effective if you and the client haven't established a strong working relationship. MI is no exception to this. Miller and Rollnick (2013) define engaging in MI "as the process of establishing a mutually trusting and respectful helping relationship" (p. 40). Research supports the link between your ability to develop this kind of helping relationship and positive treatment outcomes such as reduced drinking (Moyers et al., 2016; Romano & Peters, 2016).

Opening strategies

Opening strategies promote engagement in MI by emphasizing OARS in the following ways:

- Ask open questions instead of closed questions.
- Offer affirmations of client self-efficacy, hope, and confidence in the client's ability to change.

TIP 35: *Enhancing Motivation for Change in Substance Use Disorder Treatment*
Chapter 3—Motivational Interviewing as a Counseling Style

October 2019

- Emphasize reflective listening.
- Summarize to reinforce that you are listening and genuinely interested in the client's perspective.
- Determine the client's readiness to change or and specific stage in the SOC (see Chapters 1 and 2).
- Avoid prematurely focusing on taking action.
- Try not to identify the client's treatment goals until you have sufficiently explored the client's readiness. Then you can address the client's ambivalence.

These opening strategies ensure support for the client and help the client explore ambivalence in a safe setting. In the following initial conversation, the counselor uses OARS to establish rapport and address the client's drinking through reflective listening and asking open questions:

- **Counselor:** Jerry, thanks for coming in. *(Affirmation)* What brings you here today? *(Open question)*
- **Client:** My wife thinks I drink too much. She says that's why we argue all the time. She also thinks that my drinking is ruining my health.
- **Counselor:** So your wife has some concerns about your drinking interfering with your relationship and harming your health. *(Reflection)*
- **Client:** Yeah, she worries a lot.
- **Counselor:** You wife worries a lot about the drinking. *(Reflection)* What concerns **you** about it? *(Open question)*
- **Client:** I'm not sure I'm *concerned* about it, but I do wonder sometimes if I'm drinking too much.
- **Counselor:** You are wondering about the drinking. *(Reflection)* Too much for...? *(Open question that invites the client to complete the sentence)*
- **Client:** For my own good, I guess. I mean it's not like it's really serious, but sometimes when I wake up in the morning, I feel really awful, and I can't think straight most of the morning.
- **Counselor:** It messes up your thinking, your concentration. *(Reflection)*
- **Client:** Yeah, and sometimes I have trouble remembering things.
- **Counselor:** And you wonder if these problems are related to drinking too much. *(Reflection)*
- **Client:** Well, I know it is sometimes.
- **Counselor:** You're certain that sometimes drinking too much hurts you. *(Reflection)* Tell me what it's like to lose concentration and have trouble remembering. *(Open question in the form of a statement)*
- **Client:** It's kind of scary. I am way too young to have trouble with my memory. And now that I think about it, that's what usually causes the arguments with my wife. She'll ask me to pick up something from the store and when I forget to stop on my way home from work, she starts yelling at me.
- **Counselor:** You're scared that drinking is starting to have some negative effects on what's important to you like your ability to think clearly and good communication with your wife. *(Reflection)*
- **Client:** Yeah. But I don't think I'm an alcoholic or anything.
- **Counselor:** You don't think you're that bad off, but you do wonder if maybe you're overdoing it and hurting yourself and your relationship with your wife. *(Reflection)*
- **Client:** Yeah.
- **Counselor:** You know, Jerry, it takes courage to come talk to a stranger about something that's scary to talk about. *(Affirmation)* What do you think? *(Open question)*
- **Client:** I never thought of it like that. I guess it **is** important to figure out what to do about my drinking.

TIP 35: *Enhancing Motivation for Change in Substance Use Disorder Treatment*
Chapter 3—Motivational Interviewing as a Counseling Style

October 2019

- **Counselor:** So, Jerry, let's take a minute to review where we are today. Your wife is concerned about how much you drink. You have been having trouble concentrating and remembering things and are wondering if that has to do with how much you are drinking. You are now thinking that you need to figure out what to do about the drinking. Did I miss anything? *(Summary)*

Avoiding traps

Identify and avoid traps to help preserve client engagement. The above conversation shows use of core MI skills to engage the client and help him feel heard, understood, and respected while moving the conversation toward change. The counselor avoids common traps that increase disengagement.

Common traps to avoid include the following (Miller & Rollnick, 2013):

- **The Expert Trap:** People often see a professional, like primary care physician or nurse practitioner, to get answers to questions and to help them make important decisions. But relying on another person (even a professional) to have all the answers is contrary to the spirit of MI and the principles of person-centered care. **Both you and the client have expertise.** You have knowledge and skills in listening and interviewing; the client has knowledge based on his or her life experience. In your conversations with a client, remember that you do not have to have all the answers, and trust that the client has knowledge about what is important to him or her, what needs to change, and what steps need to be taken to make those changes. Avoid falling into the expert trap by:
  - **Refraining from acting on the "righting reflex,"** the natural impulse to jump into action and direct the client toward a specific change. Such a directive style is likely to produce sustain talk and discord in the counseling relationship.
  - **Not arguing with the client.** If you try to prove a point, the client predictably takes the opposite side. Arguments with the client can rapidly degenerate into a power struggle and do not enhance motivation for change.
- **The Labeling Trap:** Diagnoses and labels like "alcoholic" or "addict" can evoke shame in clients. **There is no evidence that forcing a client to accept a label is helpful; in fact, it usually evokes discord in the counseling relationship.** In the conversation above, the counselor didn't argue with Jerry about whether he is an "alcoholic." If the counselor had done so, the outcome would likely have been different:
  - **Client:** But I don't think I'm an alcoholic or anything.
  - **Counselor:** Well, based on what you've told me, I think we should do a comprehensive assessment to determine whether or not you are.
  - **Client:** Wait a minute. That's not what I came for. I don't think counseling is going to help me.
- **The Question-and-Answer Trap:** When your focus is on getting information from a client, particularly during an assessment, you and the client can easily fall into the question-and-answer trap. This can feel like an interrogation rather than a conversation. In addition, a pattern of asking closed questions and giving short answers sets you up in the expert role, and the client becomes a passive recipient of the treatment intervention instead of an active partner in the process. Remember to ask open questions, and follow them with reflective listening responses to avoid the question-and-answer trap.
- **The Premature Focus Trap:** You can fall into this trap when you focus on an agenda for change before the client is ready—for example, jumping into solving problems before developing a strong working alliance. When you focus on an issue that is important to **you** (e.g., admission to an inpatient treatment program) but not to the client, discord will occur. Remember that your approach should match where the client is with regard to his or her readiness to change.

TIP 35: *Enhancing Motivation for Change in Substance Use Disorder Treatment*
Chapter 3—Motivational Interviewing as a Counseling Style

October 2019

- **The Blaming Trap:** Clients often enter treatment focused on who is to blame for their substance use problem. They may feel guarded and defensive, expecting you to judge them harshly as family, friends, coworkers, or others may have. Avoid the blame trap by immediately reassuring clients that you are uninterested in blaming anyone and that your role is to listen to what troubles them.

Focusing

Once you have engaged the client, the next step in MI is to find a direction for the conversation and the counseling process as a whole. This is called focusing in MI. With the client, you develop a mutually agreed-on agenda that promotes change and then identify a specific target behavior to discuss. Without a clear focus, conversations about change can be unwieldy and unproductive (Miller & Rollnick, 2013).

Deciding on an agenda

MI is essentially a conversation you and the client have about change. The direction of the conversation is influenced by the client, the counselor, and the clinical setting (Miller & Rollnick, 2013). For example, a client walking through the door of an outpatient SUD treatment program understand that his or her use of alcohol and other drugs will be on the agenda.

Clients, however, may be mandated to treatment and may not see their substance use as a problem, or they may have multiple issues (e.g., child care, relational, financial, legal problems) that interfere with recovery and that need to be addressed. When clients bring multiple problems to the table or are confused or uncertain about the direction of the conversation, you can engage in agenda mapping, which is a process consistent with MI that helps you and clients decide on the counseling focus. Exhibit 3.7 displays the components in an agenda map.

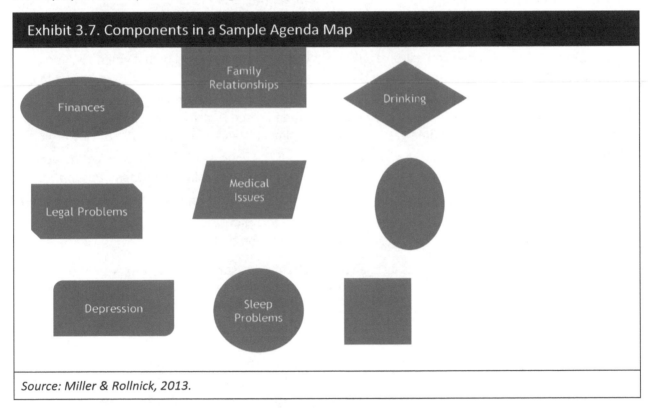

Exhibit 3.7. Components in a Sample Agenda Map

Source: Miller & Rollnick, 2013.

To engage in agenda mapping (Miller & Rollnick, 2013):

TIP 35: *Enhancing Motivation for Change in Substance Use Disorder Treatment*
Chapter 3—Motivational Interviewing as a Counseling Style

October 2019

- Have an empty agenda map handout handy, or draw 8 to 10 empty circles or shapes on a blank paper.

- Present the empty agenda map or the sheet of paper to the client by saying, "I know you were referred here to address [name the problem, such as drinking], but you may have other concerns you want to discuss. I'd like to take a few minutes and write down things you may want to talk about. That way, we'll have a map we can look at to see whether we're headed in the right direction. How does that sound?"

- Write a different concern or issue in each circle. Leave two or three circles blank so that you can add a new client concern or suggest a topic that may be important to discuss. If you suggest a topic, frame it in a way that asks permission and leaves the choice to the client: "You've mentioned a few different concerns that are important to discuss. Would it be okay to also talk about [name the problem, such as drug use] because that's why you were referred to treatment?"

- Ask the client what the most pressing concern is: "You've mentioned several things you'd like to talk about. (Summarize) Where would you like to start?"

- Leave time to guide the client back to the substance use concern if not discussed during the session.

- Keep the map as a visual record, and refer back to it with the client as a reminder of the focus and direction of the counseling process. Add and delete topics as needed.

- Remember to use OARS throughout this process to move the conversation along.

Identifying a target behavior

Once you and the client agree on a general direction, focus on a specific behavior the client is ready to discuss. Change talk links to a specific behavior change target (Miller & Rollnick, 2010); you can't evoke change talk until you identify a target behavior. For example, if the client is ready to discuss drinking, guide the conversation toward details specific to that concern. A sample of such a conversation follows:

- **Counselor:** Marla, you said you'd like to talk about your drinking. It would help if you'd give me a sense of what your specific concerns are about drinking. *(Open question in the form of a statement)*

- **Client:** Well, after work I go home to my apartment and I am so tired; I don't want to do anything but watch TV, microwave a meal, and drink till I fall asleep. Then I wake up with a big hangover in the morning and have a hard time getting to work on time. My supervisor has given me a warning.

- **Counselor:** You're worried that the amount you drink affects your sleep and ability to get to work on time. *(Reflection)* What do you think you'd like to change about the drinking? *(Open question)*

- **Client:** I think I need to stop drinking completely for a while, so I can get into a healthy sleep pattern.

- **Counselor:** So I'd like to put stop drinking for a while on the map, is that okay? *[Asks permission. Pauses. Waits for permission.]* Let's focus our conversations on that goal.

Notice that this client is already expressing change talk about her alcohol use. By narrowing the focus from drinking as a general concern to stopping drinking as a possible target behavior, the counselor moved into the MI process of evoking.

Evoking

Evoking elicits client motivations for change. It shapes conversations in ways that encourage clients, not counselors, to argue for change. Evoking is the core of MI and differentiates it from other counseling methods (Miller & Rollnick, 2013). The following sections explore evoking change talk, responding to change talk and sustain talk, developing discrepancy, evoking hope and confidence to support self-efficacy, recognizing signs of readiness to change, and asking key questions.

TIP 35: *Enhancing Motivation for Change in Substance Use Disorder Treatment*
Chapter 3—Motivational Interviewing as a Counseling Style

October 2019

Evoking change talk

Engaging the client in the process of change is the fundamental task of MI. Rather than identifying the problem and promoting ways to solve it, your task is to help clients recognize that their use of substances may be contributing to their distress and that they have a choice about how to move forward in life in ways that enhance their health and well-being. **One signal that clients' ambivalence about change is decreasing is when they start to express change talk.**

The first step to evoking change talk is to ask open questions. There are seven kinds of change talk, reflected in the DARN acronym. DARN questions can help you generate open questions that evoke change talk. Exhibit 3.8 provides examples of open questions that elicit change talk in preparation for taking steps to change.

Exhibit 3.8. Examples of Open Questions to Evoke Change Talk Using DARN	
Desire	"How would you **like** for things to change?"
	"What do you **hope** our work together will accomplish?"
	"What don't you **like** about how things are now?"
	"What don't you **like** about the effects of drinking or drug use?"
	"What do you **wish** for your relationship with _____?"
	"How do you **want** your life to be different a year from now?"
	"What are you **looking for** from this program?"
Ability	"If you decided to quit drinking, how **could** you do it?"
	"What do you think you might be **able** to change?"
	"What ideas do you have for how you **could** _____?"
	"What **encourages** you that you could **change** if you decided to?"
	"How **confident** are you that you could _____ if you made up your mind?"
	"Of the different options you've considered, what seems most **possible**?"
	"How likely are you to be **able** to _____?"
Reasons	"What are some of the reasons you have for making this change?"
	"Why would you want to stop or cut back on your use of _____?"
	"What's the downside of the way things are now?"
	"What might be the good things about quitting _____?"
	"What would make it worthwhile for you to _____?"
	"What might be some of the advantages of _____?"
	"What might be the three best reasons for _____?"
Need	"What **needs** to happen?"
	"How **important** is it for you to _____?"
	"What makes you think that you might **need** to make a change?"
	"How **serious** or **urgent** does this feel to you?"

TIP 35: *Enhancing Motivation for Change in Substance Use Disorder Treatment*
Chapter 3—Motivational Interviewing as a Counseling Style

October 2019

	"What do you think **has** to change?"

Source: Miller & Rollnick, 2013. Motivational Interviewing: Helping People Change (3rd ed.), *pp. 171–173. Adapted with permission from Guilford Press.*

Other strategies for evoking change talk (Miller & Rollnick, 2013) include:

- **Eliciting importance of change.** Ask an open question that elicits "Need" change talk (Exhibit 3.8): "How important is it for you to *[name the change in the target behavior, such as cutting back on drinking]*?" You can also use scaling questions such as those in the Importance Ruler in Exhibit 3.9 to help the client explore change talk about need more fully.

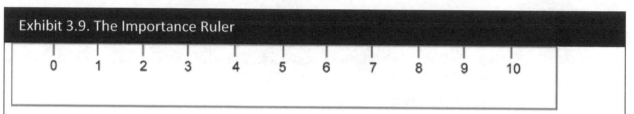

Exhibit 3.9. The Importance Ruler

0 1 2 3 4 5 6 7 8 9 10

Not Important   Extremely Important

- Initial question: "On a scale of 0 to 10, how important is it for you to change *[name the target behavior, like how much the client drinks]* if you decided to?"

- Follow-up question 1: "How are you at a *[fill in the number on the scale]* instead of a *[choose a lower number on the scale]*?" When you use a lower number, you are inviting the client to reflect on how he or she is already considering change. If you use a higher number, it will likely evoke sustain talk (Miller & Rollnick, 2013). Notice the difference in the following examples:

  Lower number
  - **Counselor:** You mention that you are at a 6 on the importance of quitting drinking. How are you at a 6 instead of a 3?
  - **Client:** I'm realizing that drinking causes more problems in my life now than when I was younger.

  Higher number
  - **Counselor:** You mention that you are at a 6 on the importance of quitting drinking. How are you at a 6 instead of a 9?
  - **Client:** Well, I am just not ready to quit right this second.

  In the higher number example, the counselor evokes sustain talk, but it is still useful information and can be the beginning of a deep conversation about the client's readiness to change.

- Follow-up question 2: "What would help move from a *[fill in the number on the scale]* to a *[choose a slightly higher number on the scale]*?" This question invites the client to reflect on reasons to increase readiness to change.

- **Exploring extremes.** Ask the client to identify the extremes of the problem; this enhances his or her motivation. For example: "What concerns you the most about *[name the target behavior, like using cocaine]*?"

- **Looking back.** To point out discrepancies and evoke change talk, ask the client about what it was like before experiencing substance use problems, and compare that response with what it is like now. For example: "What was it like before you started using heroin?"

- **Looking forward.** Ask the client to envision what he or she would like for the future. This can elicit change talk and identify goals to work toward. For example: "If you decided to *[describe the change in target behavior, such as quit smoking]*, how do you think your life would be different a month, a year, or 5 years from now?"

TIP 35: *Enhancing Motivation for Change in Substance Use Disorder Treatment*
Chapter 3—Motivational Interviewing as a Counseling Style

October 2019

Reinforce change talk by reflecting it back verbally, nodding, or making approving facial expressions and affirming statements. Encourage the client to continue exploring the possibility of change by asking for elaboration, explicit examples, or details about remaining concerns. Questions that begin with "What else" effectively invite elaboration.

Your task is to evoke change talk and selectively reinforce it via reflective listening. The amount of change talk versus sustain talk is linked to client behavior change and positive substance use outcomes (Houck et al., 2018; Lindqvist et al., 2017; Magill et al., 2014).

Responding to change talk and sustain talk

Your focus should be on evoking change talk and minimizing sustain talk. Sustain talk expresses the side of ambivalence that favors continuing one's pattern of substance use. Don't argue with the client's sustain talk, and don't try to persuade the client to take the change side of ambivalence.

There are many ways to respond to sustain talk that acknowledge it without getting stuck in it. You can use (Miller & Rollnick, 2013):

- **Simple reflections.** Acknowledge sustain talk with a simple reflective listening response. This validates what the client has said and sometimes elicits change talk. Give the client an opportunity to respond before moving on.
  - **Client:** I don't plan to quit drinking anytime soon.
  - **Counselor:** You don't think that abstinence would work for you right now.
- **Amplified reflections.** Accurately reflect the client's statement but with emphasis (and without sarcasm). An amplified reflection overstates the client's point of view, which can nudge the client to take the other side of ambivalence (i.e., change talk).
  - **Client:** But I can't quit smoking pot. All my friends smoke pot.
  - **Counselor:** So you really can't quit because you'd be too different from your friends.
- **Double-sided reflections.** A double-sided reflection acknowledges sustain talk, then pairs it with change talk either in the same client statement or in a previous statement. It acknowledges the client's ambivalence yet selectively reinforces change talk. Use "and" to join the two statements and make change talk the second statement (see Counselor Response in Exhibit 3.6).
  - **Client:** I know I should quit smoking now that I am pregnant. But I tried to go cold turkey before, and it was just too hard.
  - **Counselor:** You're worried that you won't be able to quit all at once, and you want your baby to be born healthy.
- **Agreements with a twist.** A subtle strategy is to agree, but with a slight twist or change of direction that moves the discussion forward. The twist should be said without emphasis or sarcasm.
  - **Client:** I can't imagine what I would do if I stopped drinking. It's part of who I am. How could I go to the bar and hang out with my friends?
  - **Counselor:** You just wouldn't be you without drinking. You have to keep drinking no matter how it effects your health.
- **Reframing.** Reframing acknowledges the client's experience yet suggests alternative meanings. It invites the client to consider a different perspective (Barnett, Spruijt-Metz, et al., 2014). Reframing is also a way to refocus the conversation from emphasizing sustain talk to eliciting change talk (Barnett, Spruijt-Metz, et al., 2014).
  - **Client:** My husband always nags me about my drinking and calls me an alcoholic. It bugs me.

TIP 35: *Enhancing Motivation for Change in Substance Use Disorder Treatment*
Chapter 3—Motivational Interviewing as a Counseling Style

October 2019

- **Counselor:** Although your husband expresses it in a way that frustrates you, he really cares and is concerned about the drinking.

- **A shift in focus.** Defuse discord and tension by shifting the conversational focus.
  - **Client:** The way you're talking, you think I'm an alcoholic, don't you?
  - **Counselor:** Labels aren't important to me. What I care about is how to best help you.

- **Emphasis on personal autonomy.** Emphasizing that people have choices (even if all the choices have a downside) reinforces personal autonomy and opens up the possibility for clients to choose change instead of the status quo. When you make these statements, remember to use a neutral, nonjudgmental tone, without sarcasm. A dismissive tone can evoke strong reactions from the client.
  - **Client:** I am really not interested in giving up drinking completely.
  - **Counselor:** It's really up to you. No one can make that decision for you.

All of these strategies have one thing in common: They are delivered in the spirit of MI.

Developing discrepancy: A values conversation

Developing discrepancy has been a key element of MI since its inception. It was originally one of the four principles of MI. In the current version, exploring the discrepancy between clients' values and their substance use behavior has been folded into the evoking process. When clients recognize discrepancies in their values, goals, and hopes for the future, their motivation to change increases. **Your task is to help clients focus on how their behavior conflicts with their values and goals.** The focus is on intrinsic motivation. MI doesn't work if you focus only on how clients' substance use behavior is in conflict with external pressure (e.g., family, an employer, the court) (Miller & Rollnick, 2013).

To facilitate discrepancy, have a values conversation to explore what is important to the client (e.g., good heath, positive relationships with family, being a responsible member of the community, preventing another hospitalization, staying out of jail), then highlight the conflict the client feels between his or her substance use behaviors and those values. Client experience of discrepancy between values and substance use behavior is related to better client outcomes (Apodaca & Longabaugh, 2009).

This process can raise uncomfortable feelings like guilt or shame. Frame the conversation by conveying acceptance, compassion, and affirmation. The paradox of acceptance is that it helps people tolerate more discrepancy and, instead of avoiding that tension, propels them toward change (Miller & Rollnick, 2013). However, too much discrepancy may overwhelm the client and cause him or her to think change is not possible (Miller & Rollnick, 2013).

To help a client perceive discrepancy, you can use what is sometimes termed the "Columbo approach." Initially developed by Kanfer & Schefft (1988), this approach remains a staple of MI and is particularly useful with a client who is in the Precontemplation stage and needs to be in charge of the conversation. Essentially, the counselor expresses understanding and continuously seeks clarification of the client's problem but appears unable to perceive any solution.

Expert Comment: The Columbo Approach
Sometimes I use what I refer to as the Columbo approach to develop discrepancy with clients. In the old *Columbo* television series, Peter Falk played a detective named Columbo who had a sense of what had really occurred but used a somewhat bumbling, unassuming, Socratic style of querying his prime suspect, strategically posing questions and making reflections to piece together a picture of what really happened. As the pieces began to fall into place, the object of Columbo's investigation would often reveal the real story.

TIP 35: *Enhancing Motivation for Change in Substance Use Disorder Treatment*
Chapter 3—Motivational Interviewing as a Counseling Style

October 2019

The counselor plays the role of a detective who is trying to solve a mystery but is having a difficult time because the clues don't add up. The "Columbo counselor" engages the client in solving the mystery:

Example #1: "Hmm. Help me figure this out. You've told me that keeping custody of your daughter and being a good parent are the most important things to you now. How does your heroin use fit in with that?"

Example #2: "So, sometimes when you drink during the week, you can't get out of bed to get to work. Last month, you missed 5 days. But you enjoy your work, and doing well in your job is very important to you."

In both cases, the counselor expresses confusion, which allows the client to take over and explain how these conflicting desires fit together.

The value of the Columbo approach is that it forces the client, rather than the counselor, to grapple with discrepancies and attempt to resolve them. This approach reinforces the notion that the client is the expert on his or her behavior and values. The client is truly the only one who can resolve the discrepancy. If the counselor attempts to do this instead of the client, the counselor risks making the wrong interpretation, rushing to the client to conclusions rather than listening to the client's perspective, and, perhaps most important, making the client a passive rather than an active participant in the process.

Cheryl Grills, Ph.D., Consensus Panel Member

In addition to providing personalized feedback (as discussed in Chapter 2), **you can facilitate discrepancy by** (Miller & Rollnick, 2013):

- **Identifying personal values.** For clients to feel discrepancy between their values and actions, they need to recognize what those values are. Some clients may have only a vague understanding of their values or goals. A tool to help you and clients explore values is the Values Card Sort.
  - Print different values like "Achievement—to have important accomplishments" (Miller & Rollnick, 2013, p. 80) on individual cards.
  - Invite clients to sort the cards into piles by importance; those that are most important are place in one pile, and those that are least important are in another pile.
  - Ask clients to pick up to 10 cards from the most important pile; converse about each one.
  - Use OARS to facilitate the conversations.
  - Pay attention to statements about discrepancy between these important values and clients' substance use behaviors, and reinforce these statements.
  - A downloadable, public domain version of the Value Card Sort activity is available online (www.motivationalinterviewing.org/sites/default/files/valuescardsort_0.pdf).

- **Providing information.** Avoid being the expert and treating clients as passive recipients when giving information about the negative physical, emotional, mental, social, or spiritual effects or consequences of substance misuse. Instead, engage the client in a process of mutual exchange. This process is called Elicit-Provide-Elicit (EPE) and has three steps (Miller & Rollnick, 2013):
  - **Elicit readiness or interest in the information.** Don't assume that clients are interested in hearing the information you want to offer; start by asking permission. For example: "Would it be okay if I shared some information with you about the health risks of using heroin?" Don't assume that clients lack this knowledge. Ask what they already know about the risks of using heroin. For example: "What would you most like to know about the health risks of heroin use?"
  - **Provide information neutrally (i.e., without judgement).** Prioritize what clients have said they would most like to know. Fill in knowledge gaps. Present the information clearly and in small chunks. Too much information can overwhelm clients. Invite them to ask more questions about the information you're providing.

TIP 35: *Enhancing Motivation for Change in Substance Use Disorder Treatment*
Chapter 3—Motivational Interviewing as a Counseling Style

October 2019

- **Elicit clients' understanding of the information.** Don't assume that you know how clients will react to the information you have provided. Ask questions:
  - "So, what do you make of this information?"
  - "What do you think about that?
  - "How does this information impact the way you might be thinking about *[name the substance use behavior, such as drinking]?*
- Allow clients plenty of time to consider and reflect on the information you presented. Invite them to ask questions for clarification. Follow clients' responses to your open questions with reflective listening statements that emphasize change talk whenever you hear it. **EPE is an MI strategy to facilitate identifying discrepancy and is an effective and respectful way to give advice to clients about behavior change strategies during the planning process.**

- **Exploring others' concerns.** Another way to build discrepancy is to explore the clients' understanding of the concerns other people have expressed about their substance use. This differs from focusing on the external pressure that a family member, an employer, or the criminal justice system may be putting on clients to reduce or abstain from substance use. The purpose is to invite clients to explore the impact of substance use behaviors on the people with whom they are emotionally connected in a nonthreatening way. Approach this conversation from a place of genuine curiosity and even a bit of confusion (Miller & Rollnick, 2013). Here is a brief example of what this conversation might look like using an open question about a significant other's concern, where reflecting sustain talk actually has the effect of eliciting change talk:
  - **Counselor:** You mentioned that your husband is concerned about your drinking. What do you think concerns him? *(Open question)*
  - **Client:** He worries about everything. The other day, he got really upset because I drove a block home from a friend's house after a party. He shouldn't worry so much. *(Sustain talk)*
  - **Counselor:** He's worried that you could crash and hurt yourself or someone else or get arrested for driving under the influence. But you think his concern is overblown. *(Complex reflection)*
  - **Client:** I can see he may have a point. I really shouldn't drive after drinking. *(Change talk)*

Evoking hope and confidence to support self-efficacy

Many clients do not have a well-developed sense of self-efficacy. They find it hard to believe that they can begin or maintain behavior change. **Improving self-efficacy requires eliciting confidence, hope, and optimism that change, in general, is possible and that clients, specifically, can change.** This positive impact on self-efficacy may be one of the ways MI promotes behavior change (Chariyeva et al., 2013).

One of the most consistent predictors of positive client behavior change is "ability" change talk (Romano & Peters, 2016). Unless a client believes change is possible, the perceived discrepancy between desire for change and feelings of hopelessness about accomplishing change is likely to result in continued sustain talk and no change. When clients express confidence in their ability to change, they are more likely to engage in behavior change (Romano & Peters, 2016).

Counselor Note: Self-Efficacy

Self-efficacy is a person's confidence in his or her ability to change a behavior (Miller & Rollnick, 2013), such as a behavior that risks one's health. Research has found that MI is effective in enhancing a client's self-efficacy and positive outcomes including treatment completion, lower substance use at the end of treatment, greater desire to quit cannabis use, and reductions in risky sexual behavior for someone with HIV (Caviness et al., 2013; Chariyeva et al., 2013; Dufett, & Ward, 2015; Moore, Flamez,, & Szirony, 2017).

TIP 35: *Enhancing Motivation for Change in Substance Use Disorder Treatment*
Chapter 3—Motivational Interviewing as a Counseling Style

October 2019

Because self-efficacy is a critical component of behavior change, it is crucial that you also believe in clients' capacity to reach their goals. You can help clients strengthen hope and confidence in MI by evoking confidence talk. Here are two strategies for evoking confidence talk (Miller & Rollnick, 2013):

- **Use the Confidence Ruler** (Exhibit 3.10) and scaling questions to assess clients' confidence level and evoke confidence talk.

Exhibit 3.10. The Confidence Ruler

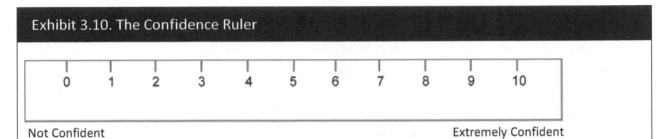

Not Confident   Extremely Confident

- Initial question: "On a scale of 0 to 10, how confident are you that you could change *[name the target behavior, like stop drinking]* if you decided to?"
- Follow-up questions:
  - "How are you at a *[fill in the number on the scale]* instead of a *[choose a lower number on the scale]*?" Using a lower number helps clients reflect on how far they've come on the confidence scale. Using a higher number with this question may discourage clients, which can elicit sustain talk. If that should happen, use strategies discussed previously for responding to sustain talk.
  - "What would help you get from a *[fill in the number on the scale]* to a *[choose a slightly higher number on the scale]*?" This open question invites clients to reflect on strategies to build confidence. Don't jump to a much higher number, which can overwhelm clients and lower confidence.

Whatever the client's response to these scaling questions, use it as an opportunity to begin a conversation about his or her confidence or perceived ability to move forward in the change process.

- **Ask open questions** that evoke client strengths and abilities. Follow the open questions with reflective listening responses. Here are some examples of open questions that elicit confidence talk:
  - "Knowing yourself as well as you do, how do you think you could [name the target behavior change, like cutting back on smoking marijuana]?"
  - "How have you made difficult changes in the past?"
  - "How could you apply what you learned then to this situation?"
  - "What gives you confidence that you could [name the target behavior change, like stopping cocaine use]?"

In addition, **you can help enhance clients' hope and confidence about change by:**

- Exploring clients' strengths and brainstorming how to apply those strengths to the current situation.
- Giving information via EPE about the efficacy of treatment to increase clients' sense of self-efficacy.
- Discussing what worked and didn't work in previous treatment episodes and offering change options based on what worked before.
- Describing how people in similar situations have successfully changed their behavior. Other clients in treatment can serve as role models and offer encouragement.
- Offering some cognitive tools, like the AA slogan "One day at a time" or "Keep it simple" to break down an overwhelming task into smaller changes that may be more manageable.
- Educating clients about the biology of addiction and the medical effects of substance use to alleviate

shame and instill hope that recovery is possible.

Engaging, focusing, and evoking set the stage for mobilizing action to change. During these MI processes, your task is to evoke DARN change talk. This moves the client along toward taking action to change substance use behaviors. At this point, your task is to evoke and respond to CAT change talk.

Recognizing signs of readiness to change

As you evoke and respond to DARN change talk, you will begin to observe these signs of readiness to change in the client's statements (Miller & Rollnick, 2013):

- **Increased change talk:** As DARN change talk increases, commitment and activation change talk begin to be expressed. The client may show optimism about change and an intention to change.

- **Decreased sustain talk:** As change talk increases, sustain talk decreases. When change talk overtakes sustain talk, it is a sign that the client is moving toward change.

- **Resolve:** The client seems more relaxed. The client talks less about the problem, and sometimes expresses a sense of resolution.

- **Questions about change:** The client asks what to do about the problem, how people change if they want to, and so forth. For example: "What do people do to get off pain pills?"

- **Envisioning:** The client begins to talk about life after a change, anticipate difficulties, or discuss the advantages of change. Envisioning requires imagining something different—not necessarily how to get to that something different, but simply imagining how things could be different.

- **Taking steps:** The client begins to experiment with small steps toward change (e.g., going to an AA meeting, going without drinking for a few days, reading a self-help book). Affirming small change steps helps the client build self-efficacy and confidence.

When you notice these signs of readiness to change, it is a good time to offer the client a recapitulation summary in which you restate his or her change talk and minimize reflections of sustain talk. **The recapitulation summary is a good way to transition into asking key questions** (Miller & Rollnick, 2013).

Asking key questions

To help a client move from preparing to mobilizing for change, ask key questions (Miller & Rollnick, 2013):

- "What do you think you will do about your drinking?"
- "After reviewing the situation, what's the next step for you?"
- "What do you want to do about your drug use?"
- "What can you do about your smoking?"
- "Where do you go from here?"
- "What you might do next?"

When the client responds with change talk (e.g., "I intend to stop using heroin"), you can move forward to the planning process. If the client responds with sustain talk (e.g., "It would be too hard for me to quit using heroin right now"), you should go back to the evoking process. Remember that change is not a linear process for most people.

Do not jump into the planning process if the client expresses enough sustain talk to indicate not being ready to take the next step. The ambivalence about taking the next step may be uncertainty about giving up the substance use behavior or a lack of confidence about being able to make the change.

TIP 35: *Enhancing Motivation for Change in Substance Use Disorder Treatment*
Chapter 3—Motivational Interviewing as a Counseling Style

October 2019

Planning

Your task in the process is to help the client develop a change plan that is acceptable, accessible, and appropriate. Once a client decides to change a substance use behavior, he or she may already have ideas about how to make that change. For example, a client may have previously stopped smoking cannabis and already knows what worked in the past. Your task is to simply reinforce the client's plan.

Don't assume that all clients need a structured method to develop a change plan. Many people can make significant lifestyle changes and initiate recovery from SUDs without formal assistance (Kelly, Bergman, Hoeppner, Vilsaint, & White, 2017). **For clients who need help developing a change plan, remember to continue using MI techniques and OARS to move the process from *why* change and *what* to change to *how* to change** (Miller & Rollnick, 2013). A change plan is like a treatment plan but broader (e.g., going to an addiction treatment program may be part of a change plan), and the client, rather than you or the treatment program, is the driver of the planning process (Miller & Rollnick, 2013).

Identifying a change goal

Part of planning is working with the client to identify or clarify a change goal. At this point, the client may have identified a change goal. For example, when you ask a key question such as "What do you want to do about the drinking?" the client might say, "I want to cut back to two drinks a day on weekends." In this situation, the focus shifts to developing a plan with specific steps the client might take to reach the change goal. If the client is vague about a change goal and says, "I really need to do something about my drinking," the first step is to help the client clarify the change goal.

Here is an example of a dialog that helps the client get more specific:

- **Counselor:** You are committed to making some changes to your drinking. *(Reflection)* What would that look like? *(Open question)*
- **Client:** Well, I tried to cut back to one drink a day, but all I could think about was going to the bar and getting drunk. I cut back for 2 days but did end up back at the bar, and then it just got worse from there. At this point, I don't think I can just cut back.
- **Counselor:** You made a good-faith effort to control the drinking and learned a lot from that experiment. *(Affirmation)* You now think that cutting back is probably not a good strategy for you. *(Reflection)*
- **Client:** Yeah. It's time to quit. But I'm not sure I can do that on my own.
- **Counselor:** You're ready to quit drinking completely and realize that you could use some help with making that kind of change. *(Reflection)*
- **Client:** Yeah. It's time to give it up.
- **Counselor:** Let's review the conversation, *(Summarization)* and then talk about next steps.

The counselor uses OARS to help the client clarify the change goal. The counselor also hears that the client lacks confidence that he or she can achieve the change goal and reinforces the client's desire for some help in making the change. The next step with this client is to develop a change plan.

Developing a change plan

Begin with the change goal identified by the client; then, explore specific steps the client can take to achieve it. In the planning process, use OARS and pay attention to CAT change talk. As you proceed, carefully note the shift from change talk that is more general to change talk that is specific to the change plan (Miller & Rollnick, 2013). (See Chapter 6 for information on a developing a change plan.) Some

TIP 35: *Enhancing Motivation for Change in Substance Use Disorder Treatment*
Chapter 3—Motivational Interviewing as a Counseling Style

October 2019

evidence shows that change talk is related to the completion of a change plan (Roman & Peters, 2016).

Here are some strategies for helping clients develop a change plan (Miller & Rollnick, 2013):

- **Confirm the change goal.** Make sure that you and the client agree on what substance use behavior the client wants to change and what the ultimate goal is (i.e., to cut back or to abstain). This goal might change as the client takes steps to achieve it. For example, a client who tries to cut back on cannabis use may find that that it is not a workable plan and may decide to abstain completely.

- **Elicit the client's ideas about how to change.** There may be many different pathways to achieve the desired goal. For example, a client whose goal is to stop drinking may go to AA or SMART Recovery meetings for support, get a prescription for naltrexone (a medication that reduces craving and the pleasurable effects of alcohol [Substance Abuse and Mental Health Services Administration & National Institute on Alcohol Abuse and Alcoholism, 2015]) from a primary care provider, enter an intensive outpatient treatment program, or try some combination of these. Before you jump in with your ideas, elicit the client's ideas about strategies to make the change. Explore pros and cons of the client's ideas; determine which appeals to the client most and is most appropriate for this client.

- **Offer a menu of options.** Use the EPE process (see the section "Developing discrepancy: A values conversation" above) to ask permission to offer suggestions about accessible treatment options, provide information about those options, and elicit the client's understanding of options and which ones seem acceptable.

- **Summarize the change plan.** Once you and the client have a clear plan, summarize the plan and the specific steps or pathways the client has identified. Listen for CAT change talk, and reinforce it through reflective listening.

- **Explore obstacles.** Once the client applies the change plan to his or her life, there will inevitably be setbacks. Try to anticipate potential obstacles and how the client might respond to them before the client takes steps to implement the plan. Then reevaluate the change plan, and help the client tweak it using the information about what did and didn't work from prior attempts.

Strengthening Commitment to Change

The planning process is just the beginning of change. Clients must commit to the plan and show that commitment by taking action. There is some evidence that client commitment change talk is associated with positive AUD outcomes (Romano & Peters, 2016). One study found that counselor efforts to elicit client commitment to change alcohol use is associated with reduced alcohol consumption and increased abstinence for clients in outpatient treatment (Magill, Stout, & Apodoaca, 2013).

Usually, people express an intention to make a change before they make a firm commitment to taking action. You can evoke the client's intention to take action by asking open questions: "What are you **willing** to do this week?" or "What specific steps of the change plan are you **ready** to take?" (Miller & Rollnick, 2013). Remember that the client may have an end goal (e.g., to quit drinking) and intermediate action steps to achieving that goal (e.g., filling a naltrexone prescription, going to an AA meeting).

Once the client has expressed an intention to change, elicit commitment change talk. Try asking an open question that invites the client to explore his or her commitment more clearly: "What would help you strengthen your commitment to _____ *[name the step or ultimate goal for change, for example, getting that prescription from your doctor for naltrexone]*?" (Miller & Rollnick, 2013).

Other strategies to strengthen commitment to action steps and change goals include (Miller & Rollnick, 2013):

- Exploring any ambivalence clients have about change goals or specific elements of change plans.

TIP 35: *Enhancing Motivation for Change in Substance Use Disorder Treatment*
Chapter 3—Motivational Interviewing as a Counseling Style

October 2019

- Reinforcing CAT change talk through reflective listening.

- Inviting clients to state their commitment to their significant others.

- Asking clients to self-monitor by recording progress toward change goals (e.g., with a drinking log).

- Exploring, with clients' consent, whether supportive significant others can help with medication adherence or other activities that reinforce commitment (e.g., getting to AA meetings).

The change plan process lends itself to using other counseling methods like CBT and MET. For example, you can encourage clients to monitor their thoughts and feelings in high-risk situations where they are more likely to return to substance use or misuse. Chapter 7 provides more information on relapse prevention. No matter what counseling strategies you use, keep to the spirit of MI by working with clients and honoring and respecting their right to and capacity for self-direction.

Benefits of MI in Treating SUDs

The number of research studies on MI has doubled about every 3 years from 1999 to 2013 (Miller & Rollnick, 2013). Many studies were randomized clinical trials reflecting a range of clinical populations, types of problems, provider settings, types of SUDs, and co-occurring substance use and mental disorders (Smedslund et al., 2011). Although some studies report mixed results, the overall scientific evidence suggests that MI is associated with small to strong (and significant) effects for positive substance use behavioral outcomes compared with no treatment. MI is as effective as other counseling approaches (DiClemente et al., 2017). A research review found strong, significant support for MI and combined MI/MET in client outcomes for alcohol, tobacco, and cannabis and some support for its use in treating cocaine and combined illicit drug use disorders (DiClemente et al., 2017). Positive outcomes included reduced alcohol, tobacco, and cannabis use; fewer alcohol-related problems; and improved client engagement and retention (DiClemente et al., 2017). MI and combined MI/MET were effective with adolescents, young adults, college students, adults, and pregnant women.

Counselor adherence to MI skills is important for producing client outcomes (Apodaca et al., 2016; Magill et al., 2013). For instance, using open questions, simple and complex reflective listening responses, and affirmations is associated with change talk (Apodaca et al., 2016; Romano & Peters, 2016). Open questions and reflective listening responses can elicit sustain talk when counselors explore ambivalence with clients (Apodaca et al., 2016). However, growing evidence suggests that the amount and strength of client change talk versus sustain talk in counseling sessions are key components of MI associated with behavior change (Gaume et al., 2016; Houck et al., 2018; Lindqvist et al., 2017; Magill et al., 2014).

Other benefits of MI include (Miller & Rollnick, 2013):

- **Cost effectiveness.** MI can be delivered in brief interventions like SBIRT (screening, brief intervention, and referral to treatment) and FRAMES (**F**eedback, **R**esponsibility, **A**dvice, **M**enu of options, **E**mpathy, and **S**elf-efficacy, see Chapter 2), which makes it cost effective. In addition, including significant others in MI interventions is also cost effective (Shepard et al., 2016).

- **Ease of use.** MI has been adapted and integrated into many settings, including primary care facilities, emergency departments, behavioral health centers, and criminal justice and social service agencies. It is useful anywhere that focuses on helping people manage substance misuse and SUDs.

- **Broad dissemination.** MI has been disseminated throughout the United States and internationally.

- **Applicability to diverse health and behavioral health problems.** Beyond substance use behaviors, MI has demonstrated benefits across a wide range of behavior change goals.

- **Effectiveness.** Positive effects from MI counseling occur across a range of real-life clinical settings.

TIP 35: *Enhancing Motivation for Change in Substance Use Disorder Treatment*
Chapter 3—Motivational Interviewing as a Counseling Style

October 2019

- **Ability to complement other treatment approaches.** MI fits well with other counseling approaches, such as CBT. It can enhance client motivation to engage in specialized addiction treatment services and stay in and adhere to treatment.
- **Ease of adoption by a range of providers.** MI can be implemented by primary care and behavioral health professionals, peer providers, criminal justice personnel, and various other professionals.
- **Role in mobilizing client resources.** MI is based on person-centered counseling principles. It focuses on mobilizing the client's own resources for change. It is consistent with the healthcare model of helping people learn to self-manage chronic illnesses like diabetes and heart disease.

Conclusion

MI is a directed, person-centered counseling style that is effective in helping clients change their substance use behaviors. When delivered in the spirit of MI, the core skills of asking open questions, affirming, using reflective listening, and summarizing enhance client motivation and readiness to change. Counselor empathy, shown through reflective listening and evoking change talk, is another important element of MI's effectiveness and is associated with positive client outcomes. MI has been adapted for use in brief interventions and across a wide range of clinical settings and client populations. It is compatible with other counseling models and theories of change, including CBT and the SOC.

TIP 35: *Enhancing Motivation for Change in Substance Use Disorder Treatment*
Chapter 3—Motivational Interviewing as a Counseling Style

October 2019

This page intentionally left blank.

TIP 35: *Enhancing Motivation for Change in Substance Use Disorder Treatment*
Chapter 3—Motivational Interviewing as a Counseling Style

October 2019

Chapter 4—From Precontemplation to Contemplation: Building Readiness

"The task for individuals in Precontemplation is to become conscious of and concerned about the current pattern of behavior and/or interested in a new behavior. From a change perspective, it is more important to recognize an individual's current views on change and address her or his reasons for not wanting to change than it is to understand how the status quo came to be."

DiClemente, 2018, p. 29

Key Messages

- In the Precontemplation stage, clients do not recognize that they have a problem with substance use or they recognize the problem but are not ready to change their substance use behaviors.

- Counselors should be nonjudgmental about clients' low motivation to change and instead focus on building a strong working alliance.

- A key strategy to helping clients move from the Precontemplation stage to contemplating change is to raise their level of concern and awareness of the risk associated with their current substance use behaviors.

- Involving family members and significant others (SOs) can increase clients' concern about substance use.

Chapter 4 discusses strategies you can use to help clients raise doubt and concern about their substance use and related health, social, emotional, mental, financial, and legal problems. It highlights areas of focus and key counseling strategies that will help clients move from the Precontemplation stage to Contemplation. This chapter also addresses issues that may arise for clients mandated to treatment.

In the Stages of Change (SOC) model, clients who are unconcerned about their current substance use or may be concerned but aren't considering change are in Precontemplation. They may remain there or in the early Contemplation stage for years, rarely or possibly never thinking about change.

You can take advantage of many opportunities and scenarios to help someone who is misusing substances start on a journey toward change—to move from Precontemplation to Contemplation. A client in Precontemplation is often moved to enter the cycle of change by extrinsic sources of motivation. The following situations might lead a person who is misusing a substance to treatment:

- A college coach refers an athlete for treatment after he tests positive for cocaine use.

- A wife worries about her husband's drinking and insists she'll file for divorce unless he gets treatment.

- A tenant is displaced from a federal housing project because of his substance use.

- A driver is referred for treatment by the court for driving while intoxicated.

- A woman tests positive for substances during a prenatal visit to a public health clinic.

- An employer sends an employee whose job performance has declined to the company's employee assistance program, and the employee is subsequently referred for substance use treatment.

- A physician in an emergency department treats a driver involved in a serious automobile crash and discovers alcohol in his system.

- A family physician screens a patient for alcohol use disorder (AUD) and suggests treatment based on

TIP 35: *Enhancing Motivation for Change in Substance Use Disorder Treatment*
Chapter 4—From Precontemplation to Contemplation: Building Readiness

October 2019

the patient's high score on the Alcohol Use Disorders Identification Test.

- A mother whose children were taken into custody by Child Protective Services because of neglect learns that she cannot get them back until she stops using substances and seeks treatment.

In each situation, someone with an important relationship to the person misusing substances stated his or her concerns about the person's substance misuse and its negative effects. The response to these concerns depends, in part, on the person's perception of the circumstances as well as the way feedback about substance misuse is presented. An individual will be better motivated to abstain from or moderate his or her substance use if these concerned others offer relevant information in a supportive and empathic manner rather than in a judgmental, dismissive, or confrontational way.

Exhibit 4.1 presents counseling strategies for Precontemplation.

Exhibit 4.1. Counseling Strategies for Precontemplation

Client Motivation	Counselor Focus	Counseling Strategies
• The client is not concerned about substance use or lacks awareness about any problems. • The client is not yet considering change or is unwilling or unable to change. • The client is often pressured by others to seek help.	• Develop rapport and build trust to establish a strong counseling alliance. • Raise doubts and concerns about the client's substance use. • Understand special motivational counseling considerations for clients mandated to treatment.	• Elicit the client's perceptions of the problem. • Explore the events that led to entering treatment. • Assess the client's stage in the SOC and readiness to change. • Commend the client for coming to treatment. • Agree on a direction. • Provide information about the effects and risks of substance misuse. • Evoke concern about the client's substance use. • Provide personalized feedback on assessment findings. • Involve SOs in treatment to raise concern about the client's substance use. • Express concern, and leave the door open.

Develop Rapport and Build Trust

Before you raise the topic of change with people who are not thinking about it, establish rapport and trust. The challenge is to create a safe and supportive environment in which clients can feel comfortable about engaging in authentic dialog. As clients become more engaged in counseling, their defensiveness and reluctance to change decreases (Prochaska, Norcross, & DiClemente, 2013). Some motivational strategies for establishing rapport in initial conversations about behavior change include:

- **Asking the client for permission** to address the topic of changing substance use behaviors; this shows respect for the client's autonomy.

- **Telling the client something about how you or your program operates and how you and the client could work together.** State how long sessions will last and what you expect to accomplish both now and over a specified time. Try not to overwhelm the new client with all the program's rules and regulations. Specify what assessments or other formal arrangements will be needed, if appropriate.

- **Raising confidentiality issues up front.** You must inform the client which information will be kept private, which can be released with permission, and which must be sent back to a referring agency.

- **Explaining that you will not tell the client what to do or how and whether to change.** Rather, you will be asking the client to do most of the talking—giving him or her perspective about what is

TIP 35: *Enhancing Motivation for Change in Substance Use Disorder Treatment*
Chapter 4—From Precontemplation to Contemplation: Building Readiness

October 2019

happening while inviting the client to share his or her own perspective. You can also invite comments about what the client expects or hopes to achieve.

- **Asking the client to tell you why he or she has come to treatment, mentioning what you know about the reasons, and asking for the client's version or elaboration** (Miller & Rollnick, 2013). If the client seems particularly hesitant or defensive, one strategy is to choose a topic of interest to the client that can be linked to substance use. (For more information about setting an agenda, see Chapter 3.) Such information might be provided by the referral source or can be learned by asking whether the client is dealing with any stressful situations, such as illness, marital discord, or extremely heavy workload. This can lead naturally to questions such as "How does your use of alcohol fit into this?" or "How does your use of heroin affect your health?"

- **Avoiding referring to the client's "problem" or "substance misuse," because this may not reflect the client's perspective about substance use** (Miller & Rollnick, 2013). You are trying to understand the context in which substances are used and the client's readiness to change. As mentioned previously, labels can raise a person's defenses.

- **Aligning your counseling approach to the client's current stage in the SOC.** For example, move to strategies more appropriate to a later stage in the SOC if you discover that the client is already contemplating or committed to change. (For more information on the later stages in the SOC, see Chapters 5 and 6.)

Counselor Note: Agency Policy About Client Intoxication

In your first session, discuss your agency's policy on having conversations with clients who are intoxicated. Be transparent about the policy and what actions you will take if the client comes to a session intoxicated. Coming to treatment intoxicated on alcohol or drugs impairs ability to participate in treatment, whether it is for an initial counseling session, assessment, or individual or group treatment (Miller, Forechimes, & Zweben, 2011).

Many programs administer breathalyzer tests for alcohol or urinalysis for drugs and reschedule counseling sessions if substances are detected at a specified level or if a client appears to be under the influence (Miller et al., 2011). If you determine that a client is intoxicated, ask the client in a nonjudgmental way to leave. Reschedule the appointment, and help the client get home safely (Miller et al., 2011).

Elicit the Client's Perception of the Problem

To engage clients, invite them to explain their understanding of the problem. Be direct, but remain nonjudgmental. You might say, "Can you tell me a bit about what brings you here today?" or "I'd like to understand your perspective on why you're here. Can we start there?" Asking these open questions invites clients to tell you their story and shows your genuine interest in their perspective.

Explore the Events That Led to Entering Treatment

Explore what brought the client to treatment, starting by recognizing his or her emotional state. The emotional state in which the client comes to treatment is an important part of the context in which counseling begins. A client referred to treatment will exhibit a range of emotions associated with the experiences that led to counseling—for example, an arrest, a confrontation with a spouse or employer, or a health crisis. People may enter treatment feeling shaken, angry, withdrawn, ashamed, terrified, or relieved and are often experiencing a combination of feelings. **Strong emotions can become obstacles to change if you do not acknowledge them through reflective listening.**

Your initial conversation with clients should focus on their recent experience. For example, an athlete is likely to be concerned about his or her continued participation in sports, as well as athletic performance; an employee may want to keep his or her job; and a driver is probably worried about the

TIP 35: *Enhancing Motivation for Change in Substance Use Disorder Treatment*
Chapter 4—From Precontemplation to Contemplation: Building Readiness

October 2019

possibility of losing his or her license, going to jail, or injuring someone. A pregnant woman wants a healthy child; a mother may want to regain custody of her children; and a concerned husband needs specific guidance on encouraging his spouse to enter treatment.

Many people with substance use problems seek treatment in response to external pressure from family, friends, employers, healthcare providers, or the legal system (Connors, DiClemente, Velasquez, & Donovan, 2013). A client sometimes blames the referring source or someone else for pressuring him or her into treatment and report that the referring provider simply doesn't view the situation accurately. **Start with these external sources of motivation as a way to raise the client's awareness about the impact of his or her substance use on others.** For example, if the client's wife has insisted he start treatment and the client denies any problem, you might ask, "What kind of things seem to bother her?" or "What do you think makes her believe there is a problem associated with your drinking?" If the wife's perceptions are inconsistent with the client's, you might suggest that the wife come to treatment so that you can explore their different perspectives.

Similarly, you may have to review and confirm a referring agency's account or the physical evidence forwarded by a healthcare provider to help you introduce alternative viewpoints to the client in nonthreatening ways. If the client thinks a probation officer is the problem, you can ask, "Why do you think your probation officer believes you have a problem?" This lets the client express the problem from the perspective of the referring party and can raise awareness. Use reflective listening responses to let the client know you are listening. **Avoid agreeing or disagreeing with the client's position.**

Assess the Client's SOC and Readiness to Change

When you first meet the client, determine his or her readiness to change and where he or she is in the SOC; this determines what counseling strategies are likely to work. It is tempting to assume that the client with obvious signs of a substance use disorder (SUD) must already be contemplating or ready for change. However, such assumptions may be wrong. The new client could be at any point on the severity continuum (from substance misuse to severe SUD), could have few or many associated health or social problems, and could be at any stage of readiness to change. The strategies you use to engage clients in initial conversations about change should be guided by your assessment of the client's motivation and readiness.

The Importance and Confidence Rulers

The simplest way to assess the client's readiness to change is to use the Importance Ruler and the Confidence Ruler described in Chapter 3 (see Exhibit 3.9 and Exhibit 3.10, respectively). The Importance Ruler indicates how important it is for the client to make a change right now. The Confidence Ruler indicates a client's sense of self-efficacy about making a change right now. Together, they indicate how ready the client is to change target behaviors. Clients in Precontemplation will typically be at the lower end of the rulers, generally between 0 and 3.

Keep in mind that these numerical assessments are neither fixed nor always linear. The client moves forward or backward across stages or jumps from one part of the continuum to another, in either direction and at various times. **Your role is to facilitate movement in the direction of positive change.**

Identification of the client's style of Precontemplation

You should tailor your counseling approach to the ways in which the client talks about being in Precontemplation. Clients will present with different expressions of sustain talk (see Chapter 3), which is the status quo side of ambivalence about changing substance use behaviors. Exhibit 4.2 describes

TIP 35: *Enhancing Motivation for Change in Substance Use Disorder Treatment*
Chapter 4—From Precontemplation to Contemplation: Building Readiness

October 2019

different styles of expressions of ambivalence about change during the Precontemplation stage (known as the 5 Rs) and counseling strategies aligned with these different expressions of sustain talk during Precontemplation.

Exhibit 4.2. Styles of Expression in the Precontemplation Stage: The 5 Rs	
Individuals with addictive behaviors who are not yet contemplating change usually express sustain talk in one or more of five different ways. Identifying each client's style of expression helps determine the counseling approach to follow.	
Reveling	Clients are still focused on good experiences about substance use and have not necessarily experienced many substance-use–related negative consequences. Providing objective, nonjudgmental feedback about their substance use and associated health risks or other negative consequences can raise doubt about their ability to avoid negative effects of substance use on their lives.
Reluctance	Clients lack knowledge about the dimensions of the problem or the personal impact it can have to think change is necessary. They often respond to nonjudgmental feedback about how substance use is affecting their lives. They also respond to reassurance that they will be able to function without the addictive behavior.
Rebellion	Clients are afraid of losing control over their lives and have a large investment in their substance of choice. Your challenge is to help them make more positive choices for themselves rather than rebel against what they view as pressure to change. Emphasizing personal choice and responsibility can work well with them.
Resignation	Clients may feel hopeless, helpless, and overwhelmed by the energy required to change. They probably have been in treatment many times before or have tried repeatedly with little success to quit on their own. These clients must regain hope and optimism about their capacity for change. Explore with them specific barriers to change and successful change attempts with other behaviors. Offer information about how treatment has helped many people who thought they couldn't change, and link them to others in recovery who can provide additional hope and support.
Rationalization	Clients think they have all the answers and that substance use may be a problem for others but not for them. Using double-sided reflection (see Chapter 3), rather than arguing for change, seems the most effective strategy for clients expressing rationalizations. Acknowledge what these clients say, but point out any reservations they may have expressed earlier about current substance use.
Source: DiClemente, 2018.	

Readiness assessment instruments

Use assessment tools to help determine the client's readiness to change and place in the SOC. These instruments can give overall scores that correspond to levels of readiness to change. You may find it useful to **explore client responses to specific questions** to raise awareness of his or her substance use and what may be getting in the way of making a change. Several assessment tools widely used in clinical and research settings are discussed briefly below and presented in full in Appendix B:

- **The University of Rhode Island Change Assessment Scale (URICA)** was originally developed to measure a client's change stage in psychotherapy (McConnaughy, Prochaska, & Velicer, 1983) in terms of four stages of the SOC: Precontemplation, Contemplation, Action, and Maintenance. It has been adapted for addiction treatment and is the most common way of measuring the client's stage of change in clinical settings (Connors et al., 2013).

- The scale has 32 items—8 items for each of the 4 stage-specific subscales. A client rates items on a 5-point scale from 1 (strong disagreement) to 5 (strong agreement). The instrument covers a range of concerns and asks clients general questions about the client's "problem." URICA subscales have good internal consistency and validity for SUDs (Field, Adinoff, Harris, Ball, & Carroll, 2009).

- To use this tool, the client is asked to identify a specific "problem" (e.g., cocaine use) and then fills out the form keeping the specific problem in mind. There may be more than one "problem" for which the client is seeking help, so you may want to have the client fill out the instrument more than once. You can use the URICA to track a client's movement through the SOC by asking the client to fill it out periodically.

- **The Stages of Change Readiness and Treatment Eagerness Scale (SOCRATES)** measures readiness to change. The original SOCRATES was a 32-item questionnaire that used a 5-point scale ranging from 5 (strongly agree) to 1 (strongly disagree). A 19-item version was developed for clinical use and is a self-administered paper-and-pencil questionnaire (Miller & Tonigan, 1996). The SOCRATES 8A is for alcohol use, and the SOCRATES 8D is for drug use. The items on the short version assess the recognition of the problem, ambivalence, and efforts to take steps.

  SOCRATES provides clients with feedback about their scores as a starting point for discussion. Changes in scores over time can help you learn the impact of an intervention on problem recognition, ambivalence, and progress on making changes.

- **The Readiness To Change Questionnaire** was developed to help healthcare providers who are not addiction treatment specialists assess the stage of change of clients misusing alcohol (Rollnick, Heather, Gold, & Hall, 1992). The 12 items, which were adapted from the URICA, are associated with 3 stages—Precontemplation, Contemplation, and Action—and reflect typical attitudes of clients in each readiness level. For example, a person not yet contemplating change would likely give a positive response to the statement "It's a waste of time thinking about my drinking because I do not have a problem," whereas a person already taking action would probably agree with the statement "I am actively working on my drinking problem." Another individual already contemplating change would likely agree with the item "Sometimes I think I should quit or cut down on my drinking." A 5-point scale is used for rating responses, from 5 (strongly agree) to 1 (strongly disagree).

Commend the Client for Coming to Treatment

Offering clients affirmations over responsible behaviors, like entering treatment, can increase their confidence that change is possible. Clients referred for treatment may feel they have little control in the process. Some will expect to be criticized or blamed; some will expect you to cure them; and still others will hope that counseling can solve all their problems without too much effort. Whatever their expectations, affirm their courage for coming to treatment by saying things like, "It took you a lot of effort to get here. You are determined to figure out what's going on and how you can change things." For example, you can praise a client's decision to come to treatment rather than risk losing custody of her child by saying, "You must care very much about your child." Such affirmations are supportive and remind clients that they are capable of making good choices that match their values.

Agree on a Direction

In helping clients who are not yet thinking seriously of changing, plan your strategies carefully and work with them to find an acceptable pathway. Some clients will agree on one option but not on another. It may be appropriate to give advice based on your own experience and concern. **However, always ask permission to offer advice and make sure that clients want to hear what you have to say.**

TIP 35: *Enhancing Motivation for Change in Substance Use Disorder Treatment*
Chapter 4—From Precontemplation to Contemplation: Building Readiness

October 2019

Asking permission demonstrates respect for client autonomy and is consistent with person-centered counseling principles and the spirit of MI (as discussed in Chapter 3). For example: "I'd like to tell you about what we could do here. Would that be all right?"

Whenever you express a different viewpoint from that of the client, do so in a way that is supportive, not authoritative or confrontational. The client still has the choice of whether to accept your advice and to agree to a plan. It is not necessary at the beginning of the process to agree on treatment goals; however, you can use motivational strategies, like the agenda mapping discussed in Chapter 3, to agree on how to proceed in the current conversation.

Throughout the process of establishing rapport and building trust, use the OARS (asking **O**pen questions, **A**ffirming, **R**eflective listening, and **S**ummarizing) approach and person-centered counseling principles (described in Chapter 3) to create a sense of safety and respect for the client, as well as a genuine interest in the client's perspective and well-being. **Emphasizing personal autonomy will go a long way toward showing the client that you are not pressuring him or her to change.**

Raise Doubts and Concerns About the Client's Substance Use

Once you have engaged the client and developed rapport, **use the following strategies to increase the client's readiness to change and move closer to Contemplation**.

Provide Information About the Effects and Risks of Substance Misuse

Psychoeducational programs can increase clients' ambivalence about substance misuse and related problems and move them toward contemplation of change (Yeh, Tung, Horng, & Sung, 2017). Be sure to:

- Provide basic information about substance use early in the treatment process if clients have not been exposed to drug and alcohol education before.

- Use the motivational strategy of Elicit-Provide-Elicit (EPE, described in Chapter 3) to engage clients in a joint discussion rather than lecture them (Miller & Rollnick, 2013).

- Ask permission, for example, "Would it be okay to tell you a bit about the effects of _____?" or ask them to describe what they know about the effects or risks of the substances used.

- Talk about what happens to any user of the substance rather than referring just to the client.

- State what **experts** have found, not what **you** think happens.

- Provide small chunks of information then elicit the client's understanding. For example, "What do you make of all this?"

- Describe the addiction process in biological terms. Understanding facts about addiction can increase hope as well as readiness to change. For example, "When you first start using substances, it provides a pleasurable sensation. As you keep using substances, your mind begins to believe that you need these substances in the same way you need life-sustaining things like food—that you need them to survive. You're not stronger than this process, but you can be smarter, and you can regain your independence from substances."

Expert Comment: Liver Transplantation—Precontemplation to Contemplation

The client in Precontemplation can appear in surprising medical settings. It is not uncommon for me to find myself sitting across from a client with end-stage liver disease being evaluated for a liver transplant. From a medical perspective, the cause of the client's liver disease appears to be alcoholic hepatitis, which led to cirrhosis. A variety of laboratory and other information further supports a history of years of alcohol misuse. The diagnosis of AUD is not only supported by the medical information but also is made clear when the person's family indicates years of alcohol misuse despite intensely negative consequences, such as being charged with driving while intoxicated and marital stress related to the drinking. Yet, despite what might seem to be an overwhelming amount of evidence, the client himself, for a variety of dynamic and motivational reasons, cannot see himself as having a problem with alcohol. The client may feel guilty that he caused his liver damage and think he doesn't deserve this life-saving intervention. Or he may be fearful that if he examines his alcohol use too closely and shares his history, he may not be considered for transplantation at all. He may even have already been told that if he is actively drinking, he will not be listed for transplantation.

It is important for me as a counselor not to be surprised or judgmental about the client not wanting to see his problematic relationship with alcohol. The simple fact is that he has never connected his health problems with his use of alcohol. To confront the client with the overwhelming evidence about his problem drinking only makes him more defensive, reinforces his denial, and strengthens his feelings of guilt and shame.

During assessment, I take every opportunity to connect with the client's history and current situation without excessive self-disclosure. Being particularly sensitive to what the client needs and what he fears, I will help support the therapeutic alliance by asking him to share the positive side of his alcohol and drug use, thus acknowledging that, from his perspective, his use serves a purpose.

In a situation such as this, it is not uncommon for me, after completing a thorough assessment, to provide the client with a medical perspective on alcohol dependence. I will talk about changes in brain chemistry, reward systems, issues of tolerance, genetic factors, and different chemical responses to alcohol, as well as other biological processes that support addictive disease, depending on the client's educational background and medical understanding. I may go into great detail. If the client has fewer years of education, I will compare addiction to other, more familiar diseases, such as diabetes. As the client asks questions, he sees a new picture of addictive disease and sees himself in that picture. By tailoring the presentation to each client and encouraging questions throughout, I provide him and his family, if present, with important information about the biological factors supporting alcohol dependence. This knowledge often leads to self-diagnosis.

This psychoeducational reframing gives the client a different view on his relationship with alcohol, taking away some of the guilt and shame that was based on him thinking of the disease as a moral failing. The very act of self-diagnosis is a movement from Precontemplation to Contemplation. It can be accomplished by a simple cognitive reframe within the context of a thorough and caring assessment completed in a professional, yet genuinely compassionate manner.

Jeffrey M. Georgi, M.Div., Consensus Panel Member

Similarly, people who have driven under the influence of alcohol may be surprised to learn how few drinks are needed to meet the definition of legal intoxication and how drinking at these levels affects their responses. Women hoping to have children may not understand how substances can diminish fertility and potentially harm the fetus even before they know they are pregnant. Clients may not realize how alcohol interacts with other medications they are taking for depression or hypertension.

Counselor Note: Use Motivational Language in Written Materials

Remember that the effective strategies for increasing motivation in face-to-face contacts also apply to written language. Brochures, fliers, educational materials, and advertisements can help a client think differently about change. However, judgmental language like "abuse" or "denial" is just as off-putting in writing as it is when spoken in counseling sessions. **You should provide all written material in plain language** with motivation in mind. If your brochure starts with a long list of rules, the client may be scared away rather than encouraged to begin treatment. **Review written materials from the viewpoint of the client**, and keep in mind your role as a partner in a change process for which the client must take ultimate responsibility.

Evoke Concern About the Client's Substance Use

You can help move clients from Precontemplation to Contemplation by raising doubts about the harmlessness of their substance use and concerns about their substance use behaviors. As clients move beyond the Precontemplation stage and become aware of or acknowledge some problems in relation to their substance use, change becomes increasingly possible. Such clients become more aware of conflict and feel greater ambivalence (Miller & Rollnick, 2013).

One way to raise concern in the client is to explore the "positive" and "less-positive" aspects of his or her substance use. For example:

- Start with the client's views on possible "benefits" of alcohol or drugs and move to less-beneficial aspects rather than simply ask about **bad things** or **problems** associated with substance use.

- Do not focus only on negative aspects of substance use because the client could end up defending his or her substance use while you push for unwanted change.

- Avoid spending too much time exploring the "good" things about substance use that may reinforce sustain talk. Higher levels of client sustain talk is associated with lower motivation to change and negative treatment outcomes (Lindqvist, Forsberg, Enebrink, Andersson, & Rosendahl, 2017; Magill et al., 2014).

- Be aware that the client may not be ready to accept he or she has experienced any harmful effects of substance use. By showing that you understand why the client "values" alcohol or drug experiences, you help the client become more open to accepting possible problems. For example, you might ask, "Help me understand what you like about your drinking. What do you enjoy about it?" Then ask, "What do you like less about drinking?" The client who cannot recognize any things that he or she "likes less" about substance use is probably not ready to consider change and may need more information.

- After this exploration, summarize the interchange in personal language so that the client can clearly hear any ambivalence that is developing.

As mentioned in Chapter 3, you can **use double-sided reflections to respond to client ambivalence and sustain talk** (Miller & Rollnick, 2013). For example, you can say, "So, drinking helps you relax. Yet, you say you sometimes resent all the money you are spending, and it's hard for you to get to work on time, especially Monday mornings." Chapter 5 provides additional guidance on working with ambivalence.

You can also **move clients toward the Contemplation stage by having them consider the many ways in which substance use can affect life experiences.** For example, you might ask, "How is your substance use affecting your studies? How is your drinking affecting your family life?"

As you explore the effects of substance use in the individual's life, use balanced reflective listening: "Help me understand. You've been saying you see no need to change, **and** you are concerned about losing your family. I don't see how this fits together. I'm wondering if this is confusing for you, too."

Provide Personalized Feedback on Assessment Findings

Another effective strategy for raising doubt and concern is to provide clients with personalized feedback about assessment findings. As mentioned in Chapter 2, giving personalized feedback about clients' substance use is effective (Davis, Houck, Rowell, Benson, & Smith, 2015; DiClemente, Corno, Graydon, Wiprovnick, & Knoblach, 2017; Field et al., 2014; Kahler et al., 2018; McDevitt-Murphy et al.; 2014; Miller et al., 2013; Walker et al., 2017). In brief interventions, the feedback is usually short and focused on screening results. In specialty addiction treatment settings, feedback can focus on results of a comprehensive assessment, which often includes:

TIP 35: *Enhancing Motivation for Change in Substance Use Disorder Treatment*
Chapter 4—From Precontemplation to Contemplation: Building Readiness

October 2019

- Substance use patterns and history.

- *Diagnostic and Statistical Manual of Mental Disorders*, Fifth Edition, diagnostic criteria for SUDs.

- General functioning and links between substance use and lowered functioning.

- Health and biomedical effects including sleep disorders, HIV, and diabetes.

- Neuropsychological effects of long-term substance use.

- Family history of mental disorders and SUDs, which put clients at risk for SUDs and co-occurring substance use and mental disorders (CODs).

- CODs and effects of substance use on mental illness.

- Functional analysis of substance use triggers.

Provide clients with personalized feedback on the risks associated with their own substance use and how their consumption compares with others of the same culture, age, or gender. When clients hear about assessment results and understand the risks and consequences, many recognize the gap between where they are and where their values lie.

To make findings from an assessment a useful part of the counseling process, make sure the client understands the value of such information and believes the results will be helpful. If possible, schedule formal assessments after the client has had at least one session with you or use a motivational interviewing (MI) assessment strategy that involves having a brief MI conversation before and after the assessment (see Chapter 8 for more information). This approach will help establish rapport, determine the client's readiness for change, and measure his or her potential response to personalized feedback.

Start a standard assessment by **explaining what types of tests or questionnaires will be administered and what information these tools will reveal.** Estimate how long the process usually takes, and give any other necessary instructions. Make sure the client is comfortable with the assessment format (e.g., have self-administered tests available in the client's first language, do a face-to-face interview instead of a self-administered assessment if the client has cognitive challenges).

Counselor Note: Description of a Typical Day

An informal way to engage clients, build rapport as part of an assessment, and encourage clients to talk about substance use patterns in a nonjudgmental framework is to ask them to describe a typical day (Rollnick, Miller, & Butler, 2008). This approach can help you understand the context of clients' substance use. For example, it may reveal how much of each day is spent trying to get drugs and how little time is left to spend with loved ones. By asking about both behaviors and feelings, you can learn much about what substance use means to clients and how difficult or simple it may be to give it up. This strategy invites clients to tell a story; that story provides important details about clients' substance use patterns and related negative effects.

- **Start by asking permission.** "It would help me to understand how *[name the substance use behavior, such as drinking or smoking cannabis]* fits into to your life. Would it be okay if we spend a few minutes going through a typical day from beginning to end? Let's start from the time you get up in the morning."

- **Be curious.**

- **Avoid the use of the word "problem"** (unless the client uses it) in relation to substance use, otherwise you might create discord (Rosengren, 2018).

- **Follow the client through the sequence of events for an entire day, focusing on both behaviors and feelings**. Keep asking, "What happens when... ?"

- **Ask questions carefully and slowly.** Do not add your own thoughts about why certain events transpired.

- **Let the client use his or her own words.**

TIP 35: *Enhancing Motivation for Change in Substance Use Disorder Treatment*
Chapter 4—From Precontemplation to Contemplation: Building Readiness

October 2019

> • **Ask for clarification** only if you do not understand a term the client uses or if some information is missing.

Once the client completes the assessment, review findings with the client. Present personalized feedback to the client in a way that is likely to increase his or her awareness and develop discrepancy between the client's substance use and values. Appendix C provides a link to the *Motivational Enhancement Therapy Manual,* which includes an example of a personal feedback report to include in a comprehensive assessment. You should adapt this report for the specific kinds of assessment information you gather at your program.

When providing extensive feedback about assessment results, divide it into small chunks, and use the EPE approach, otherwise, the client might feel overwhelmed. You may only need to provide one or two pieces of feedback to raise doubts and concerns and to move the client toward Contemplation.

Involve Significant Others

Including people with whom the client has a close relationship can make treatment more effective. Many people who misuse substances or who have SUDs respond to motivation from spouses and SOs to enter treatment (Connors et al., 2013). An SO is typically a parent, spouse, live-in partner, or other family member but can be any person with a close personal relationship to the client.

Supportive SOs can help clients become intrinsically rather than just extrinsically motivated for behavior change (Bourke, Magill, & Apodaca, 2016). Including supportive SOs is cost effective and can foster positive client outcomes, including increased client change talk; increased client commitment to change; and reduced substance use, alcohol consumption, and alcohol-related consequences (Apodaca, Magill, Longabaugh, Jackson, & Monti, 2013; Bourke et al., 2016; Monti et al., 2014; Shepard et al., 2016; Smeerdijk et al., 2015).

SOs can encourage clients to use their inner resources to identify, implement, and sustain actions leading to a lifestyle free from substance misuse. They can be important in increasing clients' readiness to change by addressing substance use in the following ways:

- Reminding clients about the importance of family, their relationship to an SO in their lives, or both
- Providing helpful feedback to clients about the negative effects of their substance use behavior
- Encouraging clients to change substance use behaviors
- Alerting clients to social and individual coping resources that support recovery
- Providing positive reinforcement for using social/coping resources to change substance use

Expert Comment: Involving an SO in the Change Process

I have found that actively involving an SO, such as a spouse, relative, or friend, in motivational counseling can affect a client's commitment to change. The SO provides helpful input for clients who are ambivalent about changing addictive behaviors. SO feedback can raise the client's awareness of the negative effects of substance use. The SO can also offer needed support in sustaining the client's commitment to change.

Before involving the SO, I determine whether the SO has a positive relationship with the client and a genuine investment in affecting the change process. SOs with strong ties to the client and an interest in helping the client change substance use can help support change; those who lack these qualities can make this process more difficult. Before involving the SO, I assess the interactions between the client and the SO. I am particularly interested in learning whether the client's motivational statements are supported by the SO.

> Following this brief assessment, I use many different commitment-enhancing strategies with the SO to help him or her affect the motivational process. I try to ask questions that will help the SO feel optimistic about the client's ability to change. For example, I may ask the SO the following questions:
>
> - "Have you noticed what efforts Jack has made to change his drinking?"
> - "What has been most helpful to you in helping Jack deal with the drinking?"
> - "What is different now that leads you to feel better about Jack's ability to change?"
>
> Through techniques such as eliciting change talk from clients, SOs can help the change process.
>
> *Allen Zweben, D.S.W., Consensus Panel Member*

Before involving an SO in the client's treatment:

- Ask the client for permission to contact the SO.
- Describe the benefits of SO support.
- Review confidentiality concerns.
- If the client agrees, obtain the necessary written releases.

Some strategies for engaging an SO in an initial meeting with you and the client include the following:

- Use MI strategies to engage the SO in the counseling process (Belmontes, 2018).
- Praise the SO for his or her willingness to participate in the client's efforts to change.
- Offer conversation guidelines (e.g., use "I" statements, don't use language that blames or shames).
- Define the SO's role (e.g., offering emotional/instrumental support, giving helpful feedback, reinforcing positive reasons for change, working with client to change substance use behavior).
- Be optimistic about how the SO's support and nonjudgmental feedback can be an important factor in increasing the client's motivation to change.
- Invite the SO to be on the client's team that is working to reduce the impact of substance misuse on the couple or family.
- Provide brief instructions to the SO on how to ask open questions, use reflective listening, and support client change talk (Smeerdijk et al., 2015).
- Invite the SO to identify the family's values and how the substance use behavior might not fit with those values (Belmontes, 2018).
- Reinforce positive comments made by the SO about the client's current change efforts. Refocus the conversation if the feedback from the SO is negative or reinforces the client's sustain talk.
- Use EPE to give the SO information on support services (e.g., Al-Anon, family peer support providers, individual counseling) that will help focus on his or her own recovery while supporting the client.
- If the SO cannot be supportive and nonconfrontational or has substance misuse or behavioral health concerns that interfere with his or her ability to participate fully and supportively in the client's treatment, consider limiting the SO's role to mainly information sharing. Refer the SO to SUD treatment or behavioral health services and a recovery support group (e.g., Al-Anon).
- If the SO cannot attend counseling sessions with the client, invite the SO to the session figuratively by evoking and reinforcing client change talk associated with the significance of family and friends in the client's motivation to change (Sarpavaara, 2015). For example, you might ask, "You have mentioned that your relationship with your daughter is very important to you. How would not drinking, impact the quality of your relationship?"

For more information on families and SUD treatment, see Treatment Improvement Protocol (TIP) 39:

TIP 35: *Enhancing Motivation for Change in Substance Use Disorder Treatment*
Chapter 4—From Precontemplation to Contemplation: Building Readiness

October 2019

Substance Abuse Treatment and Family Therapy (Substance Abuse and Mental Health Services Administration, 2015a).

Express Concern, and Leave the Door Open

In the initial engagement and assessment phase, if the client remains in Precontemplation and you cannot mutually agree on treatment goals, **express concern about the client's substance misuse and leave the door open for the client to return to treatment any time**. Do this by:

- Summarizing your concern based on screening or assessment results or feedback from SOs.
- Presenting feedback in a factual, nonjudgmental way.
- Reminding the client that you respect his or her decision, even if data suggest a different choice.
- **Emphasize personal choice to maintain rapport with clients in Precontemplation.**
- Making sure the client has your contact information and appropriate crisis or emergency contact information before ending the session.
- Asking the client's permission for you or someone at your program to contact him or her by phone in a month to check in briefly. If the client says yes, follow up. This is an opportunity to assess the situation and encourage the client to return to treatment if desired.

Understand Special Motivational Counseling Considerations for Clients Mandated to Treatment

An increasing number of clients are mandated to treatment (i.e., ordered to attend) by an employer, an employee assistance program, or the criminal justice system. In such cases, failure to enter and remain in treatment may result in punishment or negative consequences (e.g., job loss, revocation of probation or parole, prosecution, imprisonment), often for a specified time or until satisfactory completion.

Your challenge is to engage clients who are mandated to the treatment process. Although many of these clients are at the Precontemplation stage, the temptation is to use Action stage interventions immediately that are not compatible with the client's motivation level. This can be counterproductive. Clients arrive with strong emotions because of the referral process and the consequences they will face if they do not succeed in changing a pattern of use they may not believe is problematic.

In addition, evidence shows that clients mandated to treatment tend to engage in a great deal of sustain talk, which is consistent with being in the Precontemplation stage and predicts negative substance use treatment outcomes (Apodaca et al., 2014; Moyers, Houck, Glynn, Hallgren, & Manuel, 2017). **An important motivational strategy with these clients is to lessen or "soften" sustain talk before trying to evoke change talk** (Moyers et al., 2017). (See Chapter 3 for strategies for responding to sustain talk that you can apply to clients who are mandated to treatment.)

Despite these obstacles, clients mandated to treatment have similar treatment outcomes as those who attend treatment voluntarily (Kiluk et al., 2015). If you use motivational counseling strategies appropriate to their stage in the SOC, they may become invested in the change process and benefit from the opportunity to consider the consequences of use and the possibility of change.

You may have to spend your first session "decontaminating" the referral process. Some counselors say explicitly, "I'm sorry you came through the door this way." Important principles to keep in mind are to:

- Honor the client's anger and sense of powerlessness.

TIP 35: *Enhancing Motivation for Change in Substance Use Disorder Treatment*
Chapter 4—From Precontemplation to Contemplation: Building Readiness

October 2019

- Avoid assumptions about the type of treatment needed.
- Make it clear that you will help the client explore what he or she perceives is needed and useful from your time together.

When working with clients who are mandated to treatment, you are required to establish what information will be shared with the referring agency. In addition, you should:

- Formalize the release of information with clients and the agency through a written consent for release of information that adheres to federal confidentiality regulations.
- Inform clients about what information (e.g., attendance, urine test results, treatment participation) will be released, and get their consent to share this information.
- Be sure clients understand which choices they have about the information to be released and which choices are not yours or theirs to make (e.g., information related to child abuse or neglect).
- Take into account the role of the clients' attorneys (if any) in releasing information.
- Clearly delineate different levels of permission.
- Be clear with clients about consequences they may experience from the referring agency if they do not participate in treatment as required. Motivational strategies to help maintain a collaborative working alliance with clients while presenting such consequences (Stinson & Clark, 2017) include:
  - Acknowledge clients' ambivalence about participating in counseling.
  - Differentiate your role from the authority of the referring agency (e.g., "I am here to help you make some decisions about how you might want to change, not to pressure you to change").
  - Describe the consequences of not participating in treatment in a neutral, nonjudgmental tone.
  - Avoid siding with clients or the referring agency about the fairness of possible consequences and punishments. Take a neutral stance.
  - Emphasize personal choice/responsibility (e.g., "It's up to you whether you participate in treatment").

Exhibit 4.3 provides an example of an initial conversation with a client who has been required to attend counseling as a condition of parole.

Exhibit 4.3. An Opening Dialog With a Client Who Has Been Mandated to Treatment

This dialog illustrates the first meeting between a counselor and a client who is required to attend group counseling as a condition of parole. The counselor is seeking ways to affirm the client, to find incentives that matter to the client, to support the client in achieving his most important personal goals, and to help the client regain control by choosing to engage in treatment with an open mind.

The setting is an outpatient treatment program that accepts private and court-ordered referrals to a counseling group for people who use substances. The program uses a cognitive–behavioral approach. The primary interventional tool is rational behavior training. This is the first session between the counselor and the court-ordered probation client.

Counselor: Good morning. My name is Jeff. You must be Paul.

Client: Yep.

Counselor: Come on in, and sit wherever you're comfortable. I got some information from your probation officer, but what would really help me is to hear from you, Paul, a bit more about what's going on in your life, and how we might help. *(Open question in the form of a statement)*

TIP 35: *Enhancing Motivation for Change in Substance Use Disorder Treatment*
Chapter 4—From Precontemplation to Contemplation: Building Readiness

October 2019

Client: The biggest thing is this 4-year sentence hanging over me and this crap I have to do to stay out of prison.

Counselor: Well, again, Paul, it sounds like you're busy and you have a lot of pressures. *(Reflection)* But I wonder if there's something the program offers that you could use.

Client: What I need from you is to get that blasted probation officer off my back.

Counselor: I'm not exactly sure what you mean, Paul.

Client: What I mean is that, I'm already running all over the place to give urine samples and meet all the other conditions of probation, and now the court says I've got to do this treatment program to stay out of jail.

Counselor: I'm still a little confused. What is it that I can do that might help? *(Open question)*

Client: You can tell my probation officer I don't need to be here and that she should stay out of my business.

Counselor: I may be wrong, Paul, but as I understand it, that's not an option for either one of us. I want to support you so that you don't conflict with your probation officer. For you and her to be in an angry relationship seems a recipe for disaster. I get the sense from listening to you that you're really committed to yourself **and** to your family. *(Affirmation)* The last thing you want to do is to wind up in prison facing that 4-year sentence.

Client: You got that straight.

Counselor: So, it seems to me you've made some good choices so far. *(Reframe)*

Client: What do you mean?

Counselor: Well, you could have just blown this whole appointment off, but you didn't. You made a series of choices that make it clear to me that you're committed to your family, yourself, your business, and for that matter your freedom. I can respect that commitment and would like to support you in honoring the choices you've already made. *(Affirmation and emphasizing personal autonomy)*

Client: Does that mean I'm not going to have to come to these classes?

Counselor: No, I don't have the power to make that kind of decision. However, you and I can work together to figure out how you might use this course to benefit you. *(Partnership)*

Client: I can't imagine getting anything out of sitting around with a bunch of drunks, talking about our feelings, and whining about all the bad things going on in our lives.

Counselor: You just don't seem like a whiner to me. And in any case, that's not what this group is about. What we really do is give people the opportunity to learn new skills and apply those skills in their daily lives to make their lives more enjoyable and meaningful. What you've already shown me today is that you can use some of those skills to support even further the good choices that you've already made. *(Affirmation)*

Client: That's just a bunch of shrink talk. I already told you, all I need is to get my probation officer off my back and live my life the way I want to live it.

Counselor: Completing this program is going to help you do that. I think from what you've already demonstrated that you'll do well in the group. I believe you can learn something that you can use in your daily life and perhaps teach some of the other people in the group as well. I am certainly willing to work with you to help you accomplish your goal in terms of meeting the requirements of probation. My suggestion is that you take it one group at a time and see how it goes. All I would ask of you is what, in a sense, you have already demonstrated, and that is the willingness to keep your mind open and keep your goals for life clearly in front of you. I see that you're committed to your family, you're committed to yourself, and you're committed to your freedom. I want to support all three of those goals. *(Affirmation)*

Client: Well, I guess I can do this group thing, at least for now. I'm still not sure what I'm going to get from sitting around with a bunch of other guys, telling stories, but I'm willing to give it a try.

TIP 35: *Enhancing Motivation for Change in Substance Use Disorder Treatment*
Chapter 4—From Precontemplation to Contemplation: Building Readiness

October 2019

> **Counselor:** That sounds reasonable and like another good choice to me, Paul. (*Affirmation*) Let me give you a handbook that will tell you a little bit more about the group, and I'll see you tomorrow night at 6:30 at this office for our first group. It's been nice to meet you. I look forward to getting to know you better.
>
> **Client:** I'll see you tomorrow night. You know, this wasn't as bad as I thought it would be.
>
> *Jeffrey M. Georgi, M.Div., Consensus Panel Member*

Although this counseling scenario relies primarily on cognitive–behavioral therapy strategies, the counselor engages the client in the spirit of MI by emphasizing partnership and acceptance of the client. The counselor also uses affirmations and maintains a nonjudgmental, neutral tone throughout the conversation, emphasizing the client's autonomy and values. This approach is consistent with an effective way to engage a client in Precontemplation who has been mandated to treatment.

Conclusion

The first step in working with clients in the Precontemplation stage of the SOC is to develop rapport and establish a counseling alliance. The next step is to assess their readiness to change, then help them begin to develop an awareness that their use of substances is linked to problems in their lives. Motivational counseling strategies from motivational enhancement therapy (e.g., providing personalized feedback about assessment results) and MI (e.g., using reflective listening to engage, emphasizing personal choice and responsibility, exploring discrepancy) are suited to helping clients move from Precontemplation to Contemplation.

TIP 35: *Enhancing Motivation for Change in Substance Use Disorder Treatment*
Chapter 5—From Contemplation to Preparation: Increasing Commitment

October 2019

Chapter 5—From Contemplation to Preparation: Increasing Commitment

"The reasons for change need to be important and substantive enough to move the individual into deciding to make the effort to change. The task for individuals in Contemplation is to resolve their decisional balance consideration in favor of change. The decision to change marks the transition out of the Contemplation stage and into Preparation."

DiClemente, 2018, p. 29

Key Messages
• Clients in Contemplation begin to recognize concerns about substance use but are ambivalent about change. • You can use motivational counseling strategies to help clients resolve ambivalence about change. • When using a decisional balance (DB) strategy, you briefly reflect clients' reasons for continuing substance use (i.e., sustain talk) but emphasize clients' reasons for change (i.e., change talk). • Motivational counseling strategies to enhance commitment to change move clients closer to the Preparation stage and taking steps to change.

Chapter 5 describes strategies to increase clients' commitment to change by normalizing and resolving ambivalence about change and enhancing clients' decision-making capabilities. Central to most strategies is the process of evoking and exploring reasons to change through asking open question and reflective listening. The chapter begins with a discussion of ambivalence, extrinsic (external) and intrinsic (internal) motivation, and ways to help clients connect with internal motivators to enhance decision making and their commitment to change. It then focuses on DB strategies—ways to explore the costs and benefits of change and clients' values about changing substance use behaviors. Chapter 5 also addresses the importance of self-efficacy in clients' decisions to change and provides strategies for enhancing commitment to change once clients decide to change.

Exhibit 5.1 presents counseling strategies for Contemplation.

Exhibit 5.1. Counseling Strategies for Contemplation		
Client Motivation	**Counselor Focus**	**Counseling Strategies**
• The client acknowledges concerns and is considering the possibility of change but is ambivalent and uncertain. • The client begins to reflect on his or her substance use behavior and considers choices and options for change.	• Normalize and resolve client's ambivalence about change. • Help the client tip the DB scales toward change.	• Shift focus from extrinsic to intrinsic motivation. • Summarize client concerns. • Assess where the client is on the decisional scale. • Explore pros/cons of substance use and behavior change. • Reexplore values in relation to change. • Emphasize personal choice and responsibility. • Explore client's understanding of change and expectations of treatment. • Reintroduce feedback. • Explore self-efficacy. • Summarize change talk.

TIP 35: *Enhancing Motivation for Change in Substance Use Disorder Treatment*
Chapter 5—From Contemplation to Preparation: Increasing Commitment

October 2019

		• Enhance commitment to change.

Normalize and Resolve Ambivalence

You must be prepared to address ambivalence to help clients move through the Stages of Change (SOC) process. Ambivalence is a normal part of any change process. Ambivalence is uncomfortable because it involves conflicting motivations about change (Miller & Rollnick, 2013). For example, a client may enjoy drinking because it relaxes him or her but may feel guilty about losing a job because of drinking and putting his or her family in financial risk. Clients often have conflicting feelings and motivations (Miller & Rollnick, 2013). During Contemplation, ambivalence is strong. As you help clients move toward Preparation and Action, ambivalence lessens. Miller and Rollnick (2013) use the metaphor of a hill of ambivalence wherein clients move up the hill during Precontemplation/Contemplation and then journey down the hill through the resolution of ambivalence, which moves them into Preparation and Action (Exhibit 5.2). Chapter 2 provides a thorough description of DARN CAT (**D**esire, **A**bility, **R**easons, **N**eed, **C**ommitment **A**ctivation, **T**aking steps) change talk.

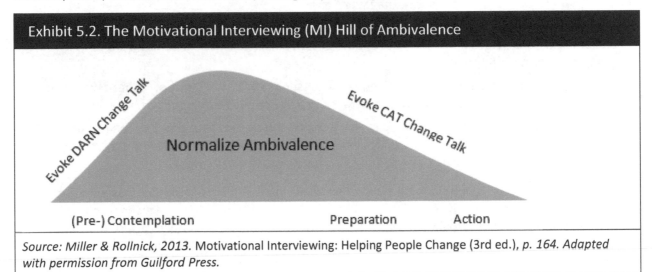

Exhibit 5.2. The Motivational Interviewing (MI) Hill of Ambivalence

Evoke DARN Change Talk

Evoke CAT Change Talk

Normalize Ambivalence

(Pre-) Contemplation   Preparation   Action

Source: Miller & Rollnick, 2013. Motivational Interviewing: Helping People Change (3rd ed.), p. 164. Adapted with permission from Guilford Press.

The two key motivational strategies you can use to resolve ambivalence in Contemplation are:

1. **Normalizing ambivalence.** As they move closer to a decision to change, clients often feel increasing conflict and doubt about whether they can or want to change. **Reassure clients that conflicting feelings, uncertainties, and reservations are common.** Normalize ambivalence by explaining that many clients experience similar strong ambivalence at this stage, even when they believe they have resolved their mixed feelings and are nearing a decision. Clients need to understand that many people go back and forth between wanting to maintain the status quo and wanting to change and yet have been able to stay on track by continuing to explore and discuss their ambivalence.

2. **Evoking DARN change talk.** DARN refers to clients' **d**esire, **a**bility, **r**easons, and **n**eed to change. During Contemplation, help clients move up the hill of ambivalence and guide them toward Preparation by evoking and reflecting DARN change talk. Use open questions: "How would you like things to change so you don't feel scared when you can't remember what happened after drinking the night before?" Exhibit 3.8 in Chapter 3 offers more examples of open questions that evoke DARN change talk. Use reflective listening responses to highlight the change talk. **Remember that the goal is to guide clients to make the arguments for change** (Miller & Rollnick, 2013). The key is to avoid jumping too quickly into evoking CAT (i.e., **c**ommitment, **a**ctivation, and **t**aking steps)

TIP 35: *Enhancing Motivation for Change in Substance Use Disorder Treatment*
Chapter 5—From Contemplation to Preparation: Increasing Commitment

October 2019

change talk, solving problems in response to ambivalence, or making a plan of action. The client has to climb up the hill of ambivalence before easing down the other side.

Shift the Focus From Extrinsic to Intrinsic Motivation

To help clients prepare for change, explore the range of both extrinsic and intrinsic motivators that have brought them to this point. Many clients move through the Contemplation stage acknowledging only the extrinsic motivators that push them to change and that brought them to treatment. External motivators may pressure clients into treatment, including a spouse, employer, healthcare provider, family member, friend, or the child welfare or criminal justice system. **Extrinsic motivators can help bring clients into and stay in treatment, but intrinsic motivators are important for significant, long-lasting change** (Flannery, 2017; Kwasnicka, Dombrowski, White, & Sniehotta, 2016; Mahmoodabad, Tonekaboni, Farmanbar, Fallahzadeh, & Kamalikhah, 2017).

You can help clients develop intrinsic motivation by assisting them in recognizing the discrepancies between "where they are" and "where they want to be":

- Invite clients to explore their life goals and values, which can strengthen internal motivation. In searching for answers, clients often reevaluate past mistakes and activities that were self-destructive or harmful to others.

- Encourage this exploration through asking open questions about client goals: "Where would you like to be in 5 years?" and "How does your substance use fit or not fit with your goals?"

- Highlight clients' recognition of discrepancies between the current situation and their hopes for the future through reflective listening. Awareness of discrepancy often evokes desire change talk, an essential source of intrinsic motivation.

Sometimes, intrinsic motivation emerges from role conflicts and family or community expectations. For example, a single mother who lost her job because of substance use may have a strong motivation to get and keep another job to provide for her children. For other clients, substance misuse has cut their cultural or community ties. For example, they stop going to church or neglect culturally affirmed roles, such as helping others or serving as role models for young people. A desire to reconnect with cultural traditions as a source of identity and strength can be a powerful motivator for some clients, as can the desire to regain others' respect. Positive change also leads to improved self-image and self-esteem.

Expert Comment: Linking Family, Community, and Cultural Values to a Desire for Change

Working with a group of Latino men in the Southwest who were mandated into treatment as a condition of parole and had spent most of their lives in prisons, we found that as these men aged, they seemed to tire of criminal life. In counseling, some expressed concerns about losing touch with their families and culture, and many reported a desire to serve as male role models for their sons and nephews. They all wanted to restore their own sense of pride and self-worth in the small community where many of their families had lived for generations.

Newly trained in MI, we recognized a large, untapped source of self-motivation in a population that we had long before decided did not want help. We had to change our previous beliefs about this population as not wanting treatment to seeing these men as requesting help and support to maintain themselves outside the prison system and in the community.

Carole Janis Otero, M.A., Consensus Panel Member

Helping clients shift from extrinsic to intrinsic motivation helps them move from contemplating change to deciding to act. Start with clients' current situations, and find a natural link between existing external motivators and intrinsic ones that they may not be aware of or find easy to describe. Through compassionate and respectful exploration, you may discover untapped intrinsic motivation.

Along with MI techniques presented in Chapter 3, use these strategies to identify and strengthen intrinsic motivation:

- **Show genuine curiosity about clients.** Show interest in their lives at the first meeting and over time. Because clients' desire to change is rarely limited to substance use, they may find it easier to talk about changing other behaviors. Most clients have concerns about several areas of their lives and wish to reconnect with their community, improve their finances, find work, or fall in love. Many are highly functional and productive in some aspects of their lives and take great pride in special skills, knowledge, or other abilities they do not want to lose.

- **Do not wait for clients to talk spontaneously about their substance use.** Show interest, and ask how their substance use affects these aspects of their lives. Even with clients who do not acknowledge any problems, question them about their lives to show concern and strengthen the counseling alliance.

- **Reframe clients' negative statements about external pressure to get treatment.** For example, help clients reframe anger expressed toward their spouse who has pressured them to enter treatment as seeing their spouse as caring and invested in the marriage

- **Identify and strengthen intrinsic motivation of clients who have been mandated to treatment.** Emphasize personal choice and responsibility with these clients. Help clients understand that they can freely choose to change because doing so makes good sense and is desirable, not because negative consequences will happen if they choose not to change.

Summarize Client Concerns

As you evoke DARN change talk and explore intrinsic and extrinsic motivations, you gather important information for helping the client resolve ambivalence about change. You have a working knowledge, and perhaps even a written list, of issues and areas about which the client has conflicting feelings and which are important intrinsic motivators for changing substance use behaviors. **A first step in helping the client to weigh the pros and cons of change is to organize the list of concerns and present them to the client in a careful summary that expresses empathy, develops discrepancy, and shifts the balance toward change.** Because you should reach agreement on these issues, the summary should end by asking whether the client agrees that these are his or her concerns about the substance use. You might ask, "Is this accurate?" or "Did I leave anything out?"

Help Tip the Decisional Balance Toward Change

For any decision, most people naturally weigh costs and benefits of the potential action. In behavioral change, these considerations are called "decisional balancing." This is a process of appraising or evaluating the "good" aspects of substance use—the reasons **not to change** (expressed through sustain talk)—and the "less-good" aspects—the reasons **to change** (expressed through change talk). DB originated with Janis and Mann (1977) as a motivational counseling strategy. It is used widely in substance use disorder (SUD) treatment to explore benefits and costs of continued substance use and of changing substance use behaviors. Research on DB in SUD treatment has shown that DB is associated with increased motivation to change in diverse client populations and favorable client outcomes (Elliot & Carey, 2013; Foster & Neighbors, 2013; Hennessy, Tanner-Smith, & Steinka-Fry, 2015).

Motivation to reduce or stop substance use increases when the costs of use outweigh the benefits and

TIP 35: *Enhancing Motivation for Change in Substance Use Disorder Treatment*
Chapter 5—From Contemplation to Preparation: Increasing Commitment

October 2019

when the pros of changing substance use outweigh the cons (Connors, DiClemente, Velasquez, & Donovan, 2013). **Your task is to help clients recognize and weigh negative aspects of substance use to tip the scale in favor of change.**

Assess Where the Client Is on the Decisional Scale

Start by getting a sense of where the client is with regard to the decision-making process. The Alcohol Decisional Balance Scale and the Drug Use Decisional Balance Scale in Appendix B are validated instruments that ask clients to rate, on a scale of 1 to 5, the importance of statements like "Having to lie to others about my drinking bothers me" in making a decision about changing substance use behaviors (Prochaska et al., 1994). The scores give you and the client a sense of where the client is with regard to reporting more pros versus more cons for continued substance use. You can also explore specific items on the measure on which the client scores high (e.g., "Some people close to me are disappointed in me because of my drug use") as a way to build discrepancy between the client's values and substance use, thus evoking change talk.

Explore the Pros and Cons of Substance Use and Behavior Change

Weighing benefits and costs of substance use and change is at the heart of DB work. To accomplish this, **invite the client to write out a list of positives and negatives of substance use and changing substance use behaviors.** This can be a homework assignment that is discussed at the next session, or the list can be generated during a session. Putting the items on paper makes it seem more "real" to the client and can help structure the conversation. You can generate a list of the pros and cons of substance use and a list of pros and cons of changing substance use behaviors separately or use a grid like the one in Exhibit 5.3.

Exhibit 5.3. Decisional Balance Sheet for Substance Use	
Reasons to Continue Substance Use (Status Quo)	Reasons to Change Substance Use (Change)
Positives of substance use	Negatives of substance use
Negatives of changing substance use	Positives of changing substance use
Source: Connors et al., 2013.	

Presenting to clients a long list of reasons to change and a short list of reasons not to change may finally upset the balance and tip the scale toward change. However, the opposite (i.e., a long list of reasons not to change and a short life of reason to change) can show how much work remains and can be used to prevent premature decision making.

Recognize that many clients find that one or two reasons to change counterbalance the weight of many reasons not to change and vice versa. Therefore, it is not just the number of reasons to change or not change but the strength of each reason that matters. **Explore the relative strength of each motivational factor, and highlight the weight clients place on each change factor.** Reasons for and against continuing substance use, or for and against aspects of change, are highly individual. Factors that shift the balance toward positive change for one person may barely matter to another. Also, the value or weight given to a particular item in this inventory of pros and cons is likely to change over time.

Whether or not you use a written worksheet, **always listen carefully when clients express ambivalence.** Both sides of ambivalence, expressed through sustain talk and change talk, are present in clients at the same time (Miller & Rollnick, 2013). You may hear both in a single client statement—for example, "I get

TIP 35: *Enhancing Motivation for Change in Substance Use Disorder Treatment*
Chapter 5—From Contemplation to Preparation: Increasing Commitment

October 2019

so energized when I snort cocaine, but it's so expensive. I'm not sure how I'll pay the bills this month." Although discussing with clients what they like about drinking or using drugs may establish rapport, increasing expressions of sustain talk is associated with negative client outcomes (Foster, Neighbors, & Pai, 2015; Houck & Moyers, 2015; Lindqvist, Forsberg, Enebrink, Andersson, & Rosendahl, 2017; Magill et al., 2014).

In DB, explore both sides of ambivalence, but avoid reinforcing sustain talk, which can be counterproductive (Krigel et al., 2017; Lindqvist et al., 2017; Miller & Rose, 2013). Once a client decides to change a substance use behavior, a DB exercise on the pros and cons of change may increase commitment to change (Miller & Rose, 2013). Carefully consider your own intention and the client's stage in the SOC before using a structured DB that explores both sides of client ambivalence equally.

Exhibit 5.4 describes other issues that may arise as clients explore pros and cons of change.

Exhibit 5.4. Other Issues in Decisional Balance	
Loss and grief	Giving up a way of life can be as intense as the loss of a close friend. Many clients need time for grieving. They have to acknowledge and mourn this loss before they are ready to build a strong attachment to recovery. Pushing them to change too fast can weaken determination. Patience and empathy are reassuring at this time.
Reservations or reluctance	Serious reservations about change can be a signal that you and clients have different views. As clients move into the Preparation stage, they may become defensive if pushed to commit to change before they are ready or if their goals conflict with yours. They may express this reluctance in behaviors rather than words. For example, some will miss appointments, sending a message that they need more time and want to slow the process. Continue to explore ambivalence with these clients, and reassess where they are in the change process.
Premature decision making	DB exercises give you a sense of whether clients are ready for change. If clients' description of pros and cons is unclear, they may express goals for change that are unrealistic or reflect a lack of understanding of their abilities and resources. Clients may say what they think you want to hear. Clients who are not ready to decide to change will let you know. Allowing clients to set themselves up for failure can result in them stopping the change process altogether or losing trust in you. Delay the commitment process, and return to Contemplation.
Keeping pace	Some clients enter treatment after they have stopped using substances on their own. Others stop substance use the day they call the program for the first appointment. They have already made a commitment to stop. If you try to elicit these clients' concerns or conduct DB exercises, you might evoke sustain talk unnecessarily and miss an important opportunity to provide the encouragement, incentives, and skills needed to help action-oriented and action-ready individuals make progress. Move with these clients immediately to create a change plan and enter the Action stage, but be alert for ambivalence that may remain or develop.
Free choice	Clients may begin using drugs or alcohol out of rebelliousness toward their family or society. Substance use may be an expression of continued freedom—freedom from the demands of others to act or live in a certain way. You may hear clients say that they cannot change because they do not want to lose their freedom. Because this belief is tied to some clients' early-forged identities, it may be a strong factor in their list of reasons not to change. However, as clients age, they may be more willing to explore whether "freedom to rebel" is actually freedom or its opposite. If you address this issue, you can reframe the rebellion as reflection of a limitation of choices (i.e., the person must do the opposite of what is expected). As clients age, they may be

TIP 35: *Enhancing Motivation for Change in Substance Use Disorder Treatment*
Chapter 5—From Contemplation to Preparation: Increasing Commitment

October 2019

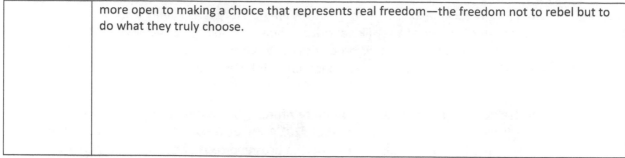

more open to making a choice that represents real freedom—the freedom not to rebel but to do what they truly choose.

Reexplore Values in Relation to Change

Use DB exercises as opportunities to help clients explore and articulate their values and to connect these values with positive change. Clients' values influence their reasons for and against change. For example, an adolescent involved in drug dealing with a neighborhood gang may say that leaving the gang is not possible because of his loyalty to the other members. Loyalty and belonging are important values to him. Relate them to other groups that inspire similar allegiance, such as a sports team or scouting—organizations that create a sense of belonging and reflect his core values. A young woman with a family history of hard work and academic achievement may wish to return to those values by finishing high school and becoming financially independent.

Hearing themselves articulate their core values helps clients increase their commitment to positive change. If they can frame the process of change within the larger context of values shared with their family, community, and culture, they may find it easier to contemplate change.

Emphasize Personal Choice and Responsibility

In a motivational approach to counseling, you don't "give" a client a choice. The choice is not yours to give; rather, it is the client's to make. Your task is to help the client make choices that are in his or her best interest and that align with his or her values and goals. Consistently emphasize the client's responsibility and freedom of choice. The client should be used to hearing you make statements such as:

- "It's up to you to decide what to do about this."
- "No one can decide this for you."
- "No one can change your drug use for you. Only you can."
- "You can decide to go on drinking or to change."

Explore the Client's Understanding of Change and Expectations of Treatment

In working toward a decision, understand what change means to clients and what their expectations of treatment are. Some clients believe that quitting or cutting down means changing their entire life—moving from their neighborhood or cutting ties with all their friends, even their family. Some believe they have to change everything overnight. This can be overwhelming. Tell clients who have never been in treatment before about the level of motivation and openness required to get the most from their treatment experience (Raylu & Kaur, 2012).

In exploring these meanings and expectations with the client, you will get a sense of which actions the client might consider and which he or she will not. For example, a client might state that she could never move from her neighborhood, a well-known drug market, because her family is there. Another says he will not consider anything but cutting down on his drinking. A third client may just as strongly state that total abstinence and a stay in a therapeutic community are the only options, as all others have failed.

TIP 35: *Enhancing Motivation for Change in Substance Use Disorder Treatment*
Chapter 5—From Contemplation to Preparation: Increasing Commitment

October 2019

By exploring treatment expectations with clients, you introduce information about the benefits of treatment and can begin a discussion about available options. When clients' expectations about treatment match what actually happens and they have positive expectations about treatment, they have better outcomes (Kuusisto, Knuuttila, & Saarnio, 2011). It is never too soon to elicit clients' expectations about treatment through reflective listening. Show that you understand their concerns, and provide accurate information about your treatment program and the benefits of treatment using motivational strategies like Elicit-Provide-Elicit (described in Chapter 3).

Reintroduce Feedback

Use personalized feedback after assessments to motivate clients. Continue to use assessment results to influence clients' decisional considerations. Objective medical, social, and neuropsychological feedback prompts many clients to contemplate change. Reviewing assessment information can refocus clients on the need for change. Reintroducing objective assessment data reminds clients of earlier insights into the need for change.

For example, a client may be intrinsically motivated to stop alcohol misuse because of health concerns yet feel overwhelmed by fear that quitting is impossible. Reintroducing feedback from the medical assessment about the risk of serious liver damage or a family history of heart disease could add significant additional weight to the DB and tip the balance in the direction of change.

Explore Self-Efficacy

By listening for self-efficacy statements from clients, you can discover what they feel they can and cannot do. Self-efficacy is a critical determinant of behavior change—it is the belief that they can act in a certain way or perform a particular task. Even clients who admit to having a serious problem are not likely to move toward positive change unless they have some hope of success. Self-efficacy can be thought of as hope or optimism, but clients do not have to have an overall optimistic view to believe a certain behavior can be changed.

Statements about self-efficacy could include the following:

- "I can't do that."
- "That is beyond my powers."
- "That would be easy."
- "I think I can manage that."

Self-efficacy is not a global measure, like self-esteem. Rather, it is behavior specific. Underlying any discussion of self-efficacy is the question "Efficacy to perform what specific behavior?" There are five categories of self-efficacy related to SUDs (DiClemente, Carbonari, Montgomery, & Hughes, 1994: Glozah, Adu, & Komesuor, 2015):

- **Coping self-efficacy** is dealing successfully with situations that tempt one to use substances, such as by being assertive with friends or talking with someone when upset rather than using the substance.
- **Treatment behavior self-efficacy** involves the client's ability to perform behaviors related to treatment, such as self-monitoring or stimulus control.
- **Recovery self-efficacy** is the ability to recover from a recurrence of the addictive behavior.
- **Control self-efficacy** is confidence in one's ability to control behavior in risky situations.
- **Abstinence self-efficacy** is confidence in one's ability to abstain despite cues or triggers to use.

Explore clients' sense of self-efficacy as they move toward Preparation. This may help you determine

TIP 35: *Enhancing Motivation for Change in Substance Use Disorder Treatment*
Chapter 5—From Contemplation to Preparation: Increasing Commitment

October 2019

more specifically whether self-efficacy is a potential support or obstacle to change. Remember, you can enhance client self-efficacy by using the Confidence Ruler (see Exhibit 3.10) and eliciting confidence talk (see the section "Evoking hope and confidence to support self-efficacy" in Chapter 3).

Summarize Change Talk

As the client transitions from Contemplation to Preparation, you will notice that the client has moved to the top of the MI Hill of Ambivalence (see Exhibit 5.2 above) and is expressing less sustain talk and more change talk. This is a good time to offer a recapitulation summary, as described in Exhibit 5.5.

Exhibit 5.5. Recapitulation Summary

At the end of DB exercises, you may sense that the client is ready to commit to change. At this point, you should summarize the client's current situation as reflected in your interactions thus far. The purpose of the summary is to draw together as many reasons for change as possible while pointing out the client's reluctance or ambivalence.

Your summary should include as many of the following elements as possible:

- A summary of the client's own perceptions of the problem
- A summary of the client's ambivalence, including what remains positive or attractive about substance use
- A review of objective evidence you have regarding the presence of risks and problems
- Your assessment of the client's situation, particularly when it aligns with the client's own concerns
- A summary of the client's change talk, emphasizing desire, ability, reasons, and need to change

Remember to recognize the client's sustain talk (i.e., reasons for staying with the status quo), but emphasize client change talk to tip the balance in favor of change.

Enhance Commitment to Change

You should still reinforce the client's commitment to change even after the client has decided to change and has begun to set goals. You should expect client indecision at any point in the change process. Additional strategies that enhance commitment at this point include asking key questions, taking small steps, going public, and envisioning.

Asking key questions

After the summary, ask a key question—for example, "What do you think you will do now?" (see the section "Asking key questions" in Chapter 3)—to help the client move over the top of the MI Hill of Ambivalence toward Preparation. Key questions will elicit CAT change talk. One of the main signs that the client is intending and committed to taking steps is an increase in CAT change talk (Miller & Rollnick, 2013). The client is making statements of **commitment** (e.g., "I will call the treatment facility to set up an intake"), **activation** (e.g., "I am willing to stop smoking marijuana for a month"), and **taking steps** (e.g., "I looked up the schedule for Narcotics Anonymous meetings on its website") (Miller & Rollnick, 2013). **Reinforce CAT change talk through reflective listening and summarizing.**

Taking small steps

You have asked the client key questions such as "What's next?" and have presented options to emphasize the client's choice to change and to select areas of focus. Remind the client that he or she has choices and can control the change process to reinforce commitment. **Reassure the client who is overwhelmed by thinking of change that he or she can set the pace and begin with small steps.** Some clients respond well to stories of others who made large, seemingly impossible life changes one step at a

TIP 35: *Enhancing Motivation for Change in Substance Use Disorder Treatment*
Chapter 5—From Contemplation to Preparation: Increasing Commitment

October 2019

time. Don't underestimate the value of such stories and models in enhancing motivation.

Going public

Sharing a commitment to change with at least one other person besides the counselor can keep clients accountable. Telling a significant other about one's desire to change usually enhances commitment to change. "Going public" can be a critical step for a client who may not have been ready to tell others until this point. Alcoholics Anonymous (AA) has applied the clinical wisdom of public commitment to change through use of the "white chip." An attendee at an AA meeting who has an intention to quit drinking can pick up a white chip. The white chip is also called a Beginner's Chip or Surrender Chip and is a public acknowledgment of the person's intention to start recovery.

Envisioning

Helping clients visualize their life after change can be a powerful motivator and an effective means of strengthening their commitment. In addition, stories about how others have successfully achieved their goals can be excellent motivators. An exercise for envisioning change is to ask clients to picture themselves after a year has passed, during which time they have made the changes they desire in the areas of their lives most hurt by their substance use. Some clients may find it valuable to write a letter to themselves that is dated in the future and describes what life will be like at that point. The letter can have the tone of a vacation postcard ("Wishing you were here!"). Others will be more comfortable describing these scenes to you. Chapter 3 provides more information MI strategies to strengthen commitment.

Conclusion

To help clients move from Contemplation to Preparation, explore and resolve ambivalence about change. Help clients climb the MI Hill of Ambivalence and journey down the other side toward commitment and change. DB exercises can help clients explore ambivalence, clarify reasons to change, and identify barriers to change (e.g., reasons to continue substance use). When tipping the balance in favor of change, emphasize reflections of change talk, minimize the focus on sustain talk, and use motivational strategies to enhance commitment and facilitate clients' movement into Preparation.

TIP 35: *Enhancing Motivation for Change in Substance Use Disorder Treatment*
Chapter 6—From Preparation to Action: Initiating Change

October 2019

Chapter 6—From Preparation to Action: Initiating Change

"The Preparation stage of change entails developing a plan of action and creating the commitment needed to implement that plan. Decisions do not translate automatically into action. To change a behavior, one needs to focus attention on breaking the old pattern and creating a new one. Planning is the activity that organizes the environment and develops the strategies for making change."

DiClemente, 2018, pp. 29–30

Key Messages

- During the Preparation stage, clients are considering possible paths toward changing substance use behaviors and beginning to take small steps to reach the final change goal.
- You can support clients' movement from Preparation to Action by exploring client change goals and helping them develop a change plan.
- You can maintain a client-centered focus by eliciting clients' change goals and not imposing goals on them.

Chapter 6 describes the process of identifying and clarifying change goals. It also focuses on how and when to develop a change plan with the client and suggests ways to ensure a sound plan by offering the client a menu of options, contracting for change, identifying and lowering barriers to action, and enlisting social support. This chapter also describes your tasks while the client moves into the Action stage, like helping the client initiate the plan and evaluating the effectiveness of the plan.

In earlier stages of the Stages of Change (SOC) approach, you use motivational strategies to increase clients' readiness. **In Preparation, you use motivational strategies to strengthen clients' commitment and help them make a firm decision to change.** Clients who commit to change and believe change is possible are prepared for the Action stage. Clients who are actively taking steps to change substance use behaviors have better long-term outcomes after treatment than clients who have not reached this stage of the SOC (Heather & McCambridge, 2013).

Your task is to help clients set clear goals for change in preparation for developing a change plan. Changing any longstanding behavior requires preparation and planning. Clients must see change as being in their best interest before they can move into the Action stage. Developing a change plan that is accessible, acceptable, and appropriate for each client is key. The negative consequences of ignoring the Preparation stage can be a brief course of action followed by rapid return to substance use. By the end of the Preparation stage, clients should have a plan for change that guides them into the Action stage.

Exhibit 6.1 presents counseling strategies for Preparation and Action.

Exhibit 6.1. Counseling Strategies for Preparation and Action			
SOC	Client Motivation	Counselor Focus	Counseling Strategies
Preparation	The client is committed and planning to make a change in the near future but is still considering what to do.	• Explore client change goals. • Develop a change plan.	• Clarify the client's own goals. • Sample goals; encourage experimenting. • Elicit change strategies from the client. • Offer a menu of change options. • Negotiate a behavioral contract.

SOC	Client Motivation	Counselor Focus	Counseling Strategies
			• Explore and lower barriers to action. • Enlist social support.
Action	The client actively takes steps to change but is not yet stable.	• Support the client's action steps. • Evaluate the change plan.	• Help the client determine which change strategies are working and which are not. • Change the strategies as needed.

Exhibit 6.1. Counseling Strategies for Preparation and Action

Explore Client Change Goals

Once the client has decided to make a positive change and the commitment is clear, goals should be set. Setting goals is part of the exploring and envisioning activities in the early and middle parts of the Preparation stage. Having summarized and reviewed the client's decisional considerations, you should now be prepared to ask about ways in which the client might want to address some of the reasons to change listed on the positive side of the decisional balance sheet. **The process of talking about and setting goals strengthens commitment to change.**

Clarify the Client's Goals

Help the client set goals that are as realistic and specific as possible and that address the concerns he or she described earlier about substance use. The client may set goals in multiple areas, not just substance use. He or she may work toward goals such as regaining custody of children, getting a job, becoming financially independent, leaving an abusive relationship, and returning to school. The client who sets several goals may need help deciding which to focus on first.

Early on, goals should be short term, measurable, and realistic so that clients can begin measuring success and feeling good about themselves as well as hopeful about the change. If goals seem unreachable to you, discuss your concerns. Use OARS (**O**pen questions, **A**ffirmations, **R**eflective listening, and **S**ummarization) to help clients clarify their goals, decide on which goal to focus first, and identify steps to achieving their goals. For example, if one goal is to get a job, you can start with an open question: "What do you think is the first step toward meeting this goal?" The goal is the vision, and the steps are the specific tasks that clients perform to meet the goal.

Setting goals is a joint process. The counselor and client work together, moving from general ideas and visions to specific goals. Seeing how the client sets goals and the types of goals he or she sets provides information on the client's sense of self-efficacy, level of commitment, and readiness for change. The more hopeful a client feels about the future, the more likely he or she is to achieve treatment goals.

Make identifying and clarifying treatment goals a client-driven process. Doing so is consistent with the principles of person-centered counseling and the spirit of motivational interviewing (MI). It is up to the client to decide what actions to take or treatment options to seek to address a substance use problem. Matching the client to the preferred substance use disorder (SUD) treatment options can help reduce alcohol consumption and improve drug-related outcomes (Friedrichs, Spies, Härter, & Buchholz, 2016). In a systematic review, brief motivational alcohol interventions for adolescents had significantly larger effects on alcohol consumption if they included goal-setting exercises (Tanner-Smith & Lipsey, 2015).

Your task is to help clients identify their preferred change goals and to enhance their decision making by teaching them about their treatment options. (See Chapter 3 for more information about and

TIP 35: *Enhancing Motivation for Change in Substance Use Disorder Treatment*
Chapter 6—From Preparation to Action: Initiating Change

October 2019

strategies for identifying change goals using MI.)

Remember that the client's preferred treatment goals may not match what you prefer. A client might choose a course of action with which you do not agree or that is not in line with the treatment agency's policies. A decision to reduce but not completely stop substance use, for example, may go against the agency's policy of zero tolerance for illicit substance use. Exhibit 6.2 offers some strategies for addressing these types of situations.

Exhibit 6.2. When Treatment Goals Differ

What do you do when the client's goals differ from yours or those of your agency? This issue arises in all behavioral health services but especially in a motivational approach, where you listen reflectively to a client and actively involve him or her in decision making. As you elicit goals for change and treatment, a client may not choose goals that you think are right for him or her.

Before exploring different ways of handling this common situation, try to clarify how the client's goals and your own (or your agency's goals) do not match. For a client, goals are by definition the objectives he or she is motivated (ready, willing, and able) to work toward. If the client is not motivated to work toward it, it is not a goal. You or your agency, however, may have specific plans or hopes for the client. You cannot push your hopes and plans onto the client. This situation can become an ethical problem if you focus too much on trying to get a client to change in the direction of your or the agency's goals (Miller & Rollnick, 2013).

What are your clinical options when goals differ? You can choose from the following strategies:

- **Negotiate** (i.e., figure out how to work out the differences)
  - Rework the agenda and be open about your concerns as well as your hopes for the client (Miller & Rollnick, 2013).
  - Find goals on which you and the client can agree, and work together on those.
  - Start with areas in which the client is motivated to change. Women with alcohol or drug use disorders, for example, often come to treatment with a wide range of other problems, many of which they see as more pressing than making a change in substance use.
  - Start with the problems that the client feels are most urgent, and then address substance use when its relationship to other problems becomes obvious.

- **Approximate** (i.e., try to find an agreed-on goal that is similar)
  - Even if a client is not willing to accept your recommendations, consider the possibility of agreeing on a goal that is still a step in the right direction. Your hope, for example, might be that the client would eventually become free from all psychoactive substance use. The client, however, is most concerned about cocaine and is not ready to talk about changing cannabis, tobacco, or alcohol use.
  - Rather than dismiss the client for not accepting a goal of immediate abstinence from all substances, focus on stopping cocaine use, and then consider next steps.

- **Refer**
  - If you can't help the client with treatment goals even after trying to negotiate or approximate, refer the client to another provider or program.
  - Work within state licensing and professional ethical codes to avoid suddenly ending treatment.
  - Offer a menu of options, and take an active role in linking the client to other treatment and community-based services.
  - Be open in a nonjudgmental and neutral way about the fact that you cannot help the client with his or her treatment goal (Moyers & Houck, 2011).

Sample Goals and Encourage Experimenting

You may need to help some clients sample or try out their goals before getting them to commit to long-term change. For instance, some clients benefit from experimenting with abstinence or cutting

TIP 35: *Enhancing Motivation for Change in Substance Use Disorder Treatment*
Chapter 6—From Preparation to Action: Initiating Change

October 2019

down their substance use for a short period. The following approaches to goal sampling may be helpful for clients who are not committed to abstinence as a change goal:

- **Sobriety sampling.** This trial period of abstinence is commonly used with clients who (Boston Center for Treatment Development and Training [BCTDT], 2016):
  - Are not interested in abstinence as a treatment goal.
  - Express significant need or desire to address misuse but are not ready to commit to abstinence.
  - Have had many past unsuccessful attempts at moderate use.

  A successful trial of sobriety sampling can enhance clients' commitment to a goal of abstinence. Even a 2-to-3–week period of abstinence before treatment can lead to positive client outcomes, including reductions in alcohol misuse (Gueorguieva et al., 2014). However, longer periods of trial abstinence may give clients more of an opportunity to experience the benefits of abstinence, like clearer thinking, a better ability to recognize substance use triggers, and more time to experience the positive feeling of living without substance use (BCTDT, 2016).

- **Tapering down.** This approach has been widely used with people who smoke to reduce physical dependence and cravings before the quit date and is an option for some substances like alcohol or cannabis. This approach consists of setting increasingly lower daily and weekly limits on use of the substance while working toward a long-range goal of abstinence. The client keeps careful daily records of consumption and schedules sessions with the counselor as needed. **Tapering off opioids, benzodiazepines, or multiple substances should be done under medical supervision.**

- **Trial moderation.** Trial moderation (i.e., clients try to reduce substance use with careful monitoring) may be the only acceptable goal for some clients who are in Precontemplation. Don't assume that clients will fail at moderation; however, if the moderation experiment fails after a reasonable effort, try to get clients to reconsider abstinence as a change goal. Clients can gain insight into their ability to reduce their substance use, and many will ultimately decide to abstain if they cannot reduce their use without negative consequences. Research indicates that clients whose goal is moderation have larger social networks of people who drink daily (Gueorguieva et al., 2014). Therefore, you should address clients' drinking social network as a potential barrier to moderation as a long-term goal.

Develop a Change Plan

Your final step in readying the client to act is to work with him or her in creating a plan for change. (Chapter 3 provides a summary of MI-specific strategies for developing a change plan.) Think of a change plan as a roadmap for the client to reach his or her change goals. A solid plan for change enhances the client's self-efficacy and provides an opportunity to consider potential barriers and the likely outcomes of each change strategy. As mentioned in Chapter 3, some clients need no structured change plan.

Use these strategies to work with clients to create a sound change plan:

- Elicit change strategies from the client.
- Offer a menu of change options.
- Negotiate a behavioral contract.
- Explore and lower barriers to action.
- Enlist social support.

Elicit Change Strategies From the Client

TIP 35: *Enhancing Motivation for Change in Substance Use Disorder Treatment*
Chapter 6—From Preparation to Action: Initiating Change

October 2019

Work with clients to develop a change plan by eliciting their own ideas about what will work for them. This approach is a particularly helpful if clients have made past attempts to address substance use behaviors or have been in treatment before. For example, you might begin with a reflection of commitment talk and follow with an open question: "You clearly think that giving up cocaine is the best thing for you right now. What steps do you think you can take to reach this goal?"

Help clients create plans to match their concerns and goals. Plans will differ among clients:

- The plan can be very general or very specific and can be short term or long term.

- Some clients can commit only to a very limited plan, like going home, thinking about change, and returning on a specific date to talk further. Even a small, short-term plan like this can include specific steps for helping clients avoid high-risk situations as well as identifying specific coping strategies.

- Some plans are very simple, such as stating only that clients will enter outpatient treatment and attend an Alcoholics Anonymous (AA) meeting every day.

- Other plans include details (e.g., transportation to treatment, new ways to spend weekends).

- Many plans include specific steps to overcome anticipated barriers to success (Exhibit 6.3). Some plans lay out a sequence of steps. For example, working mothers with children who must enter inpatient treatment may develop a sequenced plan for arranging for child care.

Exhibit 6.3. Change Plan Worksheet

The most important reasons I want to make this change are:

My main goals for myself in making this change are:

I plan to do these things to reach my goals:

Specific action	When?

The first steps I plan to take in changing are:

Other people could help me in changing in these ways:

Person	Possible ways he or she can help

These are some possible obstacles to change and ways I could handle them:

Possible obstacles to change	How to respond

I will know that my plan is working when I see these results:

TIP 35: *Enhancing Motivation for Change in Substance Use Disorder Treatment*
Chapter 6—From Preparation to Action: Initiating Change

October 2019

> *Source: Miller & Rollnick, 2002.* Motivational Interviewing: Preparing People for Change (2nd ed). *Adapted with permission from Guildford Press.*

Create a change plan using a joint process in which you and the client work together. One of your most important tasks is to ensure that the plan is realistic and can be carried out. When the client offers a plan that seems unrealistic, too ambitious, or not ambitious enough, use shared decision making to rework the plan. The following areas are often part of such discussions:

- **Intensity and amount of help needed.** Encourage participation in community-based recovery support groups (e.g., AA, Narcotics Anonymous [NA], SMART Recovery, Women for Sobriety), enrolling in intensive outpatient treatment (IOP), or entering a 2-year therapeutic community.

- **Timeframe.** Choose a short-term rather than a long-term plan and a start date for the plan.

- **Available social support.** Discuss who will be involved in treatment (e.g., family, Women for Sobriety members, community members), where it will take place (e.g., at home, in the community), and when it will occur (e.g., after work, weekends, twice a week).

- **The order of subgoals and strategies or steps in the plan.** For example:
  1. Stop dealing marijuana.
  2. Stop smoking marijuana.
  3. Call friends or family to tell them about the plan.
  4. Visit friends or family who know about the plan.
  5. Learn relaxation techniques.
  6. Use relaxation techniques when feeling stressed at work.

- **Ways to address multiple problems.** Consider legal, financial, and health problems, among others.

Clients may ask you for information and advice about specific steps to add to the plan. You should:

- Ask permission to offer advice.

- Use the Elicit-Provide-Elicit (EPE) approach to keep the client in the center of the conversation (see the section "Developing discrepancy: A values conversation" in Chapter 3).

- Provide accurate and specific facts, and always ask whether they understand them.

- Elicit responses to such information by asking, "What do you think about this?"

The last step in EPE is key to completing the information exchange between you and the client.

How specific should you be when clients ask what **you** think they should do? Providing your best advice is an important part of your role. It is also appropriate to share your own views and opinions, although it is helpful to "soften" your statements and give clients permission to disagree. For example, you might soften your suggestion by saying, "This may or may not work for you, but a lot of people find it helpful to go to NA meetings to meet others who are trying to stay away from cocaine." Other techniques of MI, such as developing discrepancy, empathizing, and avoiding arguments, also are useful during this process.

The Change Plan Worksheet in Exhibit 6.3 helps clients focus their attention on the details of the plan, increase commitment to change, enlist social support, and troubleshoot potential roadblocks to change.

Use the Importance and Confidence Rulers in Exhibit 3.9 and Exhibit 3.10 to determine the client's readiness and self-efficacy about each change goal. These tools can help you and the client determine which goals to address first and which strategies to begin with. Ideally, the top goal will be one with

TIP 35: *Enhancing Motivation for Change in Substance Use Disorder Treatment*
Chapter 6—From Preparation to Action: Initiating Change

October 2019

higher ratings on both importance and confidence. If the client rates one goal as high in importance and low in confidence, focus on exploring self-efficacy and evoking confidence talk to prepare the client for taking action.

Offer a Menu of Change Options

Enhance clients' motivation to take action by offering them a variety of treatment choices. Choices can be about treatment options or about other types of services. For example, clients who will not go to AA meetings might be willing to go to a Rational Recovery, SMART Recovery, or Women for Sobriety group; clients who will not consider abstinence might be willing to decrease their consumption. **Encourage clients to learn about their options and make informed choices to enhance their commitment to the change plan.**

Expert Comment: Treatment Options and Resources

In our alcohol treatment program, I found that having lists of both community resources and diverse treatment modules helps counselors and case managers engage clients, offer individualized programming, and meet clients' multiple needs. The following are some options we offer our clients:

Treatment Module Options

- Values clarification/decision making
- Social-skills training (e.g., assertiveness, communication)
- Anxiety management/relaxation
- Anger management
- Marital and family therapy
- Adjunctive medication (i.e., disulfiram, naltrexone, or acamprosate)
- Problem-solving groups
- Intensive group therapy

Community Treatment Resources

- Halfway houses
- Support groups (e.g., AA, NA, Rational Recovery, SMART Recovery, Women for Sobriety)
- Social services (e.g., child care, vocational rehabilitation, food, shelter)
- Medical care
- Transportation
- Legal services
- Psychiatric services
- Academic and technical schools

Carlo C. DiClemente, Ph.D., Consensus Panel Member

Know your community's treatment facilities and resources. This helps you provide clients with suitable options and makes you an invaluable resource for clients. Offer clients information on:

- Specific contact people.
- Program graduates.
- Typical space availability.
- Funding issues.
- Eligibility criteria.
- Program rules and characteristics.

TIP 35: *Enhancing Motivation for Change in Substance Use Disorder Treatment*
Chapter 6—From Preparation to Action: Initiating Change

October 2019

- Community resources in other service areas, such as:
  - Food banks
  - Job training programs
  - Special programs for clients with co-occurring medical and mental disorders
  - Safe shelters for clients experiencing intimate partner violence

In addition, knowledge about clients' resources, insurance coverage, job situation, parenting responsibilities, and other factors is crucial in considering options. Initial assessment information also helps establish treatment options and priorities.

When discussing treatment options with clients, be sure to:

- Provide basic information in simple language about levels, intensities, and appropriateness of care.
- Avoid professional jargon and technical terms for treatment types or philosophies.
- Limit options to several that are appropriate, and describe these, one at a time, in language that is understandable and matches clients' concerns.
- Describe the purpose of a particular treatment, how it works, and what clients can expect.
- Ask clients to wait to make a decision about treatment until they understand all the options.
- Ask clients if they have questions, and ask their opinions about how to handle each option.
- Review the concept of the SOC; note that it is common for people to go through the stages several times as they move closer to maintaining substance use behavior change and stable recovery.
- Remind clients that not completing a treatment program and returning to substance use are not failures, but opportunities to reevaluate which change strategies are working or not working.
- Point out that, with all the options, they are certain to find some form of treatment that will work.
- Reassure clients that you are willing to work with them until they find the right choice.

Exhibit 6.4 provides a change-planning strategy for situations with many possible change options.

Exhibit 6.4. Mapping a Path for Change When There Are Multiple Options
• **Confirm the change goal.** If there are action steps to meet the change goal, decide which step to take first. For example, the client's goal might be to stop drinking completely. Some action steps might include talking with a healthcare provider about medication, going to an AA meeting, and telling a spouse about the decision. Which step does the client think is most important?
• **Make a list of the change options available to the client** (e.g., inpatient treatment, community-based recovery support groups, IOP treatment, a sober living house or therapeutic community, medication-assisted treatment).
• **Elicit the client's feelings, preferences, or both on the best way to proceed.** For example, ask, "Here are the different options we have discussed that might work for you. Which one do you like the most?" You can also discuss the pros and cons of different options (i.e., perform a decisional balance).
• **Summarize the plan and strengthen commitment.** Summarize the action steps and change goal, then evoke and reflect CAT (**C**ommitment, **A**ctivation, and **T**aking steps) change talk.
• **Troubleshoot.** Explore barriers to taking steps; raise any concerns about how realistic the plan is. Avoid the expert trap (see Chapter 3), and elicit the client's own ideas about how to manage barriers to change.
Source: Miller & Rollnick, 2013.

Negotiate a Behavioral Contract

TIP 35: *Enhancing Motivation for Change in Substance Use Disorder Treatment*
Chapter 6—From Preparation to Action: Initiating Change

October 2019

Develop a written or oral contract to help clients start working on their change plans. A contract is a formal agreement between two parties. Clients may choose to make a signed statement at the bottom of the Change Plan Worksheet or may prefer a separate document. Be sure to:

- Explain that others have found contracts useful at this stage, and invite them to try writing one.

- Avoid writing contracts for clients. **Composing and signing it is a small but important ritual of "going public" that can enhance commitment** (Connors, DiClemente, Velasquez, & Donovan, 2013).

- Encourage clients to use their own words.

- Be flexible. With some clients, a handshake is a good substitute for a written contract, particularly with clients who have challenges with reading and writing or whose first language is not English.

Establishing a contract raises issues for discussion about the client's reasons for change. What parties does the contract involve? Some contracts include the counselor as a party in the contract, specifying the counselor's functions and responsibilities. Other clients regard the contract as a promise to themselves, to a spouse, or to other family members.

Contracts are often used in treatment programs that employ behavioral techniques, such as contingency management (CM). For many counselors, contracts mean **contingencies** (i.e., rewards and consequences), and programs often build contingencies into the structure of their programs. For example, in many methadone maintenance programs, take-home medications are contingent on substance-free urinalyses. Rewards or incentives have been shown to be highly effective external reinforcers. For instance, CM rewards are effective in reducing use and misuse of a range of substances including alcohol, tobacco, cannabis, and stimulants, as well as polysubstance use (Aisncough, McNeill, Strang, Calder, & Brose, 2017; Litt, Kadden, & Petry, 2013; Sayegh, Huey, Zara, & Jhaveri, 2017).

Clients may decide to include contingencies, especially rewards or positive incentives, in the contract. Rewards can:

- Be highly individual.

- Include enjoyable activities, favorite foods, desired objects, or rituals and ceremonies, all of which can be powerful objective markers of change and reinforcers of commitment.

- Be tied to length of abstinence, quit-date anniversaries, or achievement of subgoals. For instance:
  - A client may plan an afternoon at a baseball game with her son to celebrate a month of abstinence.
  - One client might go out to dinner with friends after attending his 50th AA meeting.
  - Another client may light a candle at church.
  - Still another client might hike to the top of a nearby mountain to mark an improvement in energy and health.

Explore and Lower Barriers to Action

One category in the Change Plan Worksheet in Exhibit 6.3 addresses possible obstacles to change and ways to handle them. Identifying barriers to action is an important part of the change plan. Potential roadblocks to taking action on change goals might include:

- A lack of non-substance–using social supports.

- Unsupportive family members.

- Co-occurring medical or mental disorders.

- Distressing side effects from medication-assisted treatment or psychiatric medications.

TIP 35: *Enhancing Motivation for Change in Substance Use Disorder Treatment*
Chapter 6—From Preparation to Action: Initiating Change

October 2019

- Physical cravings or withdrawal symptoms.
- Legal issues, money-related problems, or both.
- Lack of child care.
- Transportation issues.
- A lack of cultural responsiveness of some agencies, programs, or services.

Clients can predict some barriers better than you can, so **allow them to identify and discuss possible problems.** Specifically:

- Do not try to predict everything that could go wrong.
- Focus on events or situations that are likely to be problematic.
- Build alternatives and solutions into the plan.
- Before offering advice, explore clients' ideas about how they might handle issues as they arise.
- Explore the ways clients may have overcome these or similar barriers in the past. This is a way to open a conversation about their strengths and coping skills.

Some problems are evident immediately. For instance, a highly motivated client may plan to attend an IOP treatment program 50 miles away 3 times a week, even though this requires bus and train rides and late-night travel. Explore the pros and cons of this part of the change plan with the client, and brainstorm alternative solutions, like finding a program closer to home or a family member, case manager, peer support specialist, or program volunteer who can drive the client to the program. **Remember, the change plan should include strategies that are accessible, acceptable, and appropriate for each client.**

You may need to refer clients to another treatment program or other services following initial consultation or evaluation, but this too is another common barrier to action. When you refer clients:

- Ensure they have **information** about how to get to the program, whom and when to telephone, and what to expect on the call (e.g., what type of personal information may be requested).
- Give them any **"insider information"** you have about the program or provider, which can reduce clients' anxiety and makes the process easier. For example, you may know that the receptionist at the program is a friendly person or that many people get lost by entering the building on the wrong side or that a nearby diner serves good food.
- Use **active linkage and referral interventions**, which enhance client engagement and retention in SUD treatment and ancillary services and improve outcomes (Rapp, Van Den Noortgate, Broekaert, & Vanderplasschen, 2014). Strategies for active referral procedures include:
  - **Helping the client make the telephone call to set up the intake appointment at the chosen program.** Some clients may want to make the phone call from your office; others might wish to call from home and call you later to tell you that they made an appointment. Some clients prefer to think things over first and make the call from your office at the next session.
  - **Following up with clients and the program**, if possible and with client permission, to ensure that clients are connected to the new service.
  - **Offering a "warm handoff,"** if possible, which involves introducing clients to the new provider.
  - Linking clients to a case manager, peer recovery support specialist, program alumnus, or community-based recovery support group volunteer to act as a liaison and actively engage clients in treatment programs; social, legal, or employment services; or community-based recovery support programs.

TIP 35: *Enhancing Motivation for Change in Substance Use Disorder Treatment*
Chapter 6—From Preparation to Action: Initiating Change

October 2019

Enlist Social Support

Help clients enlist social support and build or enhance social networks that support recovery from SUDs. Positive social support for substance use behavior change is an important factor in clients' initiating and sustaining behavior change (Black & Chung, 2014; Fergie et al., 2018; Rhoades et al., 2018).

As a counselor, you are a central support for clients, but you cannot provide all the support they need. In general, a supportive person is someone who will listen and not be judgmental. This supportive person should have a helpful and encouraging attitude toward clients. Ideally, this person does not use or misuse substances and understands the processes of addiction and change. The Change Plan Worksheet (Exhibit 6.3) includes space for listing supportive individuals and describing how they can help. As discussed in Chapter 4, concerned significant others can offer support by learning some MI skills (e.g., offering simple reflective listening responses, becoming effective partners in change).

Encourage clients to include social support strategies in their change plans. These include:

- **Engaging in activities with friends that don't involve substance use.** Social support often entails participating in non-substance–use activities, so close friends with whom clients have a history of shared interests other than substance use are good candidates for this helpful role. Members of social groups who drink and use drugs are not likely to offer the support clients need in recovery.

- **Repairing or resuming connections with supportive family members and significant others.** Clients can find supportive people among their family members and close friends as well as in faith-based and spiritual organizations, recreational centers, and community volunteer organizations. To make these connections, encourage clients to explore and discuss a time in their lives before substance use became a central focus. Ask them what gave meaning to their lives at that time.

- **Participating in AA or other recovery support groups.** Recovery groups provide clients with social support for behavior change, positive role models of recovery, recovering friendship networks, and hope that recovery is possible. Research confirms that participation in AA is associated with positive alcohol-related, psychological, and social outcomes (Humphreys, Blodgett, & Wagner, 2014).

- **Connecting with addiction-focused peer support.** Peer recovery support specialists can be recovery role models and an important source of social support for clients. Client participation in peer recovery support services with a peer specialist leads to positive social support and improved substance use outcomes, including decreased alcohol use and hospitalizations as well as better adherence to treatment goals after discharge (Bassuk, Hanson, Greene, Richard, & Laudet, 2016). Oxford Houses and similar sober living housing options have built-in social support systems.

- **Connecting clients with a case manager.** For some clients, especially those with chronic medical or serious mental illness, case management teams provide a sense of safety, structure, and support. A case manager can also actively link clients to community-based social services, federal and state financial assistance, and other ancillary services that support clients' recovery efforts.

When helping clients enlist social support, be particularly alert for clients who have limited social skills or social networks. Some clients may have to learn social skills and ways to structure leisure time. Add social skill-building steps into the change plan. Some clients may not be connected to any social network that is not organized around substance use. Furthermore, addiction may have so narrowed their focus to the point where they have trouble recalling activities that once held their interest or appealed to them. However, most people have unfulfilled desires to pursue an activity at some time in their lives. Ask about these wishes. One client may want to learn ballroom dancing, another to learn a martial art, or still another to take a creative writing class. Planning for change can be a particularly productive time for clients to reconnect with this desire to find fulfilling activities, and seeking such activities provides

TIP 35: *Enhancing Motivation for Change in Substance Use Disorder Treatment*
Chapter 6—From Preparation to Action: Initiating Change

October 2019

opportunities for making new friends.

Clients with a carefully drafted change plan, knowledge of both high-risk situations and potential barriers to getting started, and a group of supportive friends, family members, or recovery supports should be fully prepared and ready to move into the Action stage.

Support the Client's Action Steps

DiClemente (2018) describes four main tasks for client in the Action stage of the SOC:

1. Breaking free of the addiction using the strategies in the change plan

2. Continuing commitment to change and establishing a new pattern of behavior

3. Managing internal/external barriers to change (e.g., physical cravings, lack of positive social support)

4. Revising and refining the change plan

Your role is to continue using motivational counseling approaches to support the client in completing these tasks and moving into the Maintenance stage and stable recovery. To support clients in breaking free of substance use behaviors:

- Encourage clients to set a specific start date for each behavior change (e.g., a smoking quit date, date to enter an inpatient addiction treatment program). Setting a start date increases commitment.

- Help clients create rituals that symbolize them leaving old behaviors behind. For example, some clients may make a ritual of burning or disposing of substance paraphernalia, cigarettes, beer mugs, or liquor. Support clients in creating personally meaningful rituals. As mentioned previously, picking up a chip at an AA meeting is a ritual that supports clients' action steps toward abstinence and a new lifestyle.

To reinforce clients' commitment to change:

- Continue to evoke and reflect CAT change talk in your ongoing conversations with clients.

- Use reflective listening, summaries, and affirmations.

- Manage barriers to change by identifying those barriers (as described above in the section "Explore and Lower Barriers to Action"), working with clients to brainstorm personally relevant strategies for lowering or reducing the impact of those barriers, and offering a menu of treatment options. For example, if a client experiences intense alcohol or drug cravings, you might explore the possibility of referring the client to a medical provider for a medication evaluation, encouraging participation in a mindfulness meditation group, or both.

- Evaluate, revise, and refine the change plan as the final step in the Action stage.

Evaluate the Change Plan

Your goal of this stage of the change cycle is to help the client sustain successful actions for a long enough time that he or she gains stability and moves into Maintenance (Connors et al., 2013). It is not likely that you and the client will be able to predict all of the issues that will come up as the client initiates the change plan. The client's circumstances likely will change (e.g., a spouse might file for divorce), unanticipated issues arise (e.g., the client's drug-using social network might put pressure on the client to return to drug use), and change strategies may not turn out to work well for the client (e.g., the client loses his or her driver's license and has to find alternative transportation to NA meetings). These unanticipated issues can become a barrier to sustaining change plan actions and may require

TIP 35: *Enhancing Motivation for Change in Substance Use Disorder Treatment*
Chapter 6—From Preparation to Action: Initiating Change

October 2019

revisions to the change plan (Connors et al., 2013).

Your task is to work with the client at each encounter to evaluate the change plan and revise it as necessary. Ask the client, "What's working?" and "What's not working?" Miller and Rollnick (2013) suggest that counselors think about this process as "flexible revisiting." The same strategies used in the planning process of MI apply to revising the change plan, including confirming the change goal, eliciting the client's ideas about how to change, offering a menu of options, summarizing the change plan, and exploring obstacles (see Chapter 3). Some strategies for change may need to be removed, whereas others can be adjusted. For example, one client's goal is to quit drinking, and her action steps include attending three AA meetings a week, including one women's meeting. The client stops going to the women's meeting because one of the regular attendees is a coworker who likes to gossip, and the client is afraid that the coworker will break her anonymity at work. Your first step is to identify the issue, and then elicit the client's ideas about what else might work for her.

Open questions to start this process if a change strategy is not working include (Miller & Rollnick, 2013):

- "What now?"
- "What else might work?"
- "What's your next step?

Avoid jumping in too quickly with your own ideas. Adjusting a change plan, like creating the initial change plan, is a joint process between you and the client; the client's own ideas and resources are key (Miller & Rollnick, 2013). Finally, summarize the new change strategy and explore how the client might respond to any new obstacles that might come up while initiating the revised change plan (Miller & Rollnick, 2013).

Conclusion

As clients move from contemplating change into preparing for change, your task is to continue to reinforce clients' commitment to change and take action. You can support clients to take this next step by working together to develop a change plan, imagining possible barriers to change that might occur, and enlisting social support for taking action. Change plans are client driven and based on clients' own goals. Continue to use motivational counseling strategies to help clients identify and clarify their change goals, develop a change plan, and refine and revise the change plan as needed. Your role is to help clients sustain their goals for change, gain stability, and move into the Maintenance stage of the SOC.

TIP 35: *Enhancing Motivation for Change in Substance Use Disorder Treatment*
Chapter 6—From Preparation to Action: Initiating Change

October 2019

This page intentionally left blank.

TIP 35: *Enhancing Motivation for Change in Substance Use Disorder Treatment*
Chapter 7—From Action to Maintenance: Stabilizing Change

October 2019

Chapter 7—From Action to Maintenance: Stabilizing Change

"To become habitual, the new behavior must become integrated into the individual's lifestyle. This is the task of the Maintenance stage of change. During this stage, the new behavior pattern becomes automatic, requiring less thought or effort to sustain it…. However, even during Maintenance there is an ever-present danger of reverting to the old pattern. In fact, the new behavior becomes fully maintained only when there is little or no energy or effort needed to continue it and the individual can terminate the cycle of change."

DiClemente, 2018, p. 31

Key Messages

- In the Maintenance stage of the Stages of Change (SOC) model, clients work toward stabilizing the substance use behavioral changes they have made.
- You can support clients in the Maintenance stage by helping them stay motivated, identify triggers that might lead to a return to substance misuse, and develop a plan for coping with situational triggers when they arise.
- Relapse prevention counseling (RPC) using a motivational counseling style can prevent a return to substance misuse and help clients reenter the cycle of change quickly if they do return to substance use.

Maintaining change is often more challenging than taking one's first steps toward change. Chapter 7 addresses ways that you can use motivational strategies to help clients maintain their success in recovering from substance use disorders (SUDs). It presents strategies for stabilizing change, supporting lifestyle changes, managing setbacks during Maintenance, and helping clients reenter the cycle of change if a relapse or a return to substance misuse occurs.

Using a motivational counseling style with clients in the Precontemplation through Preparation stages helps them move toward initiating behavioral change. Yet when clients do take action, they face the reality of stopping or reducing substance use. This obstacle is more difficult than just contemplating action. Once clients have decided to take action, they are on the downslope of the Motivational Interviewing (MI) Hill of Ambivalence presented in Exhibit 5.2.

Exhibit 7.1 presents counseling strategies for Action and Relapse.

Exhibit 7.1. Counseling Strategies for Action and Relapse			
SOC	Client Motivation	Counselor Focus	Counseling Strategies
Maintenance	The client has achieved initial goals, such as abstinence, reduced substance use behaviors, or entering treatment, and is now working to maintain these goals.	• Stabilize client change. • Support the client's lifestyle changes.	• Engage and retain the client in SUD treatment. • Create a coping plan. • Identify new behaviors that reinforce change. • Identify recovery capital (RC). • Reinforce family and social support.

Exhibit 7.1. Counseling Strategies for Action and Relapse			
SOC	Client Motivation	Counselor Focus	Counseling Strategies
Relapse and Recycle	The client returns to substance misuse and temporarily exits the change cycle.	Help the client reenter the change cycle.	• Provide RPC. • Reenter the cycle of change.

Stabilize Client Change

One of the key change goals for many clients is entry into a specialized addiction treatment program. Options include outpatient, intensive outpatient, inpatient, and short- or long-term residential treatment; methadone maintenance treatment; and office-based opioid treatment. Making the decision to enter treatment is an action step. **To maintain that behavior change, you should engage and retain clients in treatment.** Unfortunately, many clients enter and stop treatment before they achieve their other change goals. Engaging and retaining clients in treatment are important strategies for stabilizing substance use behavior change. Other stabilization strategies include identifying high-risk situations and triggers for substance use, creating a coping plan, and helping clients practice and use new coping skills.

Engage and Retain Clients in SUD Treatment

You play an important role in preventing clients from stopping or dropping out of treatment before completion—a major concern for SUD treatment providers. A consistent predictor of positive client outcomes across SUD treatment services is treatment completion (Brorson, Arnevik, Rand-Hendriksen, & Duckert, 2013). Longer lengths of stay in treatment are consistent indicators of reliable behavior change and positive treatment outcomes (Running Bear, Beals, Novins, & Manson, 2017; Jason, Salina, & Ram, 2016; Turner & Deanne, 2016).

Causes of stopping treatment early vary:

- For some clients, dropping out, missing appointments, or nonadherence with other aspects of the treatment program are clear messages of **disappointment, hopelessness, or changes of heart.**

- Some clients drop out of treatment **because their treatment or behavior change goals don't match** those of the counselor or program (Connors, DiClemente, Velasquez, & Donovan, 2013).

- Strong evidence shows that **low treatment alliance** is linked to client dropout in SUD treatment (Brorson et al., 2013).

- Clients with **co-occurring substance use and mental disorders (CODs)** and those with **cognitive problems** are especially likely to end treatment early (Running Bear et al., 2017; Brorson et al., 2013; Krawczyk et al., 2017; Teeson et al., 2015). For more information about engaging clients with CODs, see Treatment Improvement Protocol (TIP) 42: *Substance Abuse Treatment for Persons With Co-Occurring Disorders* (Substance Abuse and Mental Health Services Administration [SAMHSA], 2013).

- For others, dropping out may mean they have **successfully changed their substance use behaviors on their own** (Connors et al., 2013).

- Perhaps the strongest predictor of dropout in SUD treatment is **addiction severity at treatment entry.** For example, one study of men and women in treatment for posttraumatic stress disorder found that a diagnosis of both an alcohol use disorder (AUD) and a drug use disorder strongly predicted higher dropout rates, drug use severity predicted worse adherence to treatment, and drug use severity or a lifetime diagnosis of an alcohol or drug use disorder predicted worse treatment outcomes (Bedard-Gilligan, Garcia, Zoellner, & Feeny 2018).

TIP 35: *Enhancing Motivation for Change in Substance Use Disorder Treatment*
Chapter 7—From Action to Maintenance: Stabilizing Change

October 2019

MI and motivational enhancement therapy are effective in improving treatment adherence to and retention in SUD treatment for certain substances (e.g., cocaine), especially for clients who enter treatment with low motivation to change (DiClemente, Corno, Graydon, Wiprovnick, & Knoblach, 2017). Motivational-based strategies that increase client engagement and retention in SUD treatment and reduce client dropout are addressed below.

Build a strong counseling alliance

As noted in Chapters 3 and 4, **your counseling style is an important element for establishing rapport and building a trusting relationship with clients.** MI strategies appropriate during the engaging process (see Chapter 3) help you connect with and understand clients' unique perspectives and personal values. For example, empathy, as expressed through reflective listening, is key in developing rapport with clients and predicts positive treatment alliance and client outcomes (Anderson, Crowley, Himawan, Holmberg, & Uhlin, 2016; Miller & Moyers, 2015; Moyers, 2014; Moyers, Houck, Rice, Longabaugh, & Miller, 2016).

To help clients confide in you, make them feel comfortable and safe within the treatment setting. Clients' natural reactions may depend on such factors as their gender, age, race, ethnicity, sexual or gender identity, and previous experience. For example, some ethnic or racial groups may be hesitant to enter treatment based on negative life experiences, discrimination, or problems encountered with earlier episodes of treatment. Initially, for these clients and others who have been marginalized or experienced trauma, safety in the treatment setting is a particularly important issue. (See the section "Special Applications of Motivational Interventions" in Chapter 2 for culturally responsive ways to engage clients in treatment.) You should also consider gender differences regarding the importance of establishing a strong counseling alliance. For example, one study found that women who received intensive MI over nine sessions (versus a single session) showed significantly higher counseling alliance and better alcohol use outcomes than men did (Korcha, Polcin, Evans, Bond, & Galloway, 2015).

Inform clients about program rules and expectations

Clients must become acquainted with you and the treatment program. To accomplish this:

- Tell clients explicitly what treatment involves, what is expected of them, and what rules they must follow. If clients have not been prepared by a referring source, review exactly what will happen in treatment to eliminate and confusion.

- Use language clients understand.

- Encourage questions, and provide clarification of anything that seems confusing.

- Explain what information must be reported to a referring agency that has mandated the treatment, including what it means to consent to release of information. This discussion is part of the regular informed consent process that should happen when clients enter treatment.

Address client expectations about treatment

One of the first things you should discuss with new clients is their expectations about the treatment process. Ask clients about their past treatment experiences and what they think the current treatment experience will be like. Clients who are in SUD treatment for the first time do not know much about what the counseling process entails and tend to underestimate the level of motivation, personal commitment, and responsibility required to take action to change (Raylu & Kaur, 2012). This suggests that **clients without previous SUD treatment experience benefit from discussions about treatment expectations and the importance of being open to the counseling process** (Raylu & Kaur, 2012).

Ask clients for permission to explore their treatment expectations. Ask for elaboration on their initial impressions as well as their expectations, hopes, and fears. Some common client fears about treatment are that:

- The counselor will be confrontational and force treatment goals on them.
- Treatment will take too long and require the client to give up too much.
- The rules are too strict, and clients will be discharged for the smallest mistake.
- Medication will not be prescribed for painful withdrawal symptoms.
- The program does not understand women, members of different ethnic/racial groups, or people who use certain substances or combinations of substances.
- A spouse or other family member will be required to participate.

Many clients have negative expectations based on previous treatment. A motivational approach can help you understand their concerns, which is especially important for clients who feel forced into treatment by someone else (e.g., by an employer, the court, a spouse). When clients have unrealistic expectations, like believing the treatment program will get their driver's license reinstated or restore a marriage, be open and honest about what the program can and cannot do. **Use OARS (Open questions, Affirmations, Reflective listening, and Summarization) to explore negative expectations about treatment and the client's hopes about what treatment can accomplish.**

Explore and resolve barriers to completing treatment

Work with clients to brainstorm and explore solutions to common issues. As treatment progresses, clients may experience barriers that slow their success and could result in them stopping treatment early. Sometimes clients do not feel ready to participate or suddenly rethink their decision to enter treatment. Rethinking participation in treatment is a sign that clients may have returned to the Contemplation stage. If this is the case, reengage the client using the motivational strategies discussed in Chapter 5. **If clients are clearly not ready to participate in specialized treatment, leave the door open for them to return at another time, and provide a menu of options for referral to other services.**

During treatment, clients may have negative reactions or embarrassing moments when they:

- Share with you more than they had planned to share.
- Experience intense or overwhelming emotions.
- Realize the mismatch in information they have given you.
- Realize how they have hurt others or their own futures.

You can deal with these difficult reactions by:

- Anticipating and discussing such problems before they occur.
- Letting clients know that these reactions are a normal part of the recovery process.
- Working with clients to develop a plan to handle these difficult reactions.
- Exploring previous treatment, including their reasons for leaving early and how to better match current treatment to their needs.

If this is the client's first treatment experience, get his or her ideas about what might be a roadblock to completing treatment:

- Start with an affirmation, and ask an open question:

  "It took a lot of determination and effort for you to be here. Good for you! Sometimes things come

TIP 35: *Enhancing Motivation for Change in Substance Use Disorder Treatment*
Chapter 7—From Action to Maintenance: Stabilizing Change

October 2019

up during counseling sessions that are difficult and might make you wonder if staying in treatment is worth the effort. That's normal. What are some things you can imagine that might make it challenging for you to follow through with your commitment to completing the program?"

- Follow with reflective listening responses.
- Ask the client for ideas about strategies to deal with ambivalence about staying in treatment.
- Be culturally aware as you help the client manage or try to prevent common difficulties.

Increase congruence between intrinsic and extrinsic motivation

Exploring with clients their internal and external reasons for entering and staying in treatment can help reduce their chances of early dropout. Self-determination theory proposes that intrinsic (internal) motivation may have a stronger impact on maintaining behavior change than extrinsic (external) motivation, which may be more effective in helping clients initiate behavior change. A meta-analysis of MI (which emphasizes increasing internal motivation) and contingency management (which emphasizes external motivators) found that both approaches were effective in reducing use of a wide variety of substances (Sayegh, Huey, Zara, & Jhaveri, 2017). The analysis also found evidence to suggest that extrinsically focused counseling strategies produced short-term treatment effects, whereas intrinsically focused counseling strategies produced long-term treatment effects.

Help clients increase congruence, or agreement, between internal and external motivations. You can explore external motivations clients may view as forced or unwanted and reframe them as positive reasons that align with their internal reasons for staying in treatment to increase congruence.

Explore client nonadherence

Clients' nonadherence to treatment is often a sign that they are unhappy with the counseling process. For example, clients may miss appointments, arrive late, fail to complete required forms, or remain silent when asked to participate. Any occurrence of such behavior provides an opportunity to discuss the reasons for the behavior and learn from it. Often clients are expressing their ambivalence and are not ready to make a change. Explore the behavior in a nonjudgmental, problem-solving manner that helps you discover whether the behavior was intentional or whether a reasonable explanation for the behavior exists. For example, clients might be late as a sign of "rebelling" against what they think will be a stressful session, or it could simply be that their car broke down.

As with all motivational strategies, **you need to draw out clients' views of and thoughts about the event.** Generally, if you can get clients to voice their frustrations, they will come up with the answers themselves. Asking a question such as "What do you think is getting in the way of being here on time?" is likely to open a dialog. Respond with reflective listening, open questions that evoke change talk, and affirmations. For example, you might ask, "How does being late fit or not fit with your goal of getting the most out of this treatment experience?" Remember to praise the client for simply getting to the session.

Missed appointments or not showing up for scheduled activities require a more proactive approach. Some strategies for responding to missed appointments are listed in Exhibit 7.2.

Exhibit 7.2. Options for Responding to a Missed Appointment

- Place a telephone call.
- Send a text message.
- Write an email.
- Mail a personal letter.

TIP 35: *Enhancing Motivation for Change in Substance Use Disorder Treatment*
Chapter 7—From Action to Maintenance: Stabilizing Change

October 2019

- Contact preapproved relatives or significant or concerned others.
- Pay the client a personal visit (if appropriate for your role and agency policy).
- Contact the referral source.

As part of the informed consent process, find out from clients which contact methods they prefer, discuss confidentiality and security issues (e.g., protection of clients' personal health information, agency policies regarding email and texting), and obtain appropriate releases to contact other individuals or organizations.

Reach out and follow up

You might need to reach out to the client following certain events, such as a wedding, birth of a child, traumatic injury or illness, or several missed appointments. Doing so shows your personal concern and genuine interest in protecting the counseling relationship and enhancing the recovery process. As mentioned previously, explore the client's preferred methods for you to reach out if he or she misses appointments or drops out of treatment. Make sure to get written consent to contact relatives, friends, or others. In addition, you should be aware of and abide by the client's cultural rules and values about having contact outside the SUD setting.

If clients complete their initial treatment goals and end treatment, follow up with them periodically. Setbacks, particularly with maintenance of substance use behavior change, often occurs between 3 and 6 months after treatment, and you should plan regular follow-up sessions with clients to reinforce and support maintenance of treatment gains (Miller, Forcehimes, & Zweben, 2011).

Create a Coping Plan

To help clients move fully into Maintenance, help them stabilize actual change in their substance use behavior. Support clients' stabilization by helping them develop a coping plan that lists strategies for managing thoughts, urges, and impulses to drink or use drugs. This planning process includes:

- Assessing and enhancing self-efficacy.
- Identifying high-risk situations that trigger the impulse to drink or use drugs.
- Identifying coping strategies to manage high-risk situations.
- Helping clients practice and use effective coping skills.

Assess and enhance self-efficacy

Help clients improve their self-efficacy. Self-efficacy is important for changing substance use behaviors as well as sustaining those changes. There is a strong relationship between client self-efficacy and SUD treatment outcomes across a variety of substances (e.g., alcohol, cannabis, cocaine) and different counseling approaches. There is also evidence that a strong counseling alliance helps clients enhance self-efficacy and increase positive treatment outcomes for alcohol use (Kadden & Litt, 2011).

Clients may have high self-efficacy in some situations and low self-efficacy in others. Several validated tools can help assess clients' level of self-efficacy or confidence in how well they would cope with the temptation to use substances in high-risk situations. Scores provide feedback about clients' self-efficacy for a specific behavior over a range of high-risk situations. Some computerized versions of these instruments generate charts that present clients' scores in an easy-to-understand way. Descriptions of the Situational Confidence Questionnaire (SCQ)/Brief SCQ (BSCQ) and the Alcohol Abstinence Self-Efficacy Scale (AASES), three of the most widely used instruments, follow:

- The **SCQ** and **BSCQ** have been used with people who misuse alcohol. The 100-item SCQ asks clients to identify their level of confidence in resisting drinking in 8 circumstances (Breslin, Sobell, Sobell, &

TIP 35: *Enhancing Motivation for Change in Substance Use Disorder Treatment*
Chapter 7—From Action to Maintenance: Stabilizing Change

October 2019

Agrawal, 2000):

- Unpleasant emotions
- Physical discomfort
- Testing personal control over substance use
- Urges and temptations to drink
- Pleasant times with others
- Conflicts with others
- Pleasant emotions
- Social pressure to drink

Clients are asked to imagine themselves in each situation and rate their confidence on a 6-point scale, ranging from not at all confident (a rating of 0) to totally confident (a rating of 6), that they can resist the urge to drink heavily. The BSCQ is a shortened 8-question form that asks clients to rate these circumstances using a scale of 0% to 100%, with 0% indicating not at all confident and 100% indicating totally confident. The BSCQ and its scoring instruments are available in Appendix B.

- The **AASES** measures an individual's self-efficacy in abstaining from alcohol (DiClemente, Carbonari, Montgomery, & Hughes, 1994). Although similar to the SCQ/BSCQ, the AASES focuses on clients' confidence in their ability to abstain from drinking across 20 different situations. The AASES consists of 20 items and can be used to assess both the temptation to drink and the confidence to abstain. The AASES and its scoring instructions are available in Appendix B.

By using these tools, clients can better understand the high-risk situations in which they have low self-efficacy. This information can be helpful in setting realistic goals and developing an individualized coping plan. Clients who rank many situations as high risk (i.e., low self-efficacy) may need to identify and develop new coping strategies.

Other **strategies to enhance client self-efficacy in Maintenance include** (Miller & Rollnick, 2013):

- Expressing confidence in the client's ability to change.
- Reviewing past success with changing substance use or other health behaviors.
- Reviewing the client's current strengths.
- Using the Confidence Ruler (Exhibit 3.10) to measure coping strategies.
- Presenting a menu of coping strategies that have a high likelihood of success.

Identify high-risk situations and coping strategies

Another approach to helping clients identify high-risk situations is to use a structured interview that identifies the high-risk situation (i.e., who, where, and when), external triggers (i.e., what), and internal triggers (i.e., thoughts, feelings, and physical cravings) that led to substance use in the past. Once these situations are identified, clients explore coping strategies to manage these triggers that have worked in the past and that might work now and in the future. Understanding these triggers helps clients target specific strategies for coping with these triggers.

Strategies for conducting the interview include the following:

- **Let the client know the purpose of the interview, and ask permission to conduct it.** For example, you might say, "It can be helpful to explore some of the situations when you drank or used drugs in the past and what led to your decision to use in those situations. Sometimes those can be thoughts or feelings or the situation itself. We sometimes call what led to substance use internal and external

TIP 35: *Enhancing Motivation for Change in Substance Use Disorder Treatment*
Chapter 7—From Action to Maintenance: Stabilizing Change

October 2019

triggers. Once we know what has 'triggered' your drinking or drug use in the past, we can brainstorm ways to cope with those triggers now, instead of drinking or using. Is that okay?"

- **Draw a four-column table on a piece of paper and label the columns** High-Risk Situation, External Triggers, Internal Triggers, and Coping Strategies as in Exhibit 7.3.

Exhibit 7.3. Triggers and Coping Strategies			
High-Risk Situation (who, where, when)	External Triggers (what)	Internal Triggers (thoughts, feelings, impulses, cravings)	Coping Strategies
Example: "Watching a football game with my drinking buddies."	Example: "A beer commercial comes on."	Example: "My mouth waters, and I think about how good a beer would taste."	Example: "I could go to the refrigerator and get a cold soft drink instead of a beer."

- **Ask an open question to start the discussion.** "Tell me about situations in which you have been most likely to drink or use drugs in the past, or times when you have tended to drink or use more than expected. These might be when you were with specific people, in specific places, or at certain times of day, or perhaps when you were feeling a particular way."
- **Elicit ideas from the client about ways he or she might have resisted temptation to use in the past.**
- **Elicit ideas from the client about strategies he or she could use now** to avoid high-risk situation or external triggers as well as ways to manage the internal triggers without resorting to substance use.
- **Ask the client to elaborate on possible coping strategies.**
- **Use the Confidence Ruler** (Exhibit 3.10) to evaluate the client's confidence in applying these coping strategies. Evoke confidence talk to reinforce and enhance self-efficacy (see Chapter 3).

As you explore triggers, do not solely use reflective listening. This technique might accidentally evoke sustain talk from the client and decrease his or her commitment to engaging in coping strategies. Instead, **use affirmations and reflective listening responses to reinforce the client's commitment to engaging in coping strategies as an alternative to substance use.**

If the client has difficulty identifying coping strategies:

- Offer some ideas that others have found helpful.
- Brainstorm with the client.
- Offer a menu of possible coping strategies.
- Explore with the client which options are more likely to work as in the examples in Exhibit 7.4.

Exhibit 7.4. A Menu of Coping Strategies
Coping strategies are not mutually exclusive; different ones can be used at different times. In addition, not all are equally good; some involve getting uncomfortably close to trigger situations. Here are some examples of a menu of strategies that might help clients in different high-risk situations.
Example #1: Client X typically uses cocaine whenever his cousin, who uses regularly, drops by the house. Coping strategies to consider include (1) call the cousin and ask him not to come by anymore; (2) call the cousin and ask him not to bring cocaine when he visits; (3) if there is a pattern to when the cousin comes, plan to be out of the house at that time; or (4) if someone else lives in the house, ask him or her to be present for the cousin's visit.

TIP 35: *Enhancing Motivation for Change in Substance Use Disorder Treatment*
Chapter 7—From Action to Maintenance: Stabilizing Change

October 2019

Example #2: Client Y typically uses cocaine when she goes with a particular group of friends, one of whom often brings drugs along. She is particularly vulnerable when they all drink alcohol. Coping strategies to consider might include (1) go out with a different set of friends; (2) go along with this group only for activities that do not involve drinking; (3) leave the group as soon as drinking seems imminent; (4) tell the supplier that she is trying to stay off cocaine and would appreciate not being offered any; or (5) ask all of her friends, or one especially close friend, to help her out by not using when she is around or by telling the supplier to stop offering it to her.

Example #3: Client Z typically uses cocaine when feeling tired or stressed. Coping strategies might include (1) scheduling activities to get more sleep at night, (2) scheduling activities to have 1 hour per day of relaxation time, (3) learning and practicing specific stress reduction and relaxation techniques, or (4) learning problem-solving techniques that can reduce stress in high-risk situations.

Use the coping strategies identified in the structured interview to develop a written coping plan. This could be as simple as jotting down a few ideas for managing triggers in high-risk situations on a file card or it could be as detailed as creating a change plan using the Change Plan Worksheet in Exhibit 6.3.

Help the clients practice new coping skills

Just as you would monitor and reevaluate a change plan with clients, revisit the coping plan, and modify it as necessary. Ask clients to rehearse coping strategies in counseling sessions and to try to implement those strategies in everyday life. For example, growing evidence shows that practicing mindfulness is an effective strategy for managing cravings and urges to use substances (Grant et al., 2017). If this coping strategy is new to clients, help them develop a change plan that might include attending a mindfulness class or group and practicing mindfulness at home or in a counseling session that focuses on managing cravings. **Rehearsing new skills reinforces them and helps build self-efficacy.**

Support the Client's Lifestyle Changes

Your task in the Maintenance stage is to support and praise clients' positive lifestyle and identify behaviors that reinforce these changes. Clients must put forth ongoing and sustained effort to maintain their change of substance use behaviors. As clients successfully maintain changes, they develop a strong sense of self-efficacy. They use less effort to cope with temptations and triggers, and new behaviors become the norm (DiClemente, 2018). As substance use behavior change becomes a new lifestyle, the client develops a new sense of identity. For some, this is expressed in self-identification as a "nonsmoker" or a "recovering addict." For others, the new story of identity is about becoming an integral member of the family or community.

Identify New Behaviors that Reinforce Change

You should examine all areas of clients' life for new reinforcers, which should come from multiple sources and be of various types. A setback in one area can be counterbalanced by a positive reinforcer from another area. As the motivation for positive change becomes harder to sustain, clients need strong reasons for overcoming the challenges they will face. Help them select positive reinforcers that will prevail over substance use over time.

Small steps are helpful, but they cannot fill a whole life. Abstaining from substances is a sudden change and often leaves a large space in clients' lives. You can help clients fill this space by exploring activities that will support their healthy new identity such as:

- **Doing volunteer work** links clients to the community. Clients can fill time, decrease isolation, and improve self-efficacy through this prosocial activity, making positive contributions to the community.
- **Becoming involved in 12-Step activities.** Similar to volunteering, this fills a need to be involved with

TIP 35: *Enhancing Motivation for Change in Substance Use Disorder Treatment*
Chapter 7—From Action to Maintenance: Stabilizing Change

October 2019

a group and contributes to a worthwhile organization.

- **Setting goals** to improve work, education, health, and nutrition.
- **Spending more time with family, significant others, and friends.**
- **Participating in spiritual or cultural activities.**
- **Learning new skills or improving old ones** in such areas as sports, art, music, and hobbies.

Identify Recovery Capital

Help clients tap into and build new sources of positive RC and lessen the impact of negative sources of RC as a way to support the maintenance of change. "Recovery capital" refers to internal and external resources a person draws on to begin and sustain recovery. Internal resources include, but are not limited to, values, knowledge, skills, self-efficacy, and hope. External resources include, but are not limited to, employment; safe housing; financial resources; access to health care; and social, family, spiritual, cultural, and community supports (Granfield & Cloud, 1999). RC can be positive (e.g., drug-free social network) or negative (e.g., drug-using social network) (Hennesey, 2017). Positive and negative RC interact with each other in the recovery process and change over time (Hennessy, 2017). RC is linked with clients' natural recovery resources. (See also the "Natural Change" section in Chapter 1.)

Reinforce Family and Social Support

Family and social support are important sources of RC. They can help clients permanently break free from addiction and engage in a new lifestyle (DiClemente, 2018). Family and friends who are supportive of the clients' recovery can be especially helpful in stabilizing change because they can reinforce new behavior and provide positive incentives to continue in recovery. They can involve clients in new social and recreational activities and be a source of emotional and financial support. Other types of support they provide can be instrumental (e.g., babysitting, carpooling), romantic, spiritual, and communal (i.e., belonging to a particular group or community).

Identify different types of social supports that clients have available to help determine gaps in their support system and help them build a larger, more diverse social network. Clients with more severe AUD tend to have smaller, less diverse social networks (i.e., supports other than family or close friends) than those with no history of AUD or less severe alcohol misuse experiences (Mowbray, Quinn, & Cranford, 2014). More extensive social networks in which individuals with addiction exchange support with one another can help individuals sustain recovery over time (Panebianco, Gallupe, Carrington, & Colozzi, 2016). An extended and diverse social network might comprise:

- Family members.
- Friends.
- Peer support specialists.
- Members of recovery support groups.
- Healthcare providers.
- Employers.
- 12-Step sponsors.
- Spiritual advisors.
- Members of a church or spiritual community.
- Neighbors.
- Members of community groups.

TIP 35: *Enhancing Motivation for Change in Substance Use Disorder Treatment*
Chapter 7—From Action to Maintenance: Stabilizing Change

October 2019

- Participants in organized recreational activities.

Use motivational counseling strategies to explore current and potential sources of social support and how those supports could help clients maintain recovery and lifestyle changes. For example, family members can act as a warning system if they see early signs of possible relapse. A peer recovery support specialist can link clients to alcohol- and drug-free recreational events in the community or other recovery support. Exhibit 7.5 describes a brief clinical scenario with a client who lacks social support.

Exhibit 7.5. Susan's Story: A Client Lacking Social Support

Client context: Susan is 41 years old and has a long history of AUD and multiple treatment episodes. The longest period Susan has been able to maintain abstinence from alcohol has been 1 month. She has tried to participate in Alcoholics Anonymous (AA); however, she finds that most of the meetings she can get to without a car are primarily attended by men, and she does not feel comfortable there. Susan's mother has been diagnosed with schizophrenia. Susan reports that her father has been diagnosed with AUD. Her father sexually abused her for years when she was a child. Susan is divorced and has only one friend she talks to, infrequently. Her only source of regular support is her father.

Susan recently participated in an IOP addiction treatment program where she also attended a Seeking Safety support group for women with histories of trauma. (For more information about Seeking Safety, see Chapter 6 of TIP 57: *Trauma-Informed Care in Behavioral Health Services* [SAMHSA, 2014b].) This is the first treatment experience in which Susan's history of trauma has been addressed simultaneously with her AUD. Susan completes the program and is referred to outpatient counseling. Once she leaves the IOP treatment program, however, her only recovery support is her outpatient counselor, Arlene.

Counseling strategies: Arlene recognizes that Susan lacks an effective social support network that can help her maintain the progress she made in the IOP program. Arlene explores Susan's recent treatment experience, her prior involvement in AA, and her transportation needs. She affirms Susan's persistence in returning to treatment and completing the IOP program and then elicits from Susan what she thinks was different for her this time in treatment. Susan says that she felt safe and supported by the women in the Seeking Safety group.

Arlene works with Susan to develop a plan to re-create that experience of support now that she is back home. The plan includes introducing Susan to a peer recovery support specialist who can help Susan remove any barriers to becoming more engaged in community-based recovery support services, like transportation. Arlene also suggests a menu of social support options to Susan, including a Women for Sobriety group, a small women's AA meeting, and an outpatient trauma recovery support group. Finally, Arlene lets Susan know that she is available by phone and between sessions until Susan has connected with other women who will be part of her ongoing support network. They discuss the boundaries around between-session contact and agree on an initial plan for weekly counseling sessions for the next 12 weeks.

Arlene sees that she can't be Susan's only source of recovery support. With motivational counseling strategies, she helps Arlene build a new support network to reinforce her recovery, maintain her long-term recovery goal of abstinence, and help her heal from trauma and previous disruptions to her social support network.

Help the Client Reenter the Change Cycle

To help clients maintain substance use behavior change, you must address the issue of relapse. Historically, the term "relapse" in addiction treatment had come to mean an all-or-nothing understanding of clients' return to substance use after a period of abstinence and judgment about their lack of motivation. This TIP uses the term "relapse" in part because the SOC model uses the term to describe points in the recovery process when clients leave the change cycle and then recycle through the SOC again with more awareness and a better understanding of how to reach the Maintenance stage. In addition, addiction treatment clinical research refers to relapse prevention as a key counseling approach to supporting clients' ongoing recovery maintenance.

A return to substance use after a period of abstinence does not mean a client has failed or is no longer in recovery. The consensus panel of this TIP seeks to reconceptualize the recurrence of substance use after treatment as **a common aspect of recovery from SUDs** based on well-documented observations:

- **Recurrence of substance use is common.** Although relapse is not technically a stage in the SOC, it is a normal part of change and recovery processes.

- **The term "relapse" itself implies only two possible outcomes—success or failure—that do not fully describe what actually occurs.** Client outcomes are much more complex than this. Often in the course of recovery, clients manage to have longer and longer periods between episodes of use, and use episodes themselves grow shorter and less severe.

- **The assumption that abstinence equals success and return to use equals failure creates a self-fulfilling prophecy.** It implies that once substance use resumes, there is nothing to lose and little that can be done. Instead, the point is to get back on track as soon as possible.

- **Recurrence of symptoms is common** to substance use behaviors and chronic illness in general.

Part of a motivational approach in Maintenance has to do with your perspective on a client's return to substance misuse and how you respond to it. You should:

- Avoid the expert and labeling traps when a client returns to substance use or substance misuse.

- Avoid the "righting reflex" and any temptation to lecture, educate, blame, or judge the client (Miller & Rollnick, 2013).

- Explore the client's understanding of his or her return to substance use.

- Use the same motivational counseling approaches as in Precontemplation, Contemplation, Preparation, and Action, depending on which stage the client is in after the recurrence.

Counselor Note: The Righting Reflex

Miller and Rollnick (2013) use the term "righting reflex" to describe the natural response to "fix" a person's problems from a desire to help. This impulse can lead you to becoming overly directive and **telling** a client what to do instead of **evoking the client's own motivation and strategies** for change.

Provide Relapse Prevention Counseling

Recurrence is common in recovery; offer RPC during Maintenance. RPC is a cognitive–behavioral therapy (CBT) approach to identifying and managing triggers to use, developing coping skills, building self-efficacy, and managing setbacks. Although this is a CBT method, you can use motivational counseling strategies to engage clients in the process and help them resolve ambivalence about learning and practicing new coping skills. (Chapter 8 provides more information about blending motivational interviewing and CBT.)

The two major components of RPC are:

- **Addressing the nature of the relapse process** through education and an analysis of high-risk situations, warning signs, and other factors that contribute to relapse, as well as clients' strengths.

- **Providing coping-skills training.** Identify and develop clients' coping strategies that are useful in maintaining both cognitive and behavioral changes that promote recovery and lessen the likelihood of relapse. (See the section "Identify high-risk situations and coping strategies" above in this chapter.)

The Marlatt model (Witkiewitz & Marlatt, 2007) is the most widely researched and implemented RPC approach in behavioral health services. Many of its strategies have been applied to counseling for

TIP 35: *Enhancing Motivation for Change in Substance Use Disorder Treatment*
Chapter 7—From Action to Maintenance: Stabilizing Change

October 2019

relapse prevention with people with SUDs and CODs. The two key features of the Marlatt model are:

1. Helping clients recognize and manage high-risk situations in which they are most likely to be tempted to immediately use substances or engage in other risky behaviors.

2. Creating a relapse management plan that includes positive coping strategies to lessen the impact of a recurrence, if it happens, and avoid a full relapse.

The two elements of a high-risk situation that increase the client's risk of relapse are:

- **Internal factors**, which include the client's
    - Cognitive distortions.
    - Intense positive and negative feelings.
    - Ineffective coping responses.
    - Low self-efficacy.
    - Positive outcome expectancies (POEs): positive thoughts and associations with drinking or using drugs.
    - Abstinence violation effect (AVE) such as feelings of guilt and shame associated with recurrence.
- **Environmental factors,** which include the client's
    - Social influences.
    - Access to substances.
    - Exposure to conditioned cues for substance use or risk behaviors.

Exhibit 7.6 shows the dynamic process of relapse and how RPC strategies help clients develop effective coping mechanisms and increase self-efficacy to decrease the probability of a relapse.

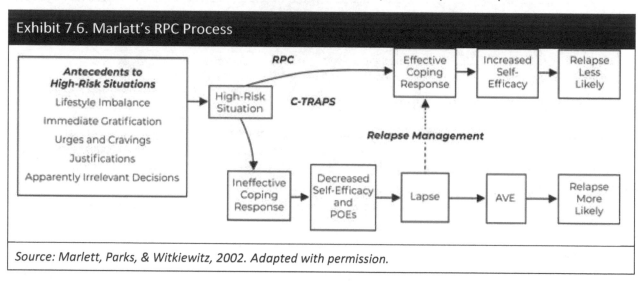

Exhibit 7.6. Marlatt's RPC Process

Source: Marlett, Parks, & Witkiewitz, 2002. Adapted with permission.

C-TRAPS

RPC has five components (Marlatt et al., 2002). C-TRAPS is a handy acronym to remember them:

- **C**ognitive traps
- **T**emptations
- **R**eplacement **A**ctivities
- **P**reparation for relapse

TIP 35: *Enhancing Motivation for Change in Substance Use Disorder Treatment*
Chapter 7—From Action to Maintenance: Stabilizing Change

October 2019

- Strategies for coping

Cognitive traps, also known as cognitive distortions, are the ways the mind works against the client's commitment to recovery and intention to refrain from substance use. They are cognitive early warning signs that a recurrence might be close at hand. They include:

- **All-or-nothing thinking** (e.g., "I got off my regular eating plan today; I'm a failure, so I might as well go all the way and eat whatever I want tonight!") and **overt justifications** (e.g., "My divorce was finalized today, and I really need something to take the edge off") for a return to substance use.

- **Minimizing the impact of a recurrence** (e.g., "Just one cigarette won't push me over the edge").

- **Apparently irrelevant decisions** or decisions that seem unimportant but set up high-risk situations where the likelihood of recurrence is very high. (For example, Ginny decides to buy a bottle of wine, just in case her friend Pam comes over to play cards. She puts the bottle in the liquor cabinet that she had just cleaned out with the help of her AA sponsor, thinking she won't be tempted.)

Cognitive traps bring clients closer to situations where temptation is strong and difficult to resist. **Help clients lessen the power of cognitive traps by:**

- Teaching them how to slow down their thinking process.

- Identifying all the steps in the process leading up to an apparently irrelevant decision.

- Inviting them to evaluate whether those choices are consistent with their recovery goals.

- Exploring possible alternative choices.

Temptations are urges or impulses closely linked to feelings or physical cravings. To distinguish between cravings and urges, note that cravings are the desire and urges are the intentions to use a substance (Witkiewitz & Marlatt, 2007). Temptation is the attraction of the immediate, positive effects of drinking or using drugs. These impulses can be powerful and seem to come out of the blue. In *Alcoholics Anonymous* (also known as "The Big Book"), the authors depicted the unpredictable lure of temptation: "Remember that we deal with alcohol—cunning, baffling, powerful!" (Alcoholics Anonymous, 2001, p. 10). **Help clients map out temptations and develop strategies for responding to them.**

Replacement activities reinforce clients' lifestyle changes through actions that support their recovery. This involves helping clients identify and engage in activities that provide fulfillment, long-term satisfaction, and a substitute for the short-term pleasure of substance use. Use OARS to ask open questions and affirm, reflect, and summarize clients' ideas for replacement activities. Brainstorming is also an effective way to help clients discover new ideas for replacement activities.

Preparation for relapse include:

- Working with clients to anticipate and prepare for this possibility.

- Taking a nonjudgmental stance with clients if they lapse.

- Explaining to them that relapse is avoidable but that they should be prepared for possible setbacks and describing how to manage a return to substance use if it occurs.

- Reframing a recurrence as a learning opportunity and reevaluating their coping strategies.

Strategies for coping are helpful ways of thinking and acting that reduce relapse risk, enhance self-efficacy, manage impulses and cravings, reduce stress, and solve problems that arise in early recovery. Elicit clients' positive coping strategies, and engage them in coping-skills training activities, such as:

- Providing psychoeducation.

- Teaching stress reduction and mindfulness practices.

TIP 35: *Enhancing Motivation for Change in Substance Use Disorder Treatment*
Chapter 7—From Action to Maintenance: Stabilizing Change

October 2019

- Brainstorming strategies with clients to avoid high-risk situations and manage impulses or cravings.
- Deconstructing negative thinking patterns.
- Sharing problem-solving skills and coping strategies that have been helpful to others.
- Modeling positive self-talk and communication skills.
- Rehearsing how to handle high-risk situations.
- Teaching alcohol and drug refusal skills.
- Exchanging in nonjudgmental feedback with other clients in RPC groups.

Relapse management strategies

If clients return to substance use, help them avoid full relapse by teaching them to (Witkiewitz & Marlatt, 2007):

- **Stop, look, and listen.** Clients can learn how to become aware of events as they are unfolding and stop the process of a recurrence before it goes further. Taking a step back from events as an observer can help clients gain perspective and allow them the emotional and cognitive space to assess the situation before reacting. The AA slogan "think…think…think" aids in relapse prevention by providing a cognitive reminder to stop, look, and listen before reacting or taking action.
- **Keep calm.** Staying calm is the emotional equivalent of stop, look, and listen. Thoughts, feelings, and behaviors are often tightly intertwined. Sometimes, clients don't remember that, just because they feel anxious or have an impulse to use substances or reengage in risk behaviors, they don't have to act on those feelings or impulses. Practicing calmness and not overreacting emotionally to a recurrence can help clients break this pattern of impulsivity.
- **Renew their commitment to recovery.** People are often discouraged by a recurrence, which can lower motivation and confidence about continuing on the recovery journey. To allay hopelessness, remind clients of previous successes with behavior change (no matter how "small"). Keep them looking forward by exploring their reasons for recovery and hopes, dreams, and goals for the future.
- **Review what led up to the recurrence.** Review the events leading up to the recurrence and do a mini-relapse assessment taking into account lifestyle imbalance, thoughts of immediate gratification, urges and cravings, justifications, apparently irrelevant decisions, and the nature of the high-risk situation that triggered the lapse. Review early warning signs clients may have noticed but disregarded and explore the cognitive traps that led to disregarding the warning signs.
- **Make an immediate plan for recovery.** Work with clients to develop an immediate action plan for recommitting to recovery. The plan should include specific action steps clients can take to avoid a full relapse that are acceptable, accessible, and appropriate from their point of view. Write the plan on paper or a file card. Include client-generated strategies for handling a recurrence, such as:
  - **Call a sponsor or recovery support person.** Include specific names and phone numbers.
  - **Go to a recovery support meeting.** Include specific meeting times and locations.
  - Engage in cognitive, emotional, physical, and behavioral strategies for managing cravings.
  - Engage in specific self-care or stress reduction activities.
  - **Return to medication** (if applicable). Include adherence strategies and names of prescribers.
  - **Call you or the treatment program** to schedule a counseling session.
- **Deal with the AVE.** Help clients deal with the emotional aftereffects of recurrence, such as guilt, shame, and the cognitive dissonance that happens when people act in ways that do not align with their values and recovery goals. This cognitive and emotional disagreement can increase the

likelihood of a return to substance use. Engage clients in exploration with compassion and understanding; encourage them to learn from recurrence and identify new coping strategies.

Reenter the Cycle of Change

If clients return to substance misuse, help them reenter the cycle as soon as possible. Most clients do not return to the Precontemplation stage (Connors et al., 2013). Rather, clients are more likely to recycle back into Contemplation, Preparation, or Action. They can use the recurrence experience as an opportunity to identify which strategies for the Maintenance stage worked and which did not work. **Your task is to debrief clients about relapse and assess where they are now in the SOC** (Connors et al., 2013). If the client has returned to Contemplation, start with resolving ambivalence and evoking change talk. Clients who have returned to Preparation or Action should revisit and revise the change plan or coping plan.

Strategies for helping clients manage a return to substance misuse include:

- **Helping them reenter the change cycle; affirming any willingness to reconsider positive change.**
  - Explore their perceptions and reactions to resumed use.
  - Use affirmations to praise them for reengaging in the change process.
  - Elicit DARN (**D**esire, **A**bility, **R**easons, and **N**eed) change talk; reflect on the client's reasons to get back on track.
- **Exploring the meaning of the recurrence as a learning opportunity.**
  - Explore what can be learned from the experience.
  - Remind them that the experience is a common and temporary part of the recovery process.
  - Elicit their positive experiences in recovery and the advantages of abstinence.
  - Use reflective listening.
  - Avoid the question-and-answer trap.
  - Explore their values, hopes, purpose, and goals in life. Ask, "What do you want to do now?"
- **Helping clients find and continuously review and evaluate current and alternative coping strategies.**
  - Review coping strategies that have and have not worked to maintain stated goals for change.
  - Help them identify new coping strategies.
- **Maintaining supportive contact** until clients exit the change cycle for each behavior change goal.

Conclusion

Maintaining substance use behavior change is often more challenging for clients than taking action toward change. Help clients stabilize and maintain changes made in the Preparation and Action stages by:

- Using motivational counseling strategies to engage and retain clients in treatment.
- Helping them develop and practice coping strategies for high-risk situations.
- Reinforcing social support.
- Helping them reenter the cycle of change quickly if they do return to substance use.

MI strategies are useful during all stages in the SOC and are used in conjunction with other counseling approaches, like CBT—particularly during the Preparation, Action, and Maintenance stages. An

TIP 35: *Enhancing Motivation for Change in Substance Use Disorder Treatment*
Chapter 7—From Action to Maintenance: Stabilizing Change

October 2019

important way to help clients throughout the SOC is to continuously assess and reassess which stage they are in the SOC and match your counseling approach accordingly.

TIP 35: *Enhancing Motivation for Change in Substance Use Disorder Treatment*
Chapter 7—From Action to Maintenance: Stabilizing Change

October 2019

This page intentionally left blank.

Chapter 8—Integrating Motivational Approaches in SUD Treatment Settings

"From its inception MI [motivational interviewing] has been organic, emerging, and evolving through collaborative processes....Our decision was to focus on promoting quality in MI practice and training...."

Miller & Rollnick, 2013, p. 377

Key Messages

- Motivational counseling approaches have been widely disseminated to substance use disorder (SUD) treatment programs.
- Adaptations of MI in group counseling, the use of technology, and blended counseling approaches enhance the implementation and integration of motivational interventions into standard treatment methods.
- Training and ongoing supervision of counselors are essential for workforce development and integration of motivational counseling approaches into SUD treatment.

Chapter 8 discusses adaptations for using motivational counseling approaches in group counseling, with technology, and in blended counseling approaches that are applicable to SUD treatment programs. It also addresses workforce development issues that treatment programs may face in fully integrating and sustaining motivational counseling approaches.

Over the past three decades, MI and motivational counseling approaches have been widely and successfully disseminated across the United States and internationally to specialty SUD treatment programs (Hall, Staiger, Simpson, Best, & Lubman, 2015). Research supports the integration of motivational counseling strategies into treatment as a prelude to ongoing treatment to increase client retention and enhance participation in treatment. Motivational counseling can increase adherence to treatment medication and behavioral change plans and makes achievement and maintenance of positive substance use behavior outcomes more likely (Miller & Rollnick, 2013). Depending on the SUD treatment setting, different adaptions of motivational interventions (e.g., individual or group counseling, blended with other counseling approaches) may be effective both clinically and programmatically.

Integrating motivational counseling approaches into a treatment program requires more than providing counseling staff with a few workshops on MI. It requires broad integration of the philosophy and underlying spirit of MI throughout the organization. Just as a counselor using a motivational approach works in partnership with clients to help them move through the Stages of Change (SOC) to achieve long-term behavioral change, organizations wishing to integrate a motivational counseling approach should work in partnership with staff to implement program changes. Organizations also go through a process of change until the treatment approach becomes a new "lifestyle."

Adaptations of Motivational Counseling Approaches

The most common delivery of motivational counseling approaches has been through brief or ongoing individual counseling. For example, MI in SUD treatment was specifically developed as a counseling approach to be delivered in face-to-face conversations between a counselor and a client. Depending on the treatment program, adaptations of motivational interventions may make treatment more cost effective, more accessible to clients, and easier to integrate into existing treatment approaches, as well

TIP 35: *Enhancing Motivation for Change in Substance Use Disorder Treatment*
Chapter 8—Integrating Motivational Approaches in SUD Treatment Settings

October 2019

as ease workload demands on counselors.

Chapter 8 discusses the following adaptations of motivational counseling approaches:

- Group counseling
- Technology adaptations (e.g., Internet-based applications and telephone-based MI)
- Blended counseling approaches

Group Counseling

The current context of service delivery in SUD treatment programs places heavy emphasis on group counseling. Many motivation-enhancing activities can take place in group counseling that cannot occur in individual treatment (e.g., clients can receive feedback from peers). Because social support is intrinsic to group treatment, clients in a group can reinforce and help maintain each other's substance use behavior changes (Holstad, Diiorio, Kelley, Resnicow, & Sharma, 2010).

However, several significant clinical issues arise when conducting groups using MI including (Feldstein Ewing, Walters, & Baer, 2013; Miller & Rollnick, 2013):

- The counselor's ability to translate MI skills to the group context
- The counselor's skill in managing group dynamics
- Fewer opportunities for group members to express change talk and receive reflective listening responses from the counselor
- Varying needs and experiences of group participants
- The counselor's ability to respond to various participant needs (e.g., reflecting commitment language of one participant while responding to another participant's ambivalence about changing substance use behaviors)
- Actively managing social pressures of peer interactions, which are not present in individual sessions
- Responding to and managing sustain talk in a group setting

Perhaps the most challenging aspect of group-based MI is the possibility of group members reinforcing each other's sustain talk instead of reflecting change talk (Miller & Rollnick, 2013). An important adaptation of MI in group is to minimize the opportunities for clients to evoke and reflect sustain talk and maximize opportunities to evoke and reflect change talk (Houck et al., 2015; Miller & Rollnick, 2013). Strategies for accomplishing this include:

- Teaching group members OARS (asking **O**pen question, **A**ffirming, **R**eflective listening, and **S**ummarizing) skills (Wagner & Ingersoll, 2013).
- Identifying the general parameters for group interactions that are in line with the spirit of MI (e.g., group members should support each other without pressure to change, avoid giving advice, focus on positives and possibilities for change) (Miller & Rollnick, 2013).
- Modeling MI skills in groups (Wagner & Ingersoll, 2013).
- Acknowledging sustain talk but emphasizing and reinforcing change talk (D'Amico et al., 2015).

Expert Comment: Motivational Enhancement in Group Counseling
Conducting motivational interventions in a group versus individual format is more difficult, more complex, and more challenging. Personally, however, I find it much more rewarding. In group counseling, particularly using motivational techniques and strategies, clients learn through the group. It is like a hall of mirrors; clients get the feel of how they come across. For me, when a client uses reflective listening with another client or points out

TIP 35: *Enhancing Motivation for Change in Substance Use Disorder Treatment*
Chapter 8—Integrating Motivational Approaches in SUD Treatment Settings

October 2019

> another client's ambivalence, the group is like a living, learning laboratory of experiences practiced first in a safe environment before being tried in the real world. In the end, what the members have is a common goal to reduce or stop substance misuse, and it is here that their mutual support and peer pressure is effective.
>
> *Linda C. Sobell, Ph.D., Consensus Panel Member*

Evidence shows that, despite some challenges, MI can be delivered successfully in a group context, particularly when group participants hear more change talk than sustain talk (Osilla et al., 2015). Positive outcomes from MI in groups include decreased alcohol use and alcohol misuse among adolescents, greater retention in SUD treatment after detoxification, increased retention in methadone maintenance treatment, and adherence to risk-reduction behaviors in women infected with HIV (Bachiller et al., 2015; D'Amico et al., 2015; Holstad et al., 2010; Navidian, Kermansaravi, Tabas, & Saeedinezhad, 2016).

Integrating MI into group treatment requires group counselors to have training and ongoing supervision in both MI strategies and group process. The **Assessment of Motivational Interviewing Groups— Observer Scale (AMIGOS—v 1.2)** is a validated tool that assesses counselor skills in group processes, client-centered focus, and using MI in groups (Wagner & Ingersoll, 2017). Appendix C provides a link to a downloadable version of AMIGOS. This tool may be helpful for assessing and enhancing counselor competence in delivering MI in groups.

Technology Adaptations

Some evidence shows the effectiveness of adaptations of MI and motivational enhancement therapy (MET) through interactive computer applications, Internet-based applications, and telephone or video conferencing when used selectively to deliver motivational interventions (Miller & Rollnick, 2013). For example, the "drinker's checkup," the original method to give personalized feedback in MET, has been delivered in interactive computer-based applications and has had positive outcomes in reducing alcohol misuse (Hester, Delaney, & Campbell, 2012).

Benefits of brief motivational interventions delivered by interactive computer applications include (Hester et al., 2012):

- Ease of use.
- Cost effectiveness.
- Adaptability to different client populations.
- Flexibility of design.

Although computer- or Internet-based adaptations of motivational interventions may be useful in providing personalized feedback to clients, computers cannot provide empathetic listening responses or evoke change talk. They also limit use of brief interventions that provide feedback to increase client engagement in treatment.

Telephone MI is the most widely used alternative to face-to-face MI and is effective for addressing tobacco cessation, alcohol misuse, and use of illicit drugs (Jiang, Wu, & Gao, 2017). Telephone counseling with, if possible, the addition of a video component has the advantage of reaching client populations in rural settings that do not have access to transportation to the treatment setting. Telephone MI approaches also have the added benefit over computer-based interventions of giving the counselor the opportunity to offer interactive motivational interventions like reflective listening, affirmations, and evoking change talk. For more information about using technology in SUD treatment, see Treatment Improvement Protocol (TIP) 60: *Using Technology-Based Therapeutic Tools in Behavioral Health Services* (Substance Abuse and Mental Health Services Administration [SAMHSA], 2015b).

TIP 35: *Enhancing Motivation for Change in Substance Use Disorder Treatment*
Chapter 8—Integrating Motivational Approaches in SUD Treatment Settings

October 2019

Blended Counseling Approaches

MI as a counseling style is compatible with a wide range of clinical approaches that have been used in SUD treatment including cognitive–behavioral therapy (CBT), psychoeducation, medication-assisted treatment, and case management approaches (Miller & Rollnick, 2013). When thinking about ways to integrate MI into current treatment approach, treatment staff should address some open questions like, "How does MI fit with what we already do?" and "At what points in our treatment approach are we most concerned about engaging clients in treatment, helping clients resolve ambivalence about change, and retaining clients in treatment?" (Miller & Rollnick, 2013). Three examples of blending MI with other SUD counseling approaches supported by research are motivational interviewing assessment (MIA), CBT, and recovery management checkup (RMC).

MIA

The National Institute on Drug Abuse Clinical Trials Network, in cooperation with SAMHSA, developed a protocol to incorporate MI into a one-session assessment intake to improve client engagement in SUD treatment programs (Carroll et al., 2006). This blended approach to the standard initial assessment in SUD treatment sandwiches a standard assessment between a brief MI counseling segment at the beginning and end of the session (Martino et al., 2006).

A challenge of doing a standard assessment with clients just entering treatment is that counselors and clients tend to fall into the question-and-answer trap (see Chapter 3). Counselors ask closed questions to elicit information needed for the assessment, and clients answer with yes, no, or short-answer responses. This pattern of interaction sets up an expectation that the counselor is the expert and the client is a passive recipient of services. It can become an obstacle to client engagement (Miller & Rollnick, 2013). MIA incorporates MI into typical SUD treatment program intake/assessment processes and facilitates client engagement while addressing the organization's need to collect assessment information for treatment planning and to comply with licensing and insurance requirements.

Research supports MIA as a method to blend MI with standard assessment approaches. An initial study found that clients who participated in the MIA-blended protocol were significantly more likely than clients who participated in the standard assessment to be enrolled in the program after 1 month (Martino et al., 2006). A more recent study found that incorporating MI into the initial intake and assessment processes (whether standard MI or MIA) promoted client retention (e.g., 70 percent remained in treatment after 4 weeks) and enhanced treatment outcomes (e.g., a 50 percent increase in days abstinent) (Martino et al., 2016). This same study found that supervision of counselors in both groups (standard MI and MIA) improved counselor performance of MI, but the counselors who received supervision in MIA showed significantly greater improvements in MI competency, although training and supervision in MIA was more costly. A link to a manual for training and supervising counselors in MIA, *Motivational Interviewing Assessment: Supervisor Tools for Enhancing Proficiency Manual*, is available for download at no cost in Appendix C (Martino et al., 2006). Another study found that the addition of motivational feedback to a standard assessment enhanced SUD treatment entry for a group of veterans with co-occurring disorders (Lozano, Larowe, Smith, Tuerk, & Roitzsch, 2013).

MI and CBT

Perhaps the most widely adopted counseling approach used in SUD treatment is CBT. CBT focuses on helping clients change thoughts (e.g., drinking is the only way to relax) and behaviors (e.g., drinking to intoxication) that interfere with everyday functioning. CBT strategies include helping clients identify and manage triggers for substance use and practicing new behaviors that reinforce abstinence. CBT is also an

TIP 35: *Enhancing Motivation for Change in Substance Use Disorder Treatment*
Chapter 8—Integrating Motivational Approaches in SUD Treatment Settings

October 2019

evidence-based approach that is widely used to treat mental disorders (e.g., anxiety, depression, posttraumatic stress disorder) that often co-occur with SUDs. However, some CBT providers have acknowledged difficulties with initial client engagement, low motivation, and nonadherence to CBT practices, such as completing out-of-session assignments (Arkowitz, Miller, & Rollnick, 2015). **Integrating MI strategies to address ambivalence and enhance motivation of clients with co-occurring disorders can improve client adherence to CBT treatment components.**

Strategies for blending MI and CBT include (Copeland, Gates, & Pokorski, 2017; Miller & Rollnick, 2013; Naar-King, Safren, & Miller, 2017):

- Engaging in a brief motivational conversation before a client moves into a CBT-focused component of treatment (e.g., a relapse prevention group).

- Alternating between MI and CBT, depending on the goals of each session.

- Using MI when the clinical focus is on engaging, focusing, evoking, and emphasizing the more directive style of CBT during the planning process.

- Shifting to MI during CBT interventions when counselor–client discord or client ambivalence about a specific change goal arises.

- Using the spirit of MI as a framework and interactional style in which to use CBT strategies.

Integrating MI into CBT approaches that the SUD treatment program already supports can enhance client motivation to engage in CBT and improve long-term maintenance of behavior change (Naar-King et al., 2017). Blending MI and CBT may actually create a more powerful approach for behavioral change in SUD treatment than either approach alone (Copeland et al., 2017; Naar-King et al., 2017). For example, a review of psychosocial interventions for cannabis use disorder found that the most consistent evidence for reducing cannabis use among a variety of interventions was a combination of CBT and MET (Gates, Sabioni, Copeland, Foll, & Gowing, 2016). Other research that evaluated studies on the integrated approach of CBT and MI found a clinically significant effect in treatment outcomes for co-occurring alcohol use disorder (AUD) and major depressive disorder compared with treatment as usual (Riper et al., 2014).

At times, CBT may require counselors to take on the role of a teacher or guide who is more directive, but counselors' overall stance should remain that of an empathetic partner–consultant instead of an expert. For example, in one study, counselors using CBT who explored and connected with clients in treatment for AUD were more successful in evoking discussions about behavior change than counselors who emphasized teaching clients behavior-change skills (Magill et al., 2016). Counselors' most important goal is to develop a relationship of mutual trust and respect with the client. They should view the client as the expert in his or her own recovery. Exhibit 8.1 provides a brief clinical scenario that depicts a counselor blending the spirit of MI with CBT relapse prevention strategies (see Chapter 7) in a counseling approach with a military veteran.

Exhibit 8.1. Blending the Spirit of MI With CBT

Jordan is 40 years old. He has been married for 12 years and has two young children. He served in the military and did two tours in Iraq. After discharge, he was arrested twice for driving under the influence and was mandated to alcohol and drug counseling. He was also referred for a psychiatric evaluation and was diagnosed with posttraumatic stress disorder.

Dan is a licensed clinical social worker in a co-occurring services program at a comprehensive behavioral health services program and has been seeing Jordan for 6 months for outpatient counseling. Initially, Jordan was angry

TIP 35: *Enhancing Motivation for Change in Substance Use Disorder Treatment*
Chapter 8—Integrating Motivational Approaches in SUD Treatment Settings

October 2019

about having to go to counseling and Dan's suggestion to try Alcoholics Anonymous (AA) as part of a recovery plan; however, Jordan has been attending AA meetings and asked another veteran to be his sponsor.

Jordan has returned to heavy drinking on three occasions in the past 6 months. His relapse risk is that he stops going to meetings and stops calling his sponsor. Then he finds himself at a local sports bar, thinking that he'll just watch the game (an apparently irrelevant decision), but he ends up getting drunk. Jordan now speaks highly of AA and has been working the 12 Steps with his sponsor. He tells Dan, "I am doing everything my sponsor tells me to do and am committed to my recovery now. I know that if I follow his suggestions and work the program, I will be okay. I just don't understand why I keep slipping."

Dan has established a good rapport with Jordan. He has done a relapse risk assessment, provided information to Jordan about the relapse process, and given Jordan homework to track high-risk situations and the coping strategies he uses to manage them. Jordan seems to respond well to Dan's directive approach but continues to return to drinking. Dan shifts gears in the current session and decides to explore Jordan's understanding of his pattern of disengagement from AA and his sponsor instead of cautioning him again about his behavioral pattern leading up to a return to drinking.

Dan: I'm wondering what you make of this pattern: not going to meetings, not calling your sponsor just before you have a slip. If you could name that pattern, what would you call it? *(Open question)*

Jordan: I guess I would call it my version of "Stinkin' Thinkin'." I work so hard at trying to do the right thing in my recovery, but then I start to think that I am not getting anywhere, you know? I'm not drinking, but I don't feel any better, so I feel like a failure and get tired of trying. It's like I need to take a break from recovery.

Dan: So, you work hard to do the right thing in recovery and really want to feel better, but sometimes you feel discouraged and think you need to take a break. *(Reflection)*

Jordan: Yeah. That describes where I am right now.

Dan: I am curious about that. Would you say you are taking a break from recovery or taking a break from the program? *[Reframe in the form of a question that leaves open the possibility for the client to reject the new perspective]*

Jordan: Gee, I never thought about it that way. I guess I'm still working on my recovery, even if I don't talk to my sponsor. Like the other day, I started to feel like I wanted to go to the bar to watch the game, but I remembered what you and I had talked about last time—that this is a warning flag, and that I could do something different. So, instead of going to the bar, I asked one of my sober friends over, and we watched the game at my house. We didn't talk about the program; we just watched the game.

Dan: You really worked that one out for yourself and didn't let "Stinkin' Thinkin'" take over. Good for you. *(Affirmation)*

At the end of the session, Dan summarizes Jordan's successful approach to "doing something different" and asks Jordan how their conversation was for him. Jordan responds that it was very helpful that Dan didn't lecture him, but rather asked him what he thought. This helped him realize for himself that he is still working on his recovery, even if he doesn't call his sponsor or go to a meeting. Jordan also mentioned that now he doesn't feel like he is failing at recovery, so he thinks he will get back to his AA program.

MI and RMC

RMC is a fairly new addiction treatment approach that uses motivational strategies; it is modeled after approaches used for staying connected to people with chronic medical illnesses like diabetes. RMC is a proactive strategy for monitoring a client's progress in recovery after intensive SUD treatment and for intervening quickly if the client returns to substance use. RMC involves regular telephone calls (more frequently at first, then less frequently) to the client to find out how he or she is coping with recovery.

RMC incorporates MI strategies to enhance motivation to return to treatment if needed. Counselors or

TIP 35: *Enhancing Motivation for Change in Substance Use Disorder Treatment*
Chapter 8—Integrating Motivational Approaches in SUD Treatment Settings

October 2019

peer recovery support specialists can perform RMC. Telephone-based motivational interventions are efficacious in treating and preventing substance use behaviors (Jiang et al., 2017). RMC is an effective method of monitoring clients' progress in recovery in the Action and Maintenance stages and intervening quickly to reengage clients into treatment after a substance use recurrence. It is linked to improved long-term substance use outcomes and increased participation in SUD treatment and recovery support services (Dennis & Scott, 2012; Dennis, Scott, & Laudet, 2014; Scott, Dennis, & Lurigio, 2017).

Workforce Development

MI is not only a counseling style but a conversational style that emphasizes guiding, rather than directing, clients toward changing substance use behaviors (Miller & Rollnick, 2013). Depending on the type of treatment program, an organization might provide aspects of MI training to only a few counselors, the entire clinical staff, or all staff, including support staff and peer providers. As increasingly more programs, including certified community behavioral health clinics (SAMHSA, 2016), adopt a client-centered treatment philosophy and MI as an evidence-based treatment, **organizations should train all staff in the spirit of MI.** This means all personnel—from the first person the client encounters walking through the door to the staff working in the billing department—understand the importance of client autonomy and choice, listening, and guiding instead of lecturing or directing in creating a welcoming environment and engaging clients in the treatment process (Miller & Rollnick, 2013).

> "MI is a complex skill, like playing a musical instrument. Watching others play the piano or attending a 2-day workshop is not likely in itself to turn one into a competent pianist" (Miller & Rollnick, 2014, p. 3).

MI has been widely disseminated as an evidence-based treatment, yet dissemination is not the same as implementation. Counselors lose their MI skills after a workshop if there is no supervision or coaching after training (Hall et al., 2015; Schwalbe, Oh, & Zweben, 2014). The key to workforce development of clinical staff in MI is to move beyond 1- or 2-day workshops and integrate ongoing training, supervision, and coaching of clinical staff to maintain fidelity to MI-consistent counseling techniques.

Another factor in whether a treatment program implements a motivational counseling approach is how closely the organization's mission and philosophy are aligned with the principles of motivational counseling. Counselors are more likely to adopt an MI counseling style when the organization's philosophy is aligned with MI principles (Ager et al., 2010).

Training

MI is an integrated and comprehensive set of listening and interviewing skills (Miller & Rollnick, 2013). For counselors to learn these skills and consistently integrate them into everyday practice, staff training and learning tasks should include (Miller & Rollnick, 2013):

- Understanding the spirt of MI.
- Developing skill in OARS.
- Identifying change goals.
- Exchanging information (i.e., Elicit-Provide-Elicit [EPE]) and giving advice skillfully.
- Recognizing change talk and sustain talk.
- Evoking change talk.
- Strengthening change talk.
- Responding skillfully to sustain talk and counselor–client discord.

TIP 35: *Enhancing Motivation for Change in Substance Use Disorder Treatment*
Chapter 8—Integrating Motivational Approaches in SUD Treatment Settings

October 2019

- Developing hope and confidence.
- Negotiating a change plan.
- Strengthening commitment.
- Integrating MI with other counseling approaches.

These learning tasks apply to training counselors in any motivational counseling approach, including brief interventions that use FRAMES (**F**eedback, **R**esponsibility, **A**dvice, **M**enu of options, **E**mpathy, and **S**elf-efficacy) and MET, where the counselor gives personalized feedback and advice. Some tasks are foundational, like learning reflective listening, and are best learned through face-to-face, interactive training experiences. Other tasks, like recognizing change talk and sustain talk, can be learned through reading material, like coded transcripts of counselor–client interactions (Miller & Rollnick, 2013).

An initial workshop that covers the foundational components of MI (e.g., understanding the spirit of MI, OARS, recognizing and responding to change talk and sustain talk) may be a good beginning. This workshop should include both knowledge exchange and interactive skill-building exercises. A meta-analysis of MI training found that training produces medium-to-large–sized effects in MI proficiency both before and after training and medium-sized effects in MI proficiency compared with controls (de Roten, Zimmermann, Ortega, & Despland, 2013). Furthermore, an initial 12-to-15–hour workshop of MI training that included didactic, face-to-face instruction, and interactive exercises increased counselor skills as did more enhanced workshops that used video, web-based, or computer technology (Schwalbe et al., 2014). For an initial workshop, a simple format may be appropriate and potentially more cost effective than complex formats.

Ongoing training is the key to learning and sustaining motivational counseling skills if skills learned during training are not practiced. MI counselor skills introduced in training can erode after only 3 months if they are not used and practiced (Schwalbe et al., 2014). Spreading out training activities over a 6-month period and increasing the practice training hours to 5 or more hours increase counselor skill level and enhance skill retention (Schwalbe et al., 2014). Ongoing training in MI should be integrated into SUD treatment over 24 months as part of professional development to ensure counselor competency (Hall et al., 2015).

There are multiple ways to train staff, and the path an organization chooses is based on many factors. Before implementing MI training, an organization should consider the following questions when developing a strategic plan:

- **Assessing organizational philosophy and the SOC**
  - Is a person-centered approach to service delivery a key component of the organization's mission statement and philosophy?
  - Is MI a new counseling approach for the organization or will MI be blended with current treatment approaches?
  - At what stage of the SOC is staff with regard to integrating a new approach?
  - What kind of preparation is needed to implement a training program?
- **Assessing staff needs**
  - Does support staff need an introduction to the spirit of MI?
  - Which counseling staff members have already been trained and are using MI skills in their counseling approach? Which staff need a foundational workshop?
  - Which clinical supervisors have been trained in MI and demonstrate skill competence?

TIP 35: *Enhancing Motivation for Change in Substance Use Disorder Treatment*
Chapter 8—Integrating Motivational Approaches in SUD Treatment Settings

October 2019

- **Tailoring a training program to meet staff needs**
  - How will the organization assess current counselor skill level in MI and tailor the training to different counselor skill levels?
  - Which would be most effective for the program:
    - Sending all counseling staff to a series of trainings provided by outside experts?
    - Training one or two clinical supervisors to provide in-house training and ongoing supervision of staff?
    - Bringing an outside expert into the organization to provide training?
    - A combination of outside and in-house training?
  - What strategies will the organization use to balance effective training, supervision, and professional development given cost considerations?

In developing the training plan, the organization should consider integrating a new counseling approach into the SUD treatment program a long-term project that needs buy-in by the entire organization.

Counselor Note: Implementation of MET in SUD Treatment Services in the Veterans Health Administration

In 2011, the Veterans Health Administration (VHA) implemented a national initiative to provide evidence-based MET counseling to veterans with SUDs. VHA developed a competency-based training program (Drapkin et al., 2016) that consisted of an initial 3.5-day training on MI plus assessment feedback, followed by 6 months of consultation with experienced MI training consultants (TCs). TCs provided ongoing supervision and coaching based on direct observation of counseling sessions using audio recordings. Training materials were adapted to address the specific needs of veterans. The VHA model of implementation was based on research in the training and supervision of clinical staff in MI to enhance implementation and fidelity.

Implementation of this competency-based model of training and supervision was enhanced by encouraging training participants to actively engage with the VHA MET community by becoming TCs and "MET champions," who provided information and consultation on how local VHA facilities could best disseminate and implement MET into their SUD treatment approach. TCs participate in monthly national conference calls with other TCs covering advanced MET topics. This model combines the use of outside trainers with in-house workforce development of new trainers and MET champions to create learning communities that sustain the use of MET in VHA facilities.

Supervision and Coaching

Training counselors in MI is the first step in integrating this approach into SUD treatment programs. Maintenance of skills and staying up to date with new developments in any counseling approach require ongoing supervision.

Supervision in MI should be competency based. This means supervision should address counselors' knowledge and proficiency in MI skills (e.g., the spirit of MI, OARS, EPE, recognizing and responding to change talk and sustain talk, evoking change talk, negotiating a change plan) needed to practice effectively. Competency-based supervision of MI includes directly observing counselor sessions, using feedback to monitor counselor proficiency, and coaching to help counselors continue developing their knowledge and skills (Martino et al., 2016). One study on competency-based supervision in MI found that anywhere from 4 to 20 supervision sessions were needed for doctoral-level interns to reach MI competency benchmarks (Schumaker et al., 2018).

Competency-based supervision requires direct observation of counselors, not simply a counselor's self-report or subjective evaluation. **Direct observation is one of the most effective ways of building and monitoring counselor skills** and can include use of video or audio taping sessions, live observation of

TIP 35: *Enhancing Motivation for Change in Substance Use Disorder Treatment*
Chapter 8—Integrating Motivational Approaches in SUD Treatment Settings

October 2019

counseling sessions in person or via one-way mirrors, or both (SAMHSA, 2009). For more information on competency-based supervision, see TIP 52: *Clinical Supervision and Professional Development of the Substance Abuse Counselor* (SAMHSA, 2009).

The program should get permission from clients before engaging in direct observation. Written consent forms should include the nature and purpose of the direct observation, a description of how clients' privacy and confidentiality will be maintained, and what will happen to any video or audio recordings after supervision or research is completed. Program should refer to in-house policies and state licensing board and professional ethics code requirements for the use of video and audio recordings for clinical supervision or research.

In addition to being competency based, **MI supervision should be performed in the spirit of MI.** Clinical supervisors should reach a level of skill in using MI to be able to:

- Describe the underlying theoretical foundations of MI.

- Explore and resolve counselor ambivalence about learning and integrating MI into treatment.

- Teach counselors MI skills.

- Model the spirit of MI and its skills in individual and group supervision sessions.

- Give respectful and nonjudgmental feedback to counselors to support self-efficacy and enhance professional development.

Coaching counselors in MI involves coding a recorded or live observation session for consistent (e.g., OARS responses) and inconsistent (e.g., giving unsolicited advice, confrontation) MI responses and using this information to provide feedback to the counselor (Miller & Rollnick, 2013). Because listening to and coding a full session are labor intensive, coaches can code brief sections of a session and produce reliable ratings of counselor fidelity to MI (Caperton, Atkins, & Imel, 2018). Two coding systems for MI have been widely used in research and clinical practice to evaluate counselor fidelity to MI (Miller & Rollnick, 2013):

- **MI Integrity (MITI)** focuses on counselor responses and provides global ratings and specific counts of MI-consistent responses. The most recent version of MITI (MITI 4) has added global ratings and greater accuracy in assessing counselor support for client autonomy and the use of persuasion when giving information and advice (Moyers, Manuel, & Ernst, 2014). The MITI 4 is a reliable way to assess counselor fidelity to MI in both its relational and its technical components (Moyers, Houck, Rice, Longbaugh, & Miller, 2016). Appendix C provides a link to the MITI 4 manual.

- **MI Skills Code (MISC)** counts both counselor and client responses (e.g., change talk, sustain talk) (Miller, Moyers, Ernst, & Amrhein, 2008). MISC is a reliable way to monitor counselor fidelity to MI and can provide an accurate measure of the ratio of client change talk to sustain talk (Lord et al.,2014). The MISC can provide not only feedback to counselors about their use of MI skills but also information about the effects of MI on counselor–client interactions. Appendix C provides a link to the MISC manual.

A positive aspect of using coding systems to assess counselor fidelity to MI is that they provide reliable and accurate measures of counselor skill level. A less-positive aspect of using coding systems is that they require considerable training and quality assurance checks to establish and maintain the reliability of the coach who is doing the coding (Miller & Rollnick, 2013). In addition, counselors may be ambivalent about recording client sessions and having a supervisor, who is responsible for performance evaluations, code the counselor's speech. Potential solutions to consider include:

- Addressing counselor ambivalence in supervision about having sessions coded.

TIP 35: *Enhancing Motivation for Change in Substance Use Disorder Treatment*
Chapter 8—Integrating Motivational Approaches in SUD Treatment Settings

October 2019

- Creating small learning communities in the organization where counselors, case managers, and peer providers can learn and practice coding snippets of actual sessions or uncoded audio, video, or written transcripts with one another. Appendix C provides links to uncoded transcripts, audio, and video examples of MI counseling sessions.

- Sending audio sessions or short excerpts to an outside coder who can perform the coding and return written feedback for supervisors to discuss with counselors.

- Encouraging counselors to listen to their own recorded sessions and use a simplified method of counting their use of OARS, their inconsistent responses (e.g., giving advice without permission), change talk and sustain talk prompts, and client expressions of change talk and sustain talk (Miller & Rollnick, 2013). Counselors can then review their "self-coding" with their supervisors.

Whichever strategies the SUD organization employs to enhance counselor fidelity to and proficiency in delivering MI, the organization will need to balance cost considerations with effective training, supervision, and professional development. **Administrators and supervisors should partner with counseling staff to move the organization along the SOC toward integrating motivational approaches into SUD treatment.**

Conclusion

Many different motivational approaches have been discussed in this TIP including MI; MET; motivational interventions in the SOC; brief interventions; screening, brief intervention, and referral for treatment; and blending MI with other counseling methods. A growing body of evidence demonstrates that motivational interventions can enhance client motivation and improve SUD treatment outcomes. Integrating MI and other motivational approaches into SUD treatment settings requires the entire organization to adopt a client-centered philosophy and administrative support for ongoing training and supervision of counselors. Motivational counseling approaches are respectful and culturally responsive methods for helping people break free from addiction and adopt new lifestyles that are consistent with the values of good health, well-being, and being integral member of the community.

TIP 35: *Enhancing Motivation for Change in Substance Use Disorder Treatment*
Chapter 8—Integrating Motivational Approaches in SUD Treatment Settings

October 2019

This page intentionally left blank.

Appendix A—Bibliography

Ager, R., Roahen-Harrison, S., Toriello, P. J., Kissinger, P., Morse, P., Morse, E., ... Rice, J. (2010). Predictors of adopting motivational enhancement therapy. *Research on Social Work Practice, 21*(1), 65–76. doi:10.1177/1049731509353170

Ainscough, T. S., McNeill, A., Strang, J., Calder, R., & Brose, L. S. (2017). Contingency management interventions for non-prescribed drug use during treatment for opiate addiction: A systematic review and meta-analysis. *Drug and Alcohol Dependence, 178*, 318–339.

Alcoholics Anonymous. (2001). *Alcoholics Anonymous: The story of how many thousands of men and women have recovered from alcoholism* (4th ed.). New York, NY: Alcoholics Anonymous World Services.

Aldridge, A., Dowd, W., & Bray, J. (2017). The relative impact of brief treatment versus brief intervention in primary health-care screening programs for substance use disorders. *Addiction, 112*, 54–64. doi:10.1111/add.13653

Aldridge, A., Linford, R., & Bray, J. (2017). Substance use outcomes of patients served by a large U.S. implementation of screening, brief intervention and referral to treatment (SBIRT). *Addiction, 112*, 43–53.

Alperstein, D., & Sharpe, L. (2016). The efficacy of motivational interviewing in adults with chronic pain: A meta-analysis and systematic review. *Journal of Pain, 17*(4), 393–403. doi:10.1016/j.jpain.2015.10.021

American Psychiatric Association. (2013). *Diagnostic and statistical manual of mental disorders* (5th ed.). Washington, DC: Author.

American Psychiatric Association. (1994). *Diagnostic and statistical manual of mental disorders* (4th ed.). Washington, DC: Author.

Amodeo, M. (2015). The addictive personality. *Substance Use and Misuse, 50*(8–9), 1031–1036. doi:10.3109/10826084.2015.1007646

Anderson, T., Crowley, M. E., Himawan, L., Holmberg, J. K., & Uhlin, B. D. (2016). Therapist facilitative interpersonal skills and training status: A randomized clinical trial on alliance and outcome. *Psychotherapy Research, 26*(5), 511–529. doi:10.1080/10503307.2015.1049671

Apodaca, T. R., Borsari, B., Jackson, K. M., Magill, M., Longabaugh, R., Mastroleo, N. R., & Barnett, N. P. (2014). Sustain talk predicts poorer outcomes among mandated college student drinkers receiving a brief motivational intervention. *Psychology of Addictive Behaviors, 28*(3), 631–638. doi:10.1037/a0037296

Apodaca, T. R., Jackson, K. M., Borsari, B., Magill, M., Longabaugh, R., Mastroleo, N. R., & Barnett, N. P. (2016). Which individual therapist behaviors elicit client change talk and sustain talk in motivational interviewing? *Journal of Substance Abuse Treatment, 61*, 60–65. doi:10.1016/j.jsat.2015.09.001

Apodaca, T. R., & Longabaugh, R. (2009). Mechanisms of change in motivational interviewing: A review and preliminary evaluation of the evidence. *Addiction,104*(5), 705–715. doi:10.1111/j.1360-0443.2009.02527.x

Apodaca, T. R., Magill, M., Longabaugh, R., Jackson, K. M., & Monti, P. M. (2013). Effect of a significant other on client change talk in motivational interviewing. *Journal of Consulting and Clinical Psychology,81*(1), 35–46. doi:10.1037/a0030881

Appiah-Brempong, E., Okyere, P., Owusu-Addo, E., & Cross, R. (2014). Motivational interviewing interventions and alcohol abuse among college students: A systematic review. *American Journal of Health Promotion, 29*(1). doi:10.4278/ajhp.130502-lit-222

Arkowitz, H., Miller, W. R., & Rollnick, S. (2015). *Motivational interviewing in the treatment of psychological problems* (2nd ed.). New York, NY: Guilford Publications.

Babor, T. F., Del Boca, F. D., & Bray, J. W. (2017). Screening, brief intervention and referral to treatment: Implications of SAMHSA's SBIRT initiative for substance abuse policy and practice. *Addiction, 112*, 110–117. doi:10.1111/add.13675

Babor, T. F., Higgins-Biddle, J. C., & Robaina, K. (2016). *USAUDIT: The Alcohol Use Disorders Identification Test, Adapted for use in the United States: A guide for primary care practitioners.* Retrieved from www.ct.gov/dmhas/lib/dmhas/publications/USAUDIT-2017.pdf

Babor, T. F., Higgins-Biddle, J. C., Saunders, J. B., & Monteiro, M. G. (2001). *The Alcohol Use Disorders Identification Test: Guidelines for use in primary care* (2nd ed.). Geneva, Switzerland: World Health Organization.

Bachiller, D., Grau-López, L., Barral, C., Daigre, C., Alberich, C., Rodríguez-Cintas, L., … Roncero C. (2015). Motivational interviewing group at inpatient detoxification: Its influence in maintaining abstinence and treatment retention after discharge. *Adicciones, 27*(2), 109–118.

Baker, A. L., Kavanagh, D. J., Kay-Lambkin, F. J., Hunt, S. A., Lewin, T. J., Carr, V. J., & McElduff, P. (2014). Randomized controlled trial of MICBT for co-existing alcohol misuse and depression: Outcomes to 36-months. *Journal of Substance Abuse Treatment, 46*(3), 281–290.

Baker, A. L., Thornton, L. K., Hiles, S., Hides, L., & Lubman, D. I. (2012). Psychological interventions for alcohol misuse among people with co-occurring depression or anxiety disorders: A systematic review. *Journal of Affective Disorders, 139*(3), 217–229. doi:10.1016/j.jad.2011.08.004

Bandura, A. (1977). Self-efficacy: Toward a unifying theory of behavioral change. *Psychological Review, 84,* 191–215.

Barata, I. A., Shandro, J. R., Montgomery, M., Polansky, R., Sachs, C. J., Duber, H. C., … Macias-Konstantopoulos, W. (2017). Effectiveness of SBIRT for alcohol use disorders in the emergency department: A systematic review. *Western Journal of Emergency Medicine, 18*(6), 1143–1152.

Barbosa, C., Cowell, A., Dowd, W., Landwehr, J., Aldridge, A., & Bray, J. (2017). The cost-effectiveness of brief intervention versus brief treatment of screening, brief intervention and referral to treatment (SBIRT) in the United States. *Addiction, 112,* 73–81. doi:10.1111/add.13658

Barnes, R. D., & Ivezaj, V. (2015). A systematic review of motivational interviewing for weight loss among adults in primary care. *Obesity Reviews, 16*(4), 304–318. doi:10.1111/obr.12264

Barnett, E., Moyers, T. B., Sussman, S., Smith, C., Rohrbach, L. A., Sun, P., & Spruijt-Metz, D. (2014). From counselor skill to decreased marijuana use: Does change talk matter? *Journal of Substance Abuse Treatment, 46,* 498–505.

Barnett, E., Spruijt-Metz, D., Moyers, T. B., Smith, C., Rohrbach, L. A., Sun, P., & Sussman, S. (2014). Bidirectional relationships between client and counselor speech: The importance of reframing. *Psychology of Addictive Behaviors, 28*(4), 1212–1219. doi:10.1037/a0036227

Barrio, P., & Gual, A. (2016). Patient-centered care interventions for the management of alcohol use disorders: A systematic review of randomized controlled trials. *Patient Preference and Adherence, 10,* 1823–1845. doi:10.2147/PPA.S109641

Bassuk, E. L., Hanson, J., Greene, R. N., Richard, M., & Laudet, A. (2016). Peer-delivered recovery support services for addictions in the United States: A systematic review. *Journal of Substance Abuse Treatment, 63,* 1–9. doi:10.1016/j.jsat.2016.01.003

Bedard-Gilligan, M., Garcia, N., Zoellner, L. A., & Feeny, N. C. (2018). Alcohol, cannabis, and other drug use: Engagement and outcome in PTSD treatment. *Psychology of Addictive Behaviors, 32*(3), 277–288.

Belmontes, K. C. (2018). When family gets in the way of recovery. *Family Journal, 26*(1), 99–104. doi:10.1177/1066480717753013

Bernstein, S. L., & D'Onofrio, G. (2017). Screening, treatment initiation, and referral for substance use disorders. *Addiction Science and Clinical Practice, 12*(1). doi:10.1186/s13722-017-0083-z

Bertholet, N., Palfai, T., Gaume, J., Daeppen, J., & Saitz, R. (2013). Do brief alcohol motivational interventions work like we think they do? *Alcoholism: Clinical and Experimental Research, 38*(3), 853–859. doi:10.1111/acer.12274

Beutler, L. E., Harwood, T. M., Michelson, A., Song, A., & Holman, J. (2011). Resistance/reactance level. *Journal of Clinical Psychology, 67*(2), 133–142.

Black, J. J., & Chung, T. (2014). Mechanisms of change in adolescent substance use treatment: How does treatment work? *Substance Abuse, 35*(4), 344–351.

Blow, F. C., Walton, M. A., Bohnert, A. S., Ignacio, R. V., Chermack, S., Cunningham, R. M., … Barry, K. L. (2017). A randomized controlled trial of brief interventions to reduce drug use among adults in a low-income urban emergency department: The HealthiER You study. *Addiction, 112*(8), 1395–1405. doi:10.1111/add.13773

Bohnert, A. S. B., Bonar, E. E., Cunningham, R., Greenwald, M. K., Thomas, L., Chermack, S., … Walton, M. (2016). A pilot randomized clinical trial of an intervention to reduce overdose risk behaviors among emergency department patients at risk for prescription drug overdose. *Drug and Alcohol Dependence, 163,* 40–47.

Borsari, B., Apodaca, T. R., Jackson, K. M., Fernandez, A., Mastroleo, N. R., Magill, M., … Carey, K. B. (2018). Trajectories of in-session change language in brief motivational interventions with mandated college students. *Journal of Consulting and Clinical Psychology, 86*(2), 158–168. doi:10.1037/ccp0000255

Boston Center for Treatment Development and Training. (2016). *Module 10: Sobriety sampling*. Retrieved from www.mass.gov/files/documents/2016/07/ty/bt-manual-module10.pdf

Bourke, E., Magill, M., & Apodaca, T. R. (2016). The in-session and long-term role of a significant other in motivational enhancement therapy for alcohol use disorders. *Journal of Substance Abuse Treatment, 64*, 35–43. doi:10.1016/j.jsat.2016.01.008

Bray, J. W., Aden, B., Eggman, A. A., Hellerstein, L., Wittenberg, E., Nosyk, B., … Schackman, B. R. (2017). Quality of life as an outcome of opioid use disorder treatment: A systematic review. *Journal of Substance Abuse Treatment, 76*, 88–93.

Breslin, F. C., Sobell, L. C., Sobell, M. B., & Agrawal, S. (2000). A comparison of a brief and long version of the Situational Confidence Questionnaire. *Behaviour Research and Therapy, 38*(12), 1211–1220.

Brorson, H. H., Arnevik, E. A., Rand-Hendriksen, K., & Duckert, F. (2013). Drop-out from addiction treatment: A systematic review of risk factors. *Clinical Psychology Review, 33*(8), 1010–1024. doi:10.1016/j.cpr.2013.07.007

Caperton, D. D., Atkins, D. C., & Imel, Z. E. (2018). Rating motivational interviewing fidelity from thin slices. *Psychology of Addictive Behaviors, 32*(4), 434–441. doi:10.1037/adb0000359

Carey, K. B., Leontieva, L., Dimmock, J., Maisto, S. A., & Batki, S. L. (2007). Adapting motivational interventions for comorbid schizophrenia and alcohol use disorders. *Clinical Psychology, 14*(1), 39–57.

Carroll, K. M., Ball, S. A., Nich, C., Martino, S., Frankforter, T. L., Farentinos, C., … Woody, G. E. (2006). Motivational interviewing to improve treatment engagement and outcome in individuals seeking treatment for substance abuse: A multisite effectiveness study. *Drug and Alcohol Dependence, 81*, 301–312.

Caviness, C. M., Hagerty, C. E., Anderson, B. J., Dios, M. A., Hayaki, J., Herman, D., & Stein, M. D. (2013). Self-efficacy and motivation to quit marijuana use among young women. *American Journal on Addictions, 22*(4), 373–380. doi:10.1111/j.1521-0391.2013.12030

Chariyeva, Z., Golin, C. E., Earp, J. A., Maman, S., Suchindran, C., & Zimmer, C. (2013). The role of self-efficacy and motivation to explain the effect of motivational interviewing time on changes in risky sexual behavior among people living with HIV: A mediation analysis. *AIDS and Behavior, 17*(2), 813–823. doi:10.1007/s10461-011-0115-8

Coffin, P. O., Santos, G.-M., Matheson, T., Behar, E., Rowe, C., Rubin, T., … Vittinghoff, E. (2017). Behavioral intervention to reduce opioid overdose among high-risk persons with opioid use disorder: A pilot randomized controlled trial. *PLOS One, 12*(10), 1–15. Retrieved from www.ncbi.nlm.nih.gov/pubmed/29049282

Connors, G. J., DiClemente, C. C., Velasquez, M. M., & Donovan, D. M. (2013). *Substance abuse treatment and the stages of change: Selecting and planning interventions*. New York, NY: Guilford Press.

Copeland, J., Gates, P., & Pokorski, I. (2017). A narrative review of psychological cannabis use treatments with and without pharmaceutical adjunct. *Current Pharmaceutical Design, 22*(42), 6397–6408. doi:10.2174/1381612822666160831094811

Copeland, L., McNamara, R., Kelson, M., & Simpson, S. (2015). Mechanisms of change within motivational interviewing in relation to health behaviors outcomes: A systematic review. *Patient Education and Counseling, 98*(4), 401–411. doi:10.1016/j.pec.2014.11.022

Cunningham, J. A., Sobell, L. C., Gavin, D. R., Sobell, M. B., & Breslin, F. C. (1997). Assessing motivation for change: Preliminary development and evaluation of a scale measuring the costs and benefits of changing alcohol or drug use. *Psychology of Addictive Behaviors, 11*(2), 107–114.

D'Amico, E. J., Houck, J. M., Hunter, S. B., Miles, J. N., Osilla, K. C., & Ewing, B. A. (2015). Group motivational interviewing for adolescents: Change talk and alcohol and marijuana outcomes. *Journal of Consulting and Clinical Psychology, 83*(1), 68–80. doi:10.1037/a0038155

Davis, J. P., Houck, J. M., Rowell, L. N., Benson, J. G., & Smith, D. C. (2015). Brief motivational interviewing and normative feedback for adolescents: Change language and alcohol use outcomes. *Journal of Substance Abuse Treatment, 65*, 66–73.

Deci, E. L., & Ryan, R. M. (2012). Overview of self-determination theory: An organismic dialectical perspective. In E. Deci & R. M. Ryan (Eds.), *Handbook of self-determination research* (pp. 3–38). Rochester, NY: University of Rochester Press.

Dennis, M. L., & Scott, C. K. (2012). Four-year outcomes from the Early Re-Intervention (ERI) experiment using Recovery Management Checkups (RMCs). *Drug and Alcohol Dependence, 121*(1–2), 10–17. doi:10.1016/j.drugalcdep.2011.07.026

Dennis, M. L., Scott, C. K., & Laudet, A. (2014). Beyond bricks and mortar: Recent research on substance use disorder recovery management. *Current Psychiatry Reports, 16*(4). doi:10.1007/s11920-014-0442-3

de Roten, Y., Zimmermann, G., Ortega, D., & Despland, J.-N. (2013). Meta-analysis of the effects of MI training on clinicians' behavior. *Journal of Substance Abuse Treatment, 45*(2), 155–162. Retrieved from www.ncbi.nlm.nih.gov/pubmed/23537923

DiClemente, C. C. (2018). *Addiction and change: How addictions develop and addicted people recover* (2nd ed.). Guilford, NY: Guilford Publications.

DiClemente, C. C., Carbonari, J. P., Montgomery, R. P. G., & Hughes, S. O. (1994). The Alcohol Abstinence Self-Efficacy Scale. *Journal of Studies on Alcohol, 55*(2), 141–148.

DiClemente, C. C., Corno, C. M., Graydon, M. M., Wiprovnick, A. E., & Knoblach, D. J. (2017). Motivational interviewing, enhancement, and brief interventions over the last decade: A review of reviews of efficacy and effectiveness. *Psychology of Addictive Behaviors, 31*(8), 862–887. doi:10.1037/adb0000318

Dillard, P. K., Zuniga, J. A., & Holstad, M. M. (2017). An integrative review of the efficacy of motivational interviewing in HIV management. *Patient Education and Counseling, 100*(4), 636–646. doi:10.1016/j.pec.2016.10.029

Drapkin, M. L., Wilbourne, P., Manuel, J. K., Baer, J., Karlin, B., & Raffa, S. (2016). National dissemination of motivation enhancement therapy in the Veterans Health Administration: Training program design and initial outcomes. *Journal of Substance Abuse Treatment, 65*, 83–87. doi:10.1016/j.jsat.2016.02.002

Dufett, I., & Ward, C. I. (2015). Can a motivational-interviewing-based outpatient substance abuse treatment achieve success? A theory-based evaluation. *African Journal of Drug and Alcohol Studies, 14*(1), 1–12.

Ekong, G., & Kavookjian, J. (2016). Motivational interviewing and outcomes in adults with type 2 diabetes: A systematic review. *Patient Education and Counseling, 99*(6), 944–952. doi:10.1016/j.pec.2015.11.022

Elliott, J. C., & Carey, K. B. (2013). Pros and cons: Prospective predictors of marijuana use on a college campus. *Psychology of Addictive Behaviors, 27*(1), 230–235. doi:10.1037/a0029835

Elliott, R., Bohart, A. C., Watson, J. C., & Murphy, D. (2018). Therapist empathy and client outcome: An updated meta-analysis. *Psychotherapy, 55*(4), 399–410. Retrieved from www.researchgate.net/publication/324562138_Therapist_Empathy_and_Client_Outcome_An_Updated_Meta-Analysis

Ewing, S. W., Wray, A. M., Mead, H. K., & Adams, S. K. (2012). Two approaches to tailoring treatment for cultural minority adolescents. *Journal of Substance Abuse Treatment, 43*(2), 190–203. doi:10.1016/j.jsat.2011.12.005

Feldstein Ewing, S. W., Walters, S., & Baer, J. C. (2013). Motivational interviewing groups for adolescents and emerging adults. In C. C. Wagner & K. S. Ingersoll (Eds.), *Motivational interviewing in groups* (pp. 387–406). New York, NY: Guilford Press.

Fergie, L., Campbell, K. A., Coleman-Haynes, T., Ussher, M., Cooper, S., & Coleman, T. (2018). Identifying effective behavior change techniques for alcohol and illicit substance use during pregnancy: A systematic review. *Annals of Behavioral Medicine*. doi:10.1093/abm/kay085

Field, C. A., Adinoff, B., Harris, T. R., Ball, S. A., & Carroll, K. M. (2009). Construct, concurrent and predictive validity of the URICA: Data from two multi-site clinical trials. *Drug and Alcohol Dependence, 101*(1–2), 115–123.

Field, C., Walters, S., Marti, C. N., Jun, J., Foreman, M., & Brown, C. (2014). A multisite randomized controlled trial of brief intervention to reduce drinking in the trauma care setting. *Annals of Surgery, 259*(5), 873–880. doi:10.1097/sla.0000000000000339

Fiszdon, J. M., Kurtz, M. M., Choi, J., Bell, M. D., & Martino, S. (2015). Motivational interviewing to increase cognitive rehabilitation adherence in schizophrenia. *Schizophrenia Bulletin, 42*(2), 327–334.

Flannery, M. (2017). Self-determination theory: Intrinsic motivation and behavioral change. *Oncology Nursing Forum, 44*(2), 155–156. Retrieved from www.ncbi.nlm.nih.gov/pubmed/28222078

Forman, D. P., & Moyers, T. B. (2019). With odds of a single session, motivational interviewing is a good bet. *Psychotherapy.* doi:10.1037/pst0000199

Foster, D., & Neighbors, C. (2013). A review of decisional balance research and directions for brief alcohol intervention among college students. *OA Alcohol, 1*(1). doi:10.13172/2053-0285-1-1-575

Foster, D. W., Neighbors, C., & Pai, A. (2015). Decisional balance: Alcohol decisional balance intervention for heavy drinking undergraduates. *Substance Use and Misuse, 50*(13), 1717–1727.

Friedrichs, A., Spies, M., Härter, M., & Buchholz, A. (2016). Patient preferences and shared decision making in the treatment of substance use disorders: A systematic review of the literature. *PLOS One, 11*(1). doi:10.1371/journal.pone.0145817

Gates, P. J., Sabioni, P., Copeland, J., Foll, B. L., & Gowing, L. (2016). Psychosocial interventions for cannabis use disorder. *Cochrane Database of Systematic Reviews.* doi:10.1002/14651858.cd005336.pub4

Gaume, J., Magill, M., Mastroleo, N. R., Longabaugh, R., Bertholet, N., Gmel, G., & Daeppen, J. (2016). Change talk during brief motivational intervention with young adult males: Strength matters. *Journal of Substance Abuse Treatment, 65*, 58–65. doi:10.1016/j.jsat.2016.01.005

Gelberg, L., Andersen, R., Vahidi, M., Rico, M., Baumeister, S., & Leake, B. (2017). A multi-component brief intervention for risky drug use among Latino patients of a federally qualified health center in East Los Angeles: A randomized controlled trial of the quit using drugs intervention trial (quit) brief intervention. *Drug and Alcohol Dependence,171.* Retrieved from https://eurekamag.com/research/064/949/064949750.php

Glozah, F. N., Adu, N. A., & Komesuor, J. (2015). Assessing alcohol abstinence self-efficacy in undergraduate students: Psychometric evaluation of the alcohol abstinence self-efficacy scale. *Health and Quality of Life Outcomes, 13*(1). doi:10.1186/s12955-015-0387-1

Gordon, T. (1970). *Parent effectiveness training: The no-lose program for raising responsible children.* New York, NY: Wyden.

Granfield, R., & Cloud, W. (1999). *Coming clean: Overcoming addiction without treatment.* New York, NY: New York University Press.

Grant, S., Colaiaco, B., Motala, A., Shanman, R., Booth, M., Sorbero, M., & Hempel, S. (2017). Mindfulness-based relapse prevention for substance use disorders: A systematic review and meta-analysis. *Journal of Addiction Medicine, 11*(5), 386–396. doi:10.1097/adm.0000000000000338

Gueorguieva, R., Wu, R., O'Connor, P. G., Weisner, C., Fucito, L. M., Hoffmann, S., … O'Malley, S. S. (2014). Predictors of abstinence from heavy drinking during treatment in COMBINE and external validation in PREDICT. *Alcoholism: Clinical and Experimental Research, 38*(10), 2647–2656.

Hall, K., Staiger, P. K., Simpson, A., Best, D., & Lubman, D. I. (2015). After 30 years of dissemination, have we achieved sustained practice change in motivational interviewing? *Addiction, 111*(7), 1144–1150. doi:10.1111/add.13014

Harley, D. A. (2017). Motivational interviewing and motivational enhancement therapy: Cultural implications in addiction intervention for African Americans. *SciFed Journal of Addiction and Therapy, 1*(1). doi:10.23959/sfjat-1000005

Harrell, P. T., Trenz, R., Scherer, M., Martins, S., & Latimer, W. (2013). A latent class approach to treatment readiness corresponds to a transtheoretical ("Stages of Change") model. *Journal of Substance Abuse Treatment, 45*(3), 249–256. doi:10.1016/j.jsat.2013.04.004

Hausotter, W. (2006). *Motivational interviewing assessment: Supervisory tools for enhancing proficiency.* Salem, OR: Northwest Frontier Addiction Technology Transfer Center, Oregon Health and Science University. Retrieved from www.motivationalinterviewing.org/sites/default/files/mia-step.pdf

Heather, N., & Honekopp, J. (2008). A revised edition of the readiness to change questionnaire (treatment version). *Addiction Research and Theory, 16*(5), 421–433.

Heather, N., & McCambridge, J. (2013). Post-treatment stage of change predicts 12-month outcome of treatment for alcohol problems. *Alcohol and Alcoholism, 48*(3), 329–336. doi:10.1093/alcalc/agt006

Hennessy, E. A. (2017). Recovery capital: A systematic review of the literature. *Addiction Research and Theory, 25*(5), 349–360. doi:10.1080/16066359.2017.1297990

Hennessy, E. A., Tanner-Smith, E. E., & Steinka-Fry, K. T. (2015). Do brief alcohol interventions reduce tobacco use among adolescents and young adults? A systematic review and meta-analysis. *Journal of Behavioral Medicine, 38*(6), 899–911.

Hester, R. K., Delaney, H. D., & Campbell, W. (2012). The college drinker's check-up: Outcomes of two randomized clinical trials of a computer-delivered intervention. *Psychology of Addictive Behaviors, 26*(1), 1–12.

Hingson, R., & Compton, W. M. (2014). Screening and brief intervention and referral to treatment for drug use in primary care: Back to the drawing board. *JAMA, 312*(5), 488. doi:10.1001/jama.2014.7863

Holstad, M. M., Diiorio, C., Kelley, M. E., Resnicow, K., & Sharma, S. (2010). Group motivational interviewing to promote adherence to antiretroviral medications and risk reduction behaviors in HIV infected women. *AIDS and Behavior, 15*(5), 885–896. doi:10.1007/s10461-010-9865-y

Houck, J. M., Hunter, S. B., Benson, J. G., Cochrum, L. L., Rowell, L. N., & Damico, E. J. (2015). Temporal variation in facilitator and client behavior during group motivational interviewing sessions. *Psychology of Addictive Behaviors, 29*(4), 941–949. doi:10.1037/adb0000107

Houck, J. M., Manuel, J. K., & Moyers, T. B. (2018). Short- and long-term effects of within-session client speech on drinking Outcomes in the COMBINE study. *Journal of Studies on Alcohol and Drugs, 79*(2), 217–222. doi:10.15288/jsad.2018.79.217

Houck, J. M., & Moyers, T. B. (2015). Within-session communication patterns predict alcohol treatment outcomes. *Drug and Alcohol Dependence, 157*, 205–209. doi:10.1016/j.drugalcdep.2015.10.025

Humphreys, K., Blodgett, J. C., & Wagner, T. H. (2014). Estimating the efficacy of Alcoholics Anonymous without self-selection bias: An instrumental variables re-analysis of randomized clinical trials. *Alcoholism: Clinical and Experimental Research, 38*(11), 2688–2694. doi:10.1111/acer.12557

Hunt, G. E., Siegfried, N., Morley, K., Sitharthan, T., & Cleary, M. (2013). Psychosocial interventions for people with both severe mental illness and substance misuse. *Cochrane Database of Systematic Reviews, 10*. Art. No.: CD001088. doi:10.1002/14651858.CD001088.pub3

Ingersoll, K. S., Ceperich, S. D., Hettema, J. E., Farrell-Carnahan, L., & Penberthy, J. K. (2013). Preconceptional motivational interviewing interventions to reduce alcohol-exposed pregnancy risk. *Journal of Substance Abuse Treatment, 44*(4), 407–416. doi:10.1016/j.jsat.2012.10.001

Jackson, L. A., Buxton, J. A., Dingwell, J., Dykeman, M., Gahagan, J., Gallant, K., … Davison, C. (2014). Improving psychosocial health and employment outcomes for individuals receiving methadone treatment: A realist synthesis of what makes interventions work. *BMC Psychology, 2*(1), 26. doi:10.1186/s40359-014-0026-3

Janis, L. L., & Mann, L. (1977). *Decision making: A psychological analysis of conflict, choice, and commitment.* London, England: Cassel and Collier Macmillan.

Jason, L. A., Salina, D., & Ram, D. (2016). Oxford recovery housing: Length of stay correlated with improved outcomes for women previously involved with the criminal justice system. *Substance Abuse, 37*(1), 248–254. doi:10.1080/08897077.2015.1037946

Jiang, S., Wu, L., & Gao, X. (2017). Beyond face-to-face individual counseling: A systematic review on alternative modes of motivational interviewing in substance abuse treatment and prevention. *Addictive Behaviors, 73*, 216–235

Joseph, J., & Basu, D. (2016). Efficacy of brief interventions in reducing hazardous or harmful alcohol use in middle-income countries: Systematic review of randomized controlled trials. *Alcohol and Alcoholism, 52*(1), 56–64. doi:10.1093/alcalc/agw054

Kadden, R. M., & Litt, M. D. (2011). The role of self-efficacy in the treatment of substance use disorders. *Addictive Behaviors, 36*(12), 1120–1126.

Kahler, C. W., Pantalone, D. W., Mastroleo, N. R., Liu, T., Bove, G., Ramratnam, B., … Mayer, K. J. (2018). Motivational interviewing with personalized feedback to reduce alcohol use in HIV-infected men who have sex with men: A randomized controlled trial. *Journal of Consulting and Clinical Psychology, 86*(8), 645–656.

Kanfer, F. H., & Schefft, B. K. (1988). *Guiding the process of therapeutic change.* Champaign, IL: Research Press.

Kelly, J. F., Bergman, B. G., Hoeppner, B., Vilsaint, C., & White, W. L. (2017). Prevalence and pathways of recovery from drug and alcohol problems in the United States population: Implications for practice, research, and policy. *Drug and Alcohol Dependence, 181*, 162–169.

Kiluk, B. D., Serafini, K., Malin-Mayor, B., Babuscio, T. A., Nich, C., & Carroll, K. M. (2015). Prompted to treatment by the criminal justice system: Relationships with treatment retention and outcome among cocaine users. *American Journal on Addictions, 24*(3), 225–232. doi:10.1111/ajad.12208

Klimas, J., Field, C., Cullen, W., O'Gorman, C., Glynn, L., Keenan, E., … Dunne, C. (2014). Psychosocial interventions to reduce alcohol consumption in concurrent problem alcohol and illicit drug users: Cochrane Review. *Drug and Alcohol Dependence, 140*. doi:10.1016/j.drugalcdep.2014.02.305

Kohler, S., & Hofmann, A. (2015). Can motivational interviewing in emergency care reduce alcohol consumption in young people? A systematic review and meta-analysis. *Alcohol and Alcoholism, 50*(2), 107–117. doi:10.1093/alcalc/agu098

Korcha, R. A., Polcin, D. L., Evans, K., Bond, J. C., & Galloway, G. P. (2015). Intensive motivational interviewing for women with alcohol problems. *Counselor (Deerfield Beach), 16*(3), 62–69.

Krawczyk, N., Feder, K. A., Saloner, B., Crum, R. M., Kealhofer, M., & Mojtabai, R. (2017). The association of psychiatric comorbidity with treatment completion among clients admitted to substance use treatment programs in a U.S. national sample. *Drug and Alcohol Dependence, 175*, 157–163. doi:10.1016/j.drugalcdep.2017.02.006

Krigel, S. W., Grobe, J. E., Goggin, K., Harris, K. J., Moreno, J. L., & Catley, D. (2017). Motivational interviewing and the decisional balance procedure for cessation induction in smokers not intending to quit. *Addictive Behaviors, 64*, 171–178. doi:10.1016/j.addbeh.2016.08.036

Kuerbis, A., Armeli, S., Muench, F., & Morgenstern, J. (2013). Motivation and self-efficacy in the context of moderated drinking: Global self-report and ecological momentary assessment. *Psychology of Addictive Behaviors, 27*(4), 934–943. doi:10.1037/a0031194

Kuusisto, K., Knuuttila, V., & Saarnio, P. (2011). Clients' self-efficacy and outcome expectations. *Addictive Disorders and Their Treatment, 10*(4), 157–168. doi:10.1097/adt.0b013e31820dd4ec

Kwasnicka, D., Dombrowski, S. U., White, M., & Sniehotta, F. (2016). Theoretical explanations for maintenance of behaviour change: A systematic review of behaviour theories. *Health Psychology Review, 10*(3), 277–296. doi:10.1080/17437199.2016.1151372

Lee, W. W., Choi, K., Yum, R. W., Yu, D. S., & Chair, S. (2016). Effectiveness of motivational interviewing on lifestyle modification and health outcomes of clients at risk or diagnosed with cardiovascular diseases: A systematic review. *International Journal of Nursing Studies, 53*, 331–341. doi:10.1016/j.ijnurstu.2015.09.010

Lenz, A. S., Rosenbaum, L., & Sheperis, D. (2016). Meta-analysis of randomized controlled trials of motivational enhancement therapy for reducing substance use. *Journal of Addictions and Offender Counseling, 37*(2), 66–86. doi:10.1002/jaoc.12017

Lindqvist, H., Forsberg, L., Enebrink, P., Andersson, G., & Rosendahl, I. (2017). Relational skills and client language predict outcome in smoking cessation treatment. *Substance Use and Misuse, 52*(1), 33–42. doi:10.1080/10826084.2016.1212892

Litt, M. D., & Kadden, R. M. (2015). Willpower versus "skillpower": Examining how self-efficacy works in treatment for marijuana dependence. *Psychology of Addictive Behaviors, 29*(3), 532–540. doi:10.1037/adb0000085

Litt, M. D., Kadden, R. M., & Petry, N. M. (2013). Behavioral treatment for marijuana dependence: Randomized trial of contingency management and self-efficacy enhancement. *Addictive Behaviors, 38*(3), 1764–1775. doi:10.1016/j.addbeh.2012.08.011

Lord, S. P., Can, D., Yi, M., Marin, R., Dunn, C. W., Imel, Z. E., … Atkins, D. C. (2014). Advancing methods for reliably assessing motivational interviewing fidelity using the motivational interviewing skills code. *Journal of Substance Abuse Treatment, 49*, 50–57.

Lozano, B. E., Larowe, S. D., Smith, J. P., Tuerk, P., & Roitzsch, J. (2013). Brief motivational feedback may enhance treatment entry in veterans with comorbid substance use and psychiatric disorders. *American Journal on Addictions, 22*(2), 132–135. doi:10.1111/j.1521-0391.2013.00315.x

Lundahl, B., Moleni, T., Burke, B. L., Butters, R., Tollefson, D., Butler, C., & Rollnick, S. (2013). Motivational interviewing in medical care settings: A systematic review and meta-analysis of randomized controlled trials. *Patient Education and Counseling, 93*(2), 157–168. doi:10.1016/j.pec.2013.07.012

Magill, M., Apodaca, T. R., Borsari, B., Gaume, J., Hoadley, A., Gordon, R. E. F., … Moyers, T. (2018). A meta-analysis of motivational interviewing process: Technical, relational, and conditional process models of change. *Journal of Consulting and Clinical Psychology, 86*(2), 140–157.

Magill, M., Gaume, J., Apodaca, T. R., Walthers, J., Mastroleo, N. R., Borsari, B., & Longabaugh, R. (2014). The technical hypothesis of motivational interviewing: A meta-analysis of MI's key causal model. *Journal of Consulting and Clinical Psychology, 82*(6), 973–983.

Magill, M., Stout, R. L., & Apodaca, T. R. (2013). Therapist focus on ambivalence and commitment: A longitudinal analysis of motivational interviewing treatment ingredients. *Psychology of Addictive Behaviors, 27*(3), 754–762. doi:10.1037/a0029639

Magill, M., Walthers, J., Mastroleo, N. R., Gaume, J., Longabaugh, R., & Apodaca, T. R. (2016). Therapist and client discussions of drinking and coping: A sequential analysis of therapy dialogues in three evidence-based alcohol use disorder treatments. *Addiction, 111*(6), 1011–1020. doi:10.1111/add.13313

Mahmoodabad, S. S., Tonekaboni, N. R., Farmanbar, R., Fallahzadeh, H., & Kamalikhah, T. (2017). The effect of motivational interviewing-based intervention using self-determination theory on promotion of physical activity among women in reproductive age: A randomized clinical trial. *Electronic Physician, 9*(5), 4461–4472. doi:10.19082/4461

Manuel, J. K., Satre, D. D., Tsoh, J., Moreno-John, G., Ramos, J. S., McCance-Katz, E. F., & Satterfield, J. M. (2015). Adapting screening, brief intervention, and referral to treatment for alcohol and drugs to culturally diverse clinical populations. *Journal of Addiction Medicine, 1.* doi:10.1097/adm.0000000000000150

Marlatt, G., A., Parks, G. A., & Witkiewitz, K. (2002*). Clinical guidelines for implementing relapse prevention therapy: A guideline developed for behavioral health recovery management project.* Chicago, IL: University of Chicago. Retrieved from www.researchgate.net/publication/235326763_Clinical_Guidelines_for_Implementing_RelapsePrevention_Thera py_A_Guideline_Developed_for_the_Behavioral_Health_Recovery_Management_Project

Martin, G. W., & Rehm, J. (2012). The effectiveness of psychosocial modalities in the treatment of alcohol problems in adults: A review of the evidence. *Canadian Journal of Psychiatry, 57*(6), 350–358. doi:10.1177/070674371205700604

Martino, S., Ball, S. A., Gallon, S. L., Hall, D., Garcia, M., Ceperich, S., … Hausotter, W. (2006). *Motivational interviewing assessment: Supervisory tools for enhancing proficiency.* Salem, OR: Northwest Frontier Addiction Technology Transfer Center, Oregon Health and Science University. Retrieved from www.motivationalinterviewing.org/sites/default/files/mia-step.pdf

Martino, S., Paris, M., Añez, L., Nich, C., Canning-Ball, M., Hunkele, K., … Carroll, K. M. (2016). The effectiveness and cost of clinical supervision for motivational interviewing: A randomized controlled trial. *Journal of Substance Abuse Treatment, 68*, 11–23.

Mattoo, S. K., Prasad, S., & Ghosh, A. (2018). Brief intervention in substance use disorders. *Indian Journal of Psychiatry, 60*(Suppl 4), S466–S472.

McCance-Katz, E. F., & Satterfield, J. (2012). SBIRT: A key to integrate prevention and treatment of substance abuse in primary care. *American Journal on Addictions, 21*(2), 176–177. doi:10.1111/j.1521-0391.2011.00213.x

McConnaughy, E. A., Prochaska, J. O., & Velicer, W. F.(1983). Stages of change in psychotherapy: Measurement and sample profiles. *Psychotherapy: Theory, Research and Practice, 20*, 368–375.

McDevitt-Murphy, M. E., Murphy, J. G., Williams, J. L., Monahan, C. J., Bracken-Minor, K. L., & Fields, J. A. (2014). Randomized controlled trial of two brief alcohol interventions for OEF/OIF veterans. *Journal of Consulting and Clinical Psychology, 82*(4), 562–568. doi:10.1037/a0036714

McQueen, J., Howe, T. E., Allan, L., Mains, D., & Hardy, V. (2011). Brief interventions for heavy alcohol users admitted to general hospital wards. *Cochrane Database of Systematic Reviews,* (8).

McQueen, J. M., Howe, T. E., Ballinger, C., & Godwin, J. (2015). Effectiveness of alcohol brief intervention in a general hospital: A randomized controlled trial. *Journal of Studies on Alcohol and Drugs, 76*(6), 838–844. doi:10.15288/jsad.2015.76.838

Merchant, R. C., Romanoff, J., Zhang, Z., Liu, T., & Baird, J. R. (2017). Impact of a brief intervention on reducing alcohol use and increasing alcohol treatment services utilization among alcohol- and drug-using adult emergency department patients. *Alcohol, 65*, 71–80. doi:10.1016/j.alcohol.2017.07.003

Miller, M. B., Leffingwell, T., Claborn, K., Meier, E., Walters, S., & Neighbors, C. (2013). Personalized feedback interventions for college alcohol misuse: An update of Walters & Neighbors (2005). *Psychology of Addictive Behaviors, 27*(4), 909–920.

Miller, W. R., Benefield, R. G., & Tonigan, J. S. (1993). Enhancing motivation for change in problem drinking: A controlled comparison of two therapist styles. *Journal of Consulting and Clinical Psychology, 61*(3), 455–461.

Miller, W. R., & Brown, J. M. (1994). *What I want from treatment* (2.0). Retrieved from https://casaa.unm.edu/inst/What%20I%20Want%20From%20Treatment.pdf

Miller, W. R., Forcehimes, A. A., & Zweben, A. (2011). *Treating addiction: A guide for professionals.* New York, NY: Guilford Press.

Miller, W. R., & Moyers, T. B. (2017). Motivational interviewing and the clinical science of Carl Rogers. *Journal of Consulting and Clinical Psychology, 85*(8), 757–766. doi:10.1037/ccp0000179

Miller, W. R., & Moyers, T. B. (2015). The forest and the trees: Relational and specific factors in addiction treatment. *Addiction, 110*(3), 401–413.

Miller, W. R., Moyers, T. B., Ernst, D. B., & Amrhein, P. C. (2008). *Manual for the Motivational Interviewing Code* (version 2.1). Albuquerque, NM: Center on Alcoholism, Substance Abuse, and Addictions, University of New Mexico. Retrieved from https://casaa.unm.edu/download/misc.pdf

Miller, W. R., & Rollnick, S. (2014). The effectiveness and ineffectiveness of complex behavioral interventions: Impact of treatment fidelity. *Contemporary Clinical Trials, 37*(2), 234–241. doi:10.1016/j.cct.2014.01.005

Miller, W. R., & Rollnick, S. (2013). *Motivational interviewing: Helping people change* (3rd ed.). New York, NY: Guilford Press.

Miller, W. R., & Rollnick, S. (2010). *Looking forward to MI-3: A work in progress* [PowerPoint slides]. Retrieved from http://motivationalinterviewing.org/sites/default/files/Forum_2010_Plenary_Bill.ppt

Miller, W. R., & Rollnick, S. (2002). *Motivational interviewing: Preparing people for change* (2nd ed.). New York, NY: Guilford Press.

Miller, W. R., & Rollnick, S. (1991). *Motivational interviewing: Preparing people to change addictive behavior.* New York, NY: Guilford Press.

Miller, W. R., & Rose, G. S. (2013). Motivational interviewing and decisional balance: Contrasting responses to client ambivalence. *Behavioural and Cognitive Psychotherapy, 43*(02), 129–141. doi:10.1017/s1352465813000878

Miller, W. R., & Sanchez, V. C. (1994). Motivating young adults for treatment and lifestyle change. In G. Howard & Nathan (Eds.), *Alcohol use and misuse by young adults* (pp. 55–82). Notre Dame, IN: University of Notre Dame Press.

Miller, W. R., & Tonigan, J. S. (1996). Assessing drinkers' motivation for change: The Stages of Change Readiness and Treatment Eagerness Scale (SOCRATES). *Psychology of Addictive Behaviors, 10*(2), 81–89.

Miller, W. R., Tonigan, J. S., & Longabaugh, R. (1995*). The Drinker Inventory of Consequences (DrInC): An instrument for assessing adverse consequences of alcohol abuse, Test manual* (vol. 4). Project MATCH Monograph Series. Rockville, MD: National Institute on Alcohol Abuse and Alcoholism. Retrieved from https://pubs.niaaa.nih.gov/publications/projectmatch/match04.pdf

Miller, W. R., & Wilbourne, P. L. (2002). Mesa Grande: A methodological analysis of clinical trials of treatments for alcohol use disorders. *Addiction, 97*(3), 265–277. doi:10.1046/j.1360-0443.2002.00019.x

Montgomery, L., Robinson, C., Seaman, E. L., & Haeny, A. M. (2017). A scoping review and meta-analysis of psychosocial and pharmacological treatments for cannabis and tobacco use among African Americans. *Psychology of Addictive Behaviors, 31*(8), 922–943. www.ncbi.nlm.nih.gov/pubmed/29199844

Monti, P. M., Colby, S. M., Mastroleo, N. R., Barnett, N. P., Gwaltney, C. J., Apodaca, T. R., … Cioffi, W. G. (2014). Individual versus significant-other-enhanced brief motivational intervention for alcohol in emergency care. *Journal of Consulting and Clinical Psychology, 82*(6), 936–948. doi:10.1037/a0037658

Moore, M., Flamez, B., & Szirony, G. M. (2017). Motivational interviewing and dual diagnosis clients: Enhancing self-efficacy and treatment completion. *Journal of Substance Use, 23*(3), 247–253. doi:10.1080/14659891.2017.1388856

Moos, R. H. (2012). Iatrogenic effects of psychosocial interventions: Treatment, life context, and personal risk factors. *Substance Use and Misuse, 47*(13–14), 1592–1598. doi:10.3109/10826084.2012.705710

Morgenstern, J., Kuerbis, A., Houser, J., Muench, F. J., Shao, S., & Treloar, H. (2016). Within-person associations between daily motivation and self-efficacy and drinking among problem drinkers in treatment. *Psychology of Addictive Behaviors, 30*(6), 630–638. doi:10.1037/adb0000204

Mowbray, O., Quinn, A., & Cranford, J. A. (2014). Social networks and alcohol use disorders: Findings from a nationally representative sample. *American Journal of Drug and Alcohol Abuse, 40*(3), 181–186. doi:10.3109/00952990.2013.860984

Moyers, T. B. (2014). The relationship in motivational interviewing. *Psychotherapy, 51*(3), 358–363. Retrieved from https://media.wcwpds.wisc.edu/motivational-interviewing/files/The-Relationship-in-Motivational-Interviewing.pdf

Moyers, T. B., & Houck, J. (2011). Combining motivational interviewing with cognitive–behavioral treatments for substance abuse: Lessons from the COMBINE research project. *Cognitive and Behavioral Practice, 18*(1), 38–45. doi:10.1016/j.cbpra.2009.09.005

Moyers, T. B., Houck, J., Glynn, L. H., Hallgren, K. A., & Manuel, J. K. (2017). A randomized controlled trial to influence client language in substance use disorder treatment. *Drug and Alcohol Dependence, 172,* 43–50. doi:10.1016/j.drugalcdep.2016.11.036

Moyers, T. B., Houck, J., Rice, S. L., Longabaugh, R., & Miller, W. R. (2016). Therapist empathy, combined behavioral intervention, and alcohol outcomes in the COMBINE research project. *Journal of Consulting and Clinical Psychology, 84*(3), 221–229. doi:10.1037/ccp0000074

Moyers, T. B., Manuel, J. K., & Ernst, D. (2014). *Motivational Interviewing Treatment Integrity Coding Manual 4.1.* Unpublished manual. Retrieved from https://motivationalinterviewing.org/sites/default/files/miti4_2.pdf

Moyers, T. B., Martin, T., & Christopher, P. (2005). *Motivational interviewing knowledge test.* Albuquerque, NM: Center on Alcoholism, Substance Abuse, and Addictions, University of New Mexico. Retrieved from https://casaa.unm.edu/download/ELICIT/MI%20Knowledge%20Test.pdf

Moyers, T. B., & Miller, W. R. (2013). Is low therapist empathy toxic? *Psychology of Addictive Behaviors, 273,* 878–884. doi:10.1037/a0030274

Mumba, M. N., Findlay, L. J., & Snow, D. E. (2018). Treatment options for opioid use disorders. *Journal of Addictions Nursing, 29*(3), 221–225.

Naar-King, S., Safren, S. A., & Miller, W. R. (2017). *Motivational interviewing and CBT: Combining strategies for maximum effectiveness.* New York, NY: Guilford Press.

Navidian, A., Kermansaravi, F., Tabas, E. E., & Saeedinezhad, F. (2016). Efficacy of group motivational interviewing in the degree of drug craving in the addicts under the methadone maintenance treatment (MMT) in South East of Iran. *Archives of Psychiatric Nursing, 30*(2), 144–149. doi:10.1016/j.apnu.2015.08.002

Norcross, J. C., Krebs, P. M., & Prochaska, J. O. (2011). Stages of Change. *Journal of Clinical Psychology, 67*(2), 143–154. Retrieved from www.researchgate.net/publication/49683193_Stages_of_Change

Novins, D. K., Croy, C. D., Moore, L. A., & Rieckmann, T. (2016). Use of evidence-based treatments in substance abuse treatment programs serving American Indian and Alaska Native communities. *Drug and Alcohol Dependence, 161,* 214–221.

Nunes, A. P., Richmond, M. K., Marzano, K., Swenson, C. J., & Lockhart, J. (2017). Ten years of implementing screening, brief intervention, and referral to treatment (SBIRT): Lessons learned. *Substance Abuse, 38*(4), 508–512. doi:10.1080/08897077.2017.1362369

Office of the Surgeon General. (2016). *Facing addiction in America: The Surgeon General's report on alcohol, drugs, and health*. Washington, DC: U.S. Department of Health and Human Services. Retrieved from https://addiction.surgeongeneral.gov/sites/default/files/surgeon-generals-report.pdf

Osilla, K. C., Ortiz, J. A., Miles, J. N., Pedersen, E. R., Houck, J. M., & Damico, E. J. (2015). How group factors affect adolescent change talk and substance use outcomes: Implications for motivational interviewing training. *Journal of Counseling Psychology, 62*(1), 79–86. doi:10.1037/cou0000049

Osterman, R., Lewis, D., & Winhusen, T. (2017). Efficacy of motivational enhancement therapy to decrease alcohol and illicit-drug use in pregnant substance users reporting baseline alcohol use. *Journal of Substance Abuse Treatment, 77*, 150–155. doi:10.1016/j.jsat.2017.02.003

Pace, B. T., Dembe, A., Soma, C. S., Baldwin, S. A., Atkins, D. C., & Imel, Z. E. (2017). A multivariate meta-analysis of motivational interviewing process and outcome. *Psychology of Addictive Behaviors, 31*(5), 524–533. doi:10.1037/adb0000280

Panebianco, D., Gallupe, O., Carrington, P. J., & Colozzi, I. (2016). Personal support networks, social capital, and risk of relapse among individuals treated for substance use issues. *International Journal of Drug Policy, 27*, 146–153. doi:10.1016/j.drugpo.2015.09.009

Polcin, D. L., Mulia, N., & Jones, L. (2012). Substance users' perspectives on helpful and unhelpful confrontation: Implications for recovery. *Journal of Psychoactive Drugs, 44*(2), 144–152.

Prochaska, J. O. (1979). *Systems of psychotherapy: A transtheoretical analysis.* Homewood, IL: Dorsey Press.

Prochaska, J. O., & DiClemente, C. C. (1984). *The transtheoretical approach: Crossing traditional boundaries of therapy.* Malabar, FL: R. E. Krieger.

Prochaska, J., Norcross, J., & DiClemente, C. (2013). Applying the Stages of Change. *Psychotherapy in Australia, 19*, 10–15. doi:10.1093/med:psych/9780199845491.003.0034

Prochaska, J. O., Velicer, W. F., Rossi, J. S., Goldstein, M. G., Marcus, B.H., Rakowski, W., … Rossi, S.R. (1994). Stages of Change and decisional balance for 12 problem behaviors. *Health Psychology, 13*, 39–46.

Rapp, R. C., Van Den Noortgate, W., Broekaert, E., & Vanderplasschen, W. (2014). The efficacy of case management with persons who have substance abuse problems: A three-level meta-analysis of outcomes. *Journal of Consulting and Clinical Psychology, 82*(4), 605–618. Retrieved from www.ncbi.nlm.nih.gov/books/NBK241643/

Raylu, N., & Kaur, I. (2012). Factors that affect treatment expectations of outpatients with substance use problems. *International Journal of Mental Health and Addiction, 10*(6), 804–817. doi:10.1007/s11469-012-9377-2

Rhoades, H., Motte-Kerr, W. L., Duan, L., Woo, D., Rice, E., Henwood, B., … Wenzel, S. L. (2018). Social networks and substance use after transitioning into permanent supportive housing. *Drug and Alcohol Dependence, 191*, 63–69. doi:10.1016/j.drugalcdep.2018.06.027

Riper, H., Andersson, G., Hunter, S. B., Wit, J. D., Berking, M., & Cuijpers, P. (2014). Treatment of comorbid alcohol use disorders and depression with cognitive–behavioural therapy and motivational interviewing: A meta-analysis. *Addiction, 109*(3), 394–406. doi:10.1111/add.12441

Rodriguez, M., Walters, S. T., Houck, J. M., Ortiz, J. A., & Taxman, F. S. (2017). The language of change among criminal justice clients: Counselor language, client language, and client substance use outcomes. *Journal of Clinical Psychology, 74*(4), 626–636. doi:10.1002/jclp.22534

Rogers, C. R. (1980). *A way of being.* Boston, MA: Houghton Mifflin.

Rogers, C. R. (1965). *Client-centered therapy.* New York, NY: Houghton Mifflin.

Rollnick, S., Heather, N., Gold, R., & Hall, W. (1992). Development of a short "readiness to change" questionnaire for use in brief, opportunistic interventions among excessive drinkers. *British Journal of Addiction, 87*, 743–754.

Rollnick, S., Miller, W. R., & Butler, C. C. (2008). *Motivational interviewing in health care: Helping patients change behavior.* New York, NY: Guilford.

Romano, M., & Peters, L. (2016). Understanding the process of motivational interviewing: A review of the relational and technical hypotheses. *Psychotherapy Research, 26*(2), 220–240. doi:10.1080/10503307.2014.954154

Rosengren, D. B. (2018). *Building motivational interviewing skills: A practitioner workbook* (2nd ed.). New York, NY: Guilford Press.

Running Bear, U. R., Beals, J., Novins, D. K., & Manson, S. M. (2017). Alcohol detoxification completion, acceptance of referral to substance abuse treatment, and entry into substance abuse treatment among Alaska Native people. *Addictive Behaviors, 65*, 25–32. doi:10.1016/j.addbeh.2016.09.009

Samson, J. E., & Tanner-Smith, E. E. (2015). Single-session alcohol interventions for heavy drinking college students: A systematic review and meta-analysis. *Journal of Studies on Alcohol and Drugs, 76*(4), 530–543.

Sarpavaara, H. (2015). Significant others in substance abusers change talk during motivational interviewing sessions in the Finnish Probation Service. *Nordic Studies on Alcohol and Drugs, 32*(1), 91–103. doi:10.1515/nsad-2015-0010

Satre, D. D., Delucchi, K., Lichtmacher, J., Sterling, S. A., & Weisner, C. (2013). Motivational interviewing to reduce hazardous drinking and drug use among depression patients. *Journal of Substance Abuse Treatment, 44*(3), 323–329.

Satre, D. D., Leibowitz, A., Sterling, S. A., Lu, Y., Travis, A., & Weisner, C. (2016). A randomized clinical trial of motivational interviewing to reduce alcohol and drug use among patients with depression. *Journal of Consulting and Clinical Psychology, 84*(7), 571–579.

Satre, D. D., Manuel, J. K., Larios, S., Steiger, S., & Satterfield, J. (2015). Cultural adaptation of screening, brief intervention and referral to treatment using motivational interviewing. *Journal of Addiction Medicine, 9*(5), 352–357. doi:10.1097/adm.0000000000000149

Sayegh, C. S., Huey, S. J., Zara, E. J., & Jhaveri, K. (2017). Follow-up treatment effects of contingency management and motivational interviewing on substance use: A meta-analysis. *Psychology of Addictive Behaviors, 31*(4), 403–414. doi:10.1037/adb0000277

Schonfeld, L., King-Kallimanis, B. L., Duchene, D. M., Etheridge, R. L., Herrera, J. R., Barry, K. L., & Lynn, N. (2010). Screening and brief intervention for substance misuse among older adults: The Florida BRITE project. *American Journal of Public Health, 100*(1), 108–114.

Schumacher, J. A., Williams, D. C., Burke, R. S., Epler, A. J., Simon, P., & Coffey, S. F. (2018). Competency-based supervision in motivational interviewing for advanced psychology trainees: Targeting an a priori benchmark. *Training and Education in Professional Psychology, 12*(3), 149–153. doi:10.1037/tep0000177

Schwalbe, C. S., Oh, H. Y., & Zweben, A. (2014). Sustaining motivational interviewing: A meta-analysis of training studies. *Addiction, 109*(8), 1287–1294. Retrieved from https://onlinelibrary.wiley.com/doi/abs/10.1111/add.12558

Scott, C. K., Dennis, M. L., & Lurigio, A. J. (2017). The effects of specialized probation and recovery management checkups (RMCs) on treatment participation, substance use, HIV risk behaviors, and recidivism among female offenders: Main findings of a 3-year experiment using subject by intervention interaction analysis. *Journal of Experimental Criminology, 13*(1), 53–77.

Shepard, D. S., Lwin, A. K., Barnett, N. P., Mastroleo, N., Colby, S. M., Gwaltney, C., & Monti, P. M. (2016). Cost-effectiveness of motivational intervention with significant others for patients with alcohol misuse. *Addiction, 111*(5), 832–839. doi:10.1111/add.13233

Skinner, H. A. (1982). The Drug Abuse Screening Test. *Addictive Behavior, 7*(4), 363–371.

Smedslund, G., Berg, R. C., Hammerstrom, K. T., Steiro, A., Leiknes, K. A., Dahl, H. M., & Karlsen, K. (2011). Motivational interviewing for substance abuse. *Cochrane Database of Systematic Reviews, 5*, CD008063

Smeerdijk, M., Keet, R., Raaij, B. V., Koeter, M., Linszen, D., Haan, L. D., & Schippers, G. (2015). Motivational interviewing and interaction skills training for parents of young adults with recent-onset schizophrenia and co-occurring cannabis use: 15-month follow-up. *Psychological Medicine, 45*(13), 2839–2848. doi:10.1017/s0033291715000793

Soderlund, P. D. (2017). Effectiveness of motivational interviewing for improving physical activity self-management for adults with type 2 diabetes: A review. *Chronic Illness, 14*(1), 54–68. doi:10.1177/1742395317699449

Steinberg, M. L., Williams, J. M., Stahl, N. F., Budsock, P. D., & Cooperman, N. A. (2015). An adaptation of motivational interviewing increases quit attempts in smokers with serious mental illness. *Nicotine and Tobacco Research, 18*(3), 243–250. doi:10.1093/ntr/ntv043

Stinson, J. D., & Clark, M. D. (2017). *Motivational interviewing with offenders: Engagement, rehabilitation, and reentry*. New York, NY: Guilford Press.

Substance Abuse and Mental Health Services Administration. (2019). *Mental health and substance use disorders.* Retrieved from www.samhsa.gov/find-help/disorders

Substance Abuse and Mental Health Services Administration. (2018). *Key substance use and mental health indicators in the United States: Results from the 2017 National Survey on Drug Use and Health.* HHS Publication No. (SMA) 18-5068, NSDUH Series H-53. Rockville, MD: Center for Behavioral Health Statistics and Quality, Substance Abuse and Mental Health Services Administration. Retrieved from www.samhsa.gov/data/

Substance Abuse and Mental Health Services Administration. (2016). *Criteria for the demonstration program to improve community mental health centers and to establish certified community behavioral health clinics.* Retrieved from Retrieved from www.samhsa.gov/sites/default/files/programs_campaigns/ccbhc-criteria.pdf

Substance Abuse and Mental Health Services Administration. (2015a). *Substance abuse treatment and family therapy.* Treatment Improvement Protocol (TIP) Series 39. HHS Publication No. (SMA) 15-4219. Rockville, MD: Substance Abuse and Mental Health Services Administration. Retrieved from https://store.samhsa.gov/product/TIP-39-Substance-Abuse-Treatment-and-Family-Therapy/SMA15-4219

Substance Abuse and Mental Health Services Administration. (2015b). *Using technology-based therapeutic tools in behavioral health services.* Treatment Improvement Protocol (TIP) Series 60. HHS Publication No. (SMA) 15-4924. Rockville, MD: Substance Abuse and Mental Health Services Administration. Retrieved from https://store.samhsa.gov/product/TIP-60-Using-Technology-Based-Therapeutic-Tools-in-Behavioral-Health-Services/SMA15-4924

Substance Abuse and Mental Health Services Administration. (2014a). *Improving cultural competence.* Treatment Improvement Protocol (TIP) Series 59. HHS Publication No. (SMA) 14-4849. Rockville, MD: Substance Abuse and Mental Health Services Administration. Retrieved from https://store.samhsa.gov/product/TIP-59-Improving-Cultural-Competence/SMA15-4849

Substance Abuse and Mental Health Services Administration. (2014b). *Trauma-informed care in behavioral health services.* Treatment Improvement Protocol (TIP) Series 60. HHS Publication No. (SMA) 14-4816. Rockville, MD: Substance Abuse and Mental Health Services Administration. Retrieved from https://store.samhsa.gov/product/TIP-57-Trauma-Informed-Care-in-Behavioral-Health-Services/SMA14-4816

Substance Abuse and Mental Health Services Administration. (2013). *Substance abuse treatment for persons with co-occurring disorders.* Treatment Improvement Protocol (TIP) Series 42. HHS Publication No. (SMA) 13-3992. Rockville, MD: Substance Abuse and Mental Health Services Administration. Retrieved from https://store.samhsa.gov/product/TIP-42-Substance-Abuse-Treatment-for-Persons-With-Co-Occurring-Disorders/SMA13-3992

Substance Abuse and Mental Health Services Administration. (2009). *Clinical supervision and professional development of the substance abuse counselor.* Treatment Improvement Protocol (TIP) Series 52. HHS Publication (SMA) 14–4435. Rockville, MD: Substance Abuse and Mental Health Services Administration. Retrieved from https://store.samhsa.gov/product/TIP-52-Clinical-Supervision-and-Professional-Development-of-the-Substance-Abuse-Counselor/SMA14-4435.html

Substance Abuse and Mental Health Services Administration. (planned). *Treating addiction in older adults.* Treatment Improvement Protocol (TIP) Series. Rockville, MD: Substance Abuse and Mental Health Services Administration.

Substance Abuse and Mental Health Services Administration, Center for the Application of Prevention Technologies. (2017). *Words matter: How language choice can reduce stigma.* Retrieved from https://facesandvoicesofrecovery.org/wp-content/uploads/2019/06/Words-Matter-How-Language-Choice-Can-Reduce-Stigma.pdf

Substance Abuse and Mental Health Services Administration & National Institute on Alcohol Abuse and Alcoholism. (2015). *Medication for the treatment of alcohol use disorder: A brief guide.* HHS Publication No. (SMA) 15-4907. Retrieved from Rockville, MD. Retrieved from https://store.samhsa.gov/product/Medication-for-the-Treatment-of-Alcohol-Use-Disorder-A-Brief-Guide/SMA15-4907

Taleff, M.J. (1997). *A handbook to assess and treat resistance in chemical dependency.* Dubuque, IA: Kendall/Hunt.

Tanner-Smith, E. E., & Lipsey, M. W. (2015). Brief alcohol interventions for adolescents and young adults: A systematic review and meta-analysis. *Journal of Substance Abuse Treatment, 51*, 1–18.

Teeson, M., Marel, C., Darke, S., Ross, J., Slade, T., Burns, L., … Mills, K. L. (2015). Long-term mortality, remission, criminality and psychiatric comorbidity of heroin dependence: 11-year findings from the Australian Treatment Outcome Study. *Addiction, 110*(6), 986–983.

Timko, C., Kong, C., Vittorio, L., & Cucciare, M. A. (2016). Screening and brief intervention for unhealthy substance use in patients with chronic medical conditions: A systematic review. *Journal of Clinical Nursing, 25*(21–22), 3131–3143. doi:10.1111/jocn.13244

Truax, C. B., & Carkhuff, R. R. (1967). *Toward effective counseling and psychotherapy.* Chicago, IL: Aldine.

Turner, B., & Deane, F. P. (2016). Length of stay as a predictor of reliable change in psychological recovery and well-being following residential substance abuse treatment. *Therapeutic Communities, 37*(3), 112–120. doi:10.1108/tc-09-2015-0022

Van Horn, D. H., Drapkin, M., Lynch, K. G., Rennert, L., Goodman, J. D., Thomas, T., … McKay, J. R. (2015). Treatment choices and subsequent attendance by substance-dependent patients who disengage from intensive outpatient treatment. *Addiction Research and Theory, 23*(5), 391–403.

Vella-Zarb, R. A., Mills, J. S., Westra, H. A., Carter, J. C., & Keating, L. (2014). A randomized controlled trial of motivational interviewing self-help versus psychoeducation self-help for binge eating. *International Journal of Eating Disorders, 48*(3), 328–332. doi:10.1002/eat.22242

Venner, K. L., Feldstein, S. W., & Tafoya, N. (2006). *Native American motivational interviewing: Weaving Native American and Western practices.* Retrieved from www.integration.samhsa.gov/clinical-practice/Native_American_MI_Manual.pdf

Venner, K. L., Sánchez, V., Garcia, J., Williams, R. L., & Sussman, A. L. (2018). Moving away from the tip of the pyramid: Screening and brief intervention for risky alcohol and opioid use in underserved patients. *Journal of the American Board of Family Medicine, 31*(2), 243–251.

Wagner, A. J., Garbers, R., Lang, A., Borgert, A. J., & Fisher, M. (2016). Increasing follow-up outcomes of at-risk alcohol patients using motivational interviewing. *Journal of Trauma Nursing, 23*(3), 165–168. doi:10.1097/jtn.0000000000000200

Wagner, C. C., & Ingersoll, K. S. (2017). Development and initial validation of the Assessment of Motivational Interviewing Groups—Observer Scales (AMIGOS). *International Journal of Group Psychotherapy, 68*(1), 69–79. doi:10.1080/00207284.2017.1315587

Wagner, C. C., & Ingersoll, K. S. (2013). *Motivational interviewing in groups.* New York, NY: Guilford Press.

Walker, D. D., Walton, T. O., Neighbors, C., Kaysen, D., Mbilinyi, L., Darnell, J., … Roffman, R. A. (2017). Randomized trial of motivational interviewing plus feedback for soldiers with untreated alcohol abuse. *Journal of Consulting and Clinical Psychology, 85*(2), 99–110. doi:10.1037/ccp0000148

White, W. L. (2014). *Slaying the dragon: The history of addiction treatment and recovery in America* (2nd ed.). Bloomington, IL: Chestnut Health Systems/Lighthouse Institute.

White, W., & Miller, W. (2007). The use of confrontation in addiction treatment: History, science and time for change. *Counselor, 8*(4), 12–30.

Wild, T. C., Yuan, Y., Rush, B. R., & Urbanoski, K. A. (2016). Client engagement in legally mandated addiction treatment: A prospective study using self-determination theory. *Journal of Substance Abuse Treatment, 69*, 35–43. doi:10.1016/j.jsat.2016.06.006

Witkiewitz, K., & Marlatt, G. A. (Eds.). (2007). *Therapist's guide to evidence-based relapse prevention.* Boston, MA: Elsevier Academic Press.

Wong-Anuchit, C., Chantamit-O-Pas, C., Schneider, J. K., & Mills, A. C. (2018). Motivational interviewing–based compliance/adherence therapy interventions to improve psychiatric symptoms of people with severe mental illness: Meta-analysis. *Journal of the American Psychiatric Nurses Association,* 107839031876179. doi:10.1177/1078390318761790

Woolard, R., Baird, J., Longabaugh, R., Nirenberg, T., Lee, C. S., Mello, M. J., & Becker, B. (2013). Project Reduce: Reducing alcohol and marijuana misuse, Effects of a brief intervention in the emergency department. *Addictive Behaviors, 38*(3), 1732–1739. doi:10.1016/j.addbeh.2012.09.006

Yeh, M., Tung, T., Horng, F., & Sung, S. (2017). Effectiveness of a psychoeducational programme in enhancing motivation to change alcohol-addictive behaviour. *Journal of Clinical Nursing, 26*(21–22), 3724–3733. doi:10.1111/jocn.13744

Yudko, E., Lozhkina, O., & Fouts, A. (2007). A comprehensive review of the psychometric properties of the Drug Abuse Screening Test. *Journal of Substance Abuse Treatment, 32,* 189–198.

Appendix B—Screening and Assessment Instruments

Appendix B presents the following tools:

1. U.S. Alcohol Use Disorders Identification Test (U.S. AUDIT)

2. Drug Abuse Screening Test (DAST-10)

3. Drinker Inventory of Consequences (DrInC) (Lifetime)

4. What I Want From Treatment (2.0)

5. Readiness to Change Questionnaire (Treatment Version) (RCQ-TV) (Revised)

6. Stages of Change Readiness and Treatment Eagerness Scale–Alcohol (SOCRATES 8A)

7. Stages of Change Readiness and Treatment Eagerness Scale–Drugs (SOCRATES 8D)

8. University of Rhode Island Change Assessment (URICA) Scale

9. Alcohol and Drug Consequences Questionnaire (ADCQ)

10. Alcohol Decisional Balance Scale

11. Drug Use Decisional Balance Scale

12. Brief Situational Confidence Questionnaire (BSCQ)

13. Alcohol Abstinence Self-Efficacy Scale (AASES)

14. Motivational Interviewing Knowledge Test

1. U.S. Alcohol Use Disorders Identification Test (AUDIT)

Instructions: Alcohol can affect your health and treatment. We ask all clients these questions. Your answers will remain confidential. Circle the best answer to each question. Think about your drinking in the past year. A drink means one beer, one small glass of wine (5 oz.), or one mixed drink containing one shot (1.5 oz.) of spirits.

1.How often do you have a drink containing alcohol? (0) Never *[Skip to Questions 9 and 10]* (1) Less than monthly (2) Monthly (3) Weekly (4) 2 to 3 times a week (5) 4 to 6 times a week (6) Daily	**6. How often during the last year have you needed an alcoholic drink first thing in the morning to get yourself going after a night of heavy drinking?** (0) Never (1) Less than monthly (2) Monthly (3) Weekly (4) Daily or almost daily
2.How many drinks containing alcohol do you have on a typical day when you are drinking? (0) 1 (1) 2 (2) 3 (3) 4 (4) 5 to 6 (5) 7 to 9 (6) 10 or more	**7. How often during the last year have you had a feeling of guilt or remorse after drinking?** (0) Never (1) Less than monthly (2) Monthly (3) Weekly (4) Daily or almost daily
3.How often do you have X (5 for men; 4 for women and men over age 65) or more drinks on one occasion? (0) Never (1) Less than monthly (2) Monthly (3) Weekly (4) 2-3 times a week (5) 4-6 times a week (6) Daily *[Skip to Questions 9 and 10 if total score for Questions 2 and 3 = 0]*	**8.How often during the last year have you been unable to remember what happened the night before because you had been drinking?** (0) Never (1) Less than monthly (2) Monthly (3) Weekly (4) Daily or almost daily
4. How often during the last year have you found that you were not able to stop drinking once you had started? (0) Never (1) Less than monthly (2) Monthly (3) Weekly (4) Daily or almost daily	9. Have you or someone else been injured as a result of your drinking? (0) No (2) Yes, but not in the last year (4) Yes, during the last year
5.How often during the last year have you failed to do what was normally expected from you because of drinking? (0) Never (1) Less than monthly (2) Monthly (3) Weekly (4) Daily or almost daily	10. Has a relative, friend, doctor, or another health professional expressed concern about your drinking or suggested you cut down? (0) No (2) Yes, but not in the last year (4) Yes, during the last year

Scoring			
Risk Level	Intervention	USAUDIT Score	Possible AUD (DSM-5, ICD-10)
Zone I	Feedback	0–6/7 (Women/Men)	None
Zone II	Feedback/brief intervention	7/8–15 (Women/Men)	Mild AUD, hazardous use
Zone III	Feedback/monitoring/brief outpatient treatment	16–24	Moderate AUD, harmful use
Zone IV	Referral to evaluation and treatment	25+	Moderate/severe AUD, alcohol dependence
Note: Questions 1 to 3 of U.S. AUDIT have been modified to reflect standard drink size in the United States and differences for men, women, and older adults.			
Source: Babor, Higgins-Biddle, & Robaina, 2016. Adapted from material in the public domain.			

2. Drug Abuse Screening Test (DAST-10)

NAME: _____   DATE: _____

DRUG USE QUESTIONNAIRE (DAST-10)

The following questions concern information about your possible involvement with drugs, not including alcoholic beverages, during the past 12 months. Carefully read each statement and decide if your answer is "Yes" or "No." Then, circle the appropriate response beside the question.

In the statements, "drug abuse" refers to (1) the use of prescribed or over-the-counter drugs in excess of the directions and (2) any non-medical use of drugs. The various classes of drugs may include: cannabis (e.g., marijuana, hash), solvents, tranquillizers (e.g., Valium), barbiturates, cocaine, stimulants (e.g., speed), hallucinogens (e.g., LSD) or narcotics (e.g., heroin). Remember that the questions **do not** include alcoholic beverages.

Please answer every question. If you have difficulty with a statement, then choose the response that is mostly right.

These questions refer to the past 12 months.	Circle your response	
1. Have you used drugs other than those required for medical reasons?	YES	NO
2. Do you abuse more than one drug at a time?	YES	NO
3. Are you always able to stop using drugs when you want to?	YES	NO
4. Have you had "blackouts" or "flashbacks" as a result of drug use?	YES	NO
5. Do you ever feel bad or guilty about your drug use?	YES	NO
6. Does your spouse (or parents) ever complain about your involvement with drugs?	YES	NO
7. Have you neglected your family because of your use of drugs?	YES	NO
8. Have you engaged in illegal activities in order to obtain drugs?	YES	NO
9. Have you ever experienced withdrawal symptoms (felt sick) when you stopped taking drugs?	YES	NO
10. Have you had medical problems as a result of your drug use (e.g., memory loss, hepatitis, convulsions, bleeding, etc.)?	YES	NO

camh

Sources: Skinner, 1982. Adapted with permission. Available online at no cost (http://adai.washington.edu/instruments/pdf/Drug_Abuse_Screening_Test_105.pdf).

3. Drinker Inventory of Consequences (DrInC) (Lifetime)

Instructions: Here are a number of events that drinkers sometimes experience. Read each one carefully and circle the number that indicates whether this has *EVER* happened to you (0 = No, 1 = Yes). If an item does not apply to you, circle zero (0).

	Has this *EVER* happened to you? Circle one answer for each item.	No	Yes
1.	I have had a hangover or felt bad after drinking.	0	1
2.	I have felt bad about myself because of my drinking.	0	1
3.	I have missed days of work or school because of my drinking.	0	1
4.	My family or friends have worried or complained about my drinking.	0	1
5.	I have enjoyed the taste of beer, wine, or liquor.	0	1
6.	The quality of my work has suffered because of my drinking.	0	1
7.	My ability to be a good parent has been harmed by my drinking.	0	1
8.	After drinking, I have had trouble with sleeping, staying asleep, or nightmares.	0	1
9.	I have driven a motor vehicle after having three or more drinks.	0	1
10.	My drinking has caused me to use other drugs more.	0	1
11.	I have been sick and vomited after drinking.	0	1
12.	I have been unhappy because of my drinking.	0	1
13.	Because of my drinking, I have not eaten properly.	0	1
14.	I have failed to do what is expected of me because of my drinking.	0	1
15.	Drinking has helped me to relax.	0	1
16.	I have felt guilty or ashamed because of my drinking.	0	1
17.	While drinking, I have said or done embarrassing things.	0	1
18.	When drinking, my personality has changed for the worse.	0	1
19.	I have taken foolish risks when I have been drinking.	0	1
20.	I have gotten into trouble because of drinking.	0	1
21.	While drinking or using drugs, I have said harsh or cruel things to someone.	0	1
22.	When drinking, I have done impulsive things that I regretted later.	0	1
23.	I have gotten into a physical fight while drinking.	0	1
24.	My physical health has been harmed by my drinking.	0	1
25.	Drinking has helped me to have a more positive outlook on life.	0	1
26.	I have had money problems because of my drinking.	0	1
27.	My marriage or love relationship has been harmed by my drinking.	0	1
28.	I have smoked tobacco more when I am drinking.	0	1
29.	My physical appearance has been harmed by my drinking.	0	1
30.	My family has been hurt by my drinking.	0	1
31.	A friendship or close relationship has been damaged by my drinking.	0	1
32.	I have been overweight because of my drinking.	0	1
33.	My sex life has suffered because of my drinking.	0	1
34.	I have lost interest in activities and hobbies because of my drinking.	0	1
35.	When drinking, my social life has been more enjoyable.	0	1
36.	My spiritual or moral life has been harmed by my drinking.	0	1
37.	Because of my drinking, I have not had the kind of life that I want.	0	1
38.	My drinking has gotten in the way of my growth as a person.	0	1

39.	My drinking has damaged my social life, popularity, or reputation.	0 1
40.	I have spent too much or lost a lot of money because of my drinking.	0 1
41.	I have been arrested for driving under the influence of alcohol.	0 1
42.	I have had trouble with the law (other than driving while intoxicated) because of drinking.	0 1
43.	I have lost a marriage or a close love relationship because of my drinking.	0 1
44.	I have been suspended/fired from or left a job or school because of drinking.	0 1
45.	I drank alcohol normally, without any problems.	0 1
46.	I have lost a friend because of my drinking.	0 1
47.	I have had an accident while drinking or intoxicated.	0 1
48.	While drinking or intoxicated, I have been physically hurt, injured, or burned.	0 1
49.	While drinking or intoxicated, I have injured someone else.	0 1
50.	I have broken things while drinking or intoxicated.	0 1

Physical	Inter-personal	Intra-personal	Impulse Control	Social Responsibility	Control Scale*
1 ____					
		2 ____		3 ____	
	4 ____				5 ____
				6 ____	
	7 ____				
8 ____			9 ____		
			10 ____		
11 ____		12 ____			
13 ____				14 ____	15 ____
		16 ____			
	17 ____	18 ____	19 ____	20 ____	
	21 ____		22 ____		
			23 ____		
24 ____					25 ____
				26 ____	
	27 ____		28 ____		
29 ____	30 ____				
	31 ____		32 ____		
33 ____		34 ____			35 ____
		36 ____			
		37 ____			
		38 ____			
	39 ____			40 ____	
			41 ____		
			42 ____		
	43 ____			44 ____	45 ____
	46 ____		47 ____		
48 ____			49 ____		
			50 ____		
____ +	____ +	____ +	____ +	____ =	____	____
Physical	Inter-personal	Intra-personal	Impulse Control	Social Responsibility	Total DrInC Score	Control Scale*

Scoring: For each item, copy the circled number from the answer sheet next to the item number above. Then sum each column to calculate scale totals. Sum these totals to calculate the Total DrInC Score.

*Zero scores on Control Scale items may indicate careless or dishonest responses. The Total DrInC Score reflects the overall number of alcohol problems that have occurred during the person's lifetime.

*See the test manual for this instrument for more information about scoring and interpreting the score. It also provides the instruments and scoring information for other versions of DrInC including one for drug use and a short version (SIP) of the instrument for alcohol and drugs.

Source: Miller, Tonigan, & Longabaugh (1995). Adapted from material in the public domain. Available online at no cost (https://pubs.niaaa.nih.gov/publications/projectmatch/match04.pdf).

4. What I Want From Treatment (2.0)

Instructions: People have different ideas about what they want, need, and expect from treatment. This questionnaire is designed to help you explain what you would *like* to have happen in your treatment. Many possibilities are listed. For each one, please indicate how much you would like for this to be part of your treatment. You can do this by circling one number (0, 1, 2, or 3) for each item. This is what the numbers mean:

0 = No   Means that you definitely do <u>NOT</u> want or need this from treatment.

1 = ?   Means that you are <u>UNSURE</u>. <u>MAYBE</u> you want this from treatment.

2 = Yes   Means that you <u>DO</u> want or need this from treatment.

3 = Yes!   Means that you <u>DEFINITELY</u> want or need this from treatment.

For example: Consider item #1, which says, "I want to receive detoxification." If you definitely do NOT want or need to receive detoxification, you would circle 0. If you are UNSURE whether you want or need detoxification, you would circle 1. If you DO want detoxification, you would circle 2. If you DEFINITELY know that detoxification is an important goal for your treatment, you would circle 3.

If you have any questions about how to use this questionnaire, ask for assistance before you begin.

Do you want this from treatment?	No 0	Maybe 1	Yes 2	Yes! 3
1. I want to receive detoxification, to ease my withdrawal from alcohol or other drugs.	0	1	2	3
2. I want to find out for sure whether I have a problem with alcohol or other drugs.	0	1	2	3
3. I want help to stop drinking alcohol completely.	0	1	2	3
4. I want help to decrease my drinking.	0	1	2	3
5. I want help to stop using drugs (other than alcohol).	0	1	2	3
6. I want help to decrease my use of drugs (other than alcohol).	0	1	2	3
7. I want to stop using tobacco.	0	1	2	3
8. I want to decrease my use of tobacco.	0	1	2	3
9. I want help with an eating problem.	0	1	2	3
10. I want help with a gambling problem.	0	1	2	3
11. I want to take Antabuse (medication to help stop drinking).	0	1	2	3
12. I want to take Trexan (medication to help stop using heroin).	0	1	2	3
13. I want to take methadone.	0	1	2	3
14. I want to learn more about alcohol/drug problems.	0	1	2	3
15. I want to learn some skills to keep from returning to alcohol or other drugs.	0	1	2	3
16. I would like to learn more about 12-Step programs like Alcoholics Anonymous (AA) or Narcotics Anonymous (NA).	0	1	2	3
17. I would like to talk about some personal problems.	0	1	2	3
18. I need to fulfill a requirement of the courts.	0	1	2	3
19. I would like help with problems in my marriage or close relationship.	0	1	2	3
20. I want help with some health problems.	0	1	2	3
21. I want help to decrease my stress and tension.	0	1	2	3
22. I would like to improve my health by learning more about nutrition and exercise.	0	1	2	3

Do you want this from treatment?	No 0	Maybe 1	Yes 2	Yes! 3
23. I want help with depression or moodiness.	0	1	2	3
24. I want to work on my spiritual growth.	0	1	2	3
25. I want to learn how to solve problems in my life.	0	1	2	3
26. I want help with angry feelings and how I express them.	0	1	2	3
27. I want to have healthier relationships.	0	1	2	3
28. I would like to discuss sexual problems.	0	1	2	3
29. I want to learn to express my feelings in a more healthy way.	0	1	2	3
30. I want to learn how to relax better.	0	1	2	3
31. I want help in overcoming boredom.	0	1	2	3
32. I want help with feelings of loneliness.	0	1	2	3
33. I want to discuss having been physically abused.	0	1	2	3
34. I want help to prevent violence at home.	0	1	2	3
35. I want to discuss having been sexually abused.	0	1	2	3
36. I want to work on having better self-esteem.	0	1	2	3
37. I want help with sleep problems.	0	1	2	3
38. I want help with legal problems.	0	1	2	3
39. I want advice about financial problems.	0	1	2	3
40. I would like help in finding a place to live.	0	1	2	3
41. I could use help in finding a job.	0	1	2	3
42. I want help in overcoming shyness.	0	1	2	3
43. Someone close to me died or left; I would like to talk about it.	0	1	2	3
44. I have thoughts about suicide, and I would like to discuss this.	0	1	2	3
45. I want help with personal fears and anxieties.	0	1	2	3
46. I want help to be a better parent.	0	1	2	3
47. I feel very confused and would like help with this.	0	1	2	3
48. I would like information about or testing for HIV/AIDS.	0	1	2	3
49. I want someone to listen to me.	0	1	2	3
50. I want to learn to have fun without drugs or alcohol.	0	1	2	3
51. I want someone to tell me what to do.	0	1	2	3
52. I want help in setting goals and priorities in my life.	0	1	2	3
53. I would like to learn how to manage my time better.	0	1	2	3
54. I want help to receive SSI/disability payments.	0	1	2	3
55. I want to find enjoyable ways to spend my free time.	0	1	2	3
56. I want help in getting my child(ren) back.	0	1	2	3
57. I would like to talk about my past.	0	1	2	3
58. I need help in getting motivated to change.	0	1	2	3
59. I would like to see a female counselor.	0	1	2	3
60. I would like to see a male counselor.	0	1	2	3
61. I would like to see the counselor I had before.	0	1	2	3
62. I would like to see a doctor or nurse about medical problems.	0	1	2	3
63. I want to receive medication.	0	1	2	3
64. I would like my spouse or partner to be in treatment with me.	0	1	2	3
65. I would like to have private, individual counseling.	0	1	2	3

Do you want this from treatment?	No 0	Maybe 1	Yes 2	Yes! 3
66. I would like to be in a group with people who are dealing with problems similar to my own.	0	1	2	3
67. I need childcare while I am in treatment.	0	1	2	3
68. I want my treatment to be short.	0	1	2	3
69. I believe I will need to be in treatment for a long time.	0	1	2	3

Is there anything else you would like from treatment? If so, please write it here.

_____

_____

_____

_____

Source: Miller & Brown, 1994. Available online at no cost (https://casaa.unm.edu/inst/What%20I%20Want%20From%20Treatment.pdf).

5. Readiness to Change Questionnaire (Treatment Version) (RCQ-TV) (Revised)

Instructions: The following questions are designed to identify how you personally feel about your drinking right now. Please think about your current situation and drinking habits, even if you have given up drinking completely. Read each question below carefully, and then decide whether you agree or disagree with the statements. Please tick the answer of your choice to each question. If you have any problems, please ask the questionnaire administrator.

Your answers are completely private and confidential.

Key: SD = Strongly disagree; **D** = Disagree; **U** = Unsure; **A** = Agree; **SA** = Strongly agree

	SD	D / A	U / SA	For office use only
1. It's a waste of time thinking about my drinking because I do not have a problem.	☐	☐ ☐	☐ ☐	PC
2. I enjoy my drinking but sometimes I drink too much.	☐	☐ ☐	☐ ☐	C
3. There is nothing seriously wrong with my drinking.	☐	☐ ☐	☐ ☐	PC
4. Sometimes I think I should quit or cut down on my drinking.	☐	☐ ☐	☐ ☐	C
5. Anyone can talk about wanting to do something about their drinking, but I'm actually doing something about it.	☐	☐ ☐	☐ ☐	A
6. I am a fairly normal drinker.	☐	☐ ☐	☐ ☐	PC
7. My drinking is a problem sometimes.	☐	☐ ☐	☐ ☐	C
8. I am actually changing my drinking habits right now (either cutting down or quitting).	☐	☐ ☐	☐ ☐	A
9. I have started to carry out a plan to cut down or quit drinking.	☐	☐ ☐	☐ ☐	A
10. There is nothing I really need to change about my drinking.	☐	☐ ☐	☐ ☐	PC
11. Sometimes I wonder if my drinking is out of control.	☐	☐ ☐	☐ ☐	C

12. I am actively working on my drinking problem.   ❑   ❑   ❑   [A]
                                                      ❑   ❑

For Office Use Only

Please enter the subject's scores below:

Scale Scores

PC Score   _____

C Score   _____

A Score   _____

Scoring: The scale score codes represent each of the Stages of Change:

- Items numbered 1,3,6,10 = Precontemplation (PC)
- Items numbered 2,4,7,11 = Contemplation (C)
- Items numbered 5,8,9,12 = Action (A)

All items should be scored on a 5-point scale ranging from:

-2 = Strongly Disagree

-1 = Disagree

0 = Unsure

+1 = Agree

+2 = Strongly Agree

To calculate the score for each scale, simply add the item scores for the scale in question. The range of each scale is -10 through 0 to +10. A negative scale score reflects an overall disagreement with items measuring the stage of change, whereas a positive score represents overall agreement. The highest scale score represents the Stage of Change Designation.

If two or more scale scores are equal, then the scale farther along the continuum of change (Precontemplation-Contemplation-Action) represents the subject's Stage of Change Designation. For example, if a subject scores 6 on the Precontemplation scale, 6 on the Contemplation scale and -2 on the Action scale, then the subject is assigned to the Contemplation stage.

If one of the five items on a scale is missing, the subject's score for that scale should be prorated (i.e., multiplied by 4/3 or 1.33). If two or more items are missing, the scale score cannot be calculated. In this case the Stage of Change Designation will be invalid.

Source: Heather & Honekopp, 2008. Adapted with permission. Source article and questionnaire are available online at no cost (https://ndarc.med.unsw.edu.au/sites/default/files/ndarc/resources/TR.019.pdf).

6. Stages of Change Readiness and Treatment Eagerness Scale–Alcohol (SOCRATES 8A)

Instructions: Please read the following statements carefully. Each one describes a way that you might (or might not) feel *about your drinking*. For each statement, circle one number from 1 to 5 to indicate how much you agree or disagree with it *right now*. Please circle one and only one number for every statement.

	No! Strongly Disagree	No Disagree	? Undecided or Unsure	Yes Agree	Yes! Strongly Agree
1. I really want to make changes in my drinking.	1	2	3	4	5
2. Sometimes I wonder if I am an alcoholic.	1	2	3	4	5
3. If I don't change my drinking soon, my problems are going to get worse.	1	2	3	4	5
4. I have already started making some changes in my drinking.	1	2	3	4	5
5. I was drinking too much at one time, but I've managed to change my drinking.	1	2	3	4	5
6. Sometimes I wonder if my drinking is hurting other people.	1	2	3	4	5
7. I am a problem drinker.	1	2	3	4	5
8. I'm not just thinking about changing my drinking, I'm already doing something about it.	1	2	3	4	5
9. I have already changed my drinking, and I am looking for ways to keep from slipping back to my old pattern.	1	2	3	4	5
10. I have serious problems with drinking.	1	2	3	4	5
11. Sometimes I wonder if I am in control of my drinking.	1	2	3	4	5
12. My drinking is causing a lot of harm.	1	2	3	4	5
13. I am actively doing things now to cut down or stop drinking.	1	2	3	4	5
14. I want help to keep from going back to the drinking problems that I had before.	1	2	3	4	5
15. I know that I have a drinking problem.	1	2	3	4	5
16. There are times when I wonder if I drink too much.	1	2	3	4	5
17. I am an alcoholic.	1	2	3	4	5
18. I am working hard to change my drinking.	1	2	3	4	5
19. I have made some changes in my drinking, and I want some help to keep from going back to the way I used to drink.	1	2	3	4	5

See the scoring and interpretation information presented in the SOCRATES 8D tool below for the SOCRATES 8A tool presented on this page.

7. Stages of Change Readiness and Treatment Eagerness Scale–Drug (SOCRATES 8D)

Instructions: Please read the following statements carefully. Each describes a way you might (or might not) feel *about your drug use*. For each statement, circle one number from 1 to 5 to indicate how much you agree or disagree with it *right now*. Please circle one and only one number for each statement.

		No! Strongly Disagree	No Disagree	? Undecided or Unsure	Yes Agree	Yes! Strongly Agree
1.	I really want to make changes in my use of drugs.	1	2	3	4	5
2.	Sometimes I wonder if I am an addict.	1	2	3	4	5
3.	If I don't change my drug use soon, my problems are going to get worse.	1	2	3	4	5
4.	I have already started making some changes in my use of drugs.	1	2	3	4	5
5.	I was using drugs too much at one time, but I've managed to change that.	1	2	3	4	5
6.	Sometimes I wonder if my drug use is hurting other people.	1	2	3	4	5
7.	I have a drug problem.	1	2	3	4	5
8.	I'm not just thinking about changing my drug use, I'm already doing something about it.	1	2	3	4	5
9.	I have already changed my drug use, and I am looking for ways to keep from slipping back to my old pattern.	1	2	3	4	5
10.	I have serious problems with drugs.	1	2	3	4	5
11.	Sometimes I wonder if I am in control of my drug use.	1	2	3	4	5
12.	My drug use is causing a lot of harm.	1	2	3	4	5
13.	I am actively doing things now to cut down or stop my use of drugs.	1	2	3	4	5
14.	I want help to keep from going back to the drug problems that I had before.	1	2	3	4	5
15.	I know that I have a drug problem.	1	2	3	4	5
16.	There are times when I wonder if I use drugs too much.	1	2	3	4	5
17.	I am a drug addict.	1	2	3	4	5
18.	I am working hard to change my drug use.	1	2	3	4	5
19.	I have made some changes in my drug use, and I want some help to keep from going back to the way I used before.	1	2	3	4	5

SOCRATES Scoring Form (19-Item Version 8A & 8D): Transfer the client's answers from questionnaire:

Recognition (Re)	Ambivalence (Am)	Taking Steps (Ts)
1 _____	2 _____	4 _____
3 _____		5 _____
	6 _____	
7 _____		8 _____
		9 _____
10 _____	11 _____	
12 _____		13 _____
		14 _____

15 _____   16 _____

17 _____   18 _____

                      19 _____

Totals: Re: _____   Am: _____   Ts: _____

Possible Range: 7–35   **4–20**   **8–40**

SOCRATES Profile Sheet (19-Item Version 8A & 8D)

Instructions: From the SOCRATES Scoring Form above (19-Item Version) transfer the Totals to the appropriate Raw Scores cells below. Then for each scale, CIRCLE the same value above it to determine the decile range.

Decile Scores	Recognition	Ambivalence	Taking Steps
90 (Very High)		19–20	39–40
80		18	37–38
70 (High)	35	17	36
60	34	16	34–35
50 (Medium)	32–33	15	33
40	31	14	31–32
30 (Low)	29–30	12–13	30
20	27–28	9–11	26–29
10 (Very Low)	7–26	4–8	8–25
Raw Scores (from Scoring Sheet)	Re=	Am=	Ts=

These interpretive ranges are based on a sample of 1,726 adult men and women presenting for treatment of alcohol problems through Project MATCH. Note that individual scores are therefore being ranked as low, medium, or high *relative to people already presenting for alcohol treatment*.

Guidelines for Interpretation of SOCRATES-8A Scores: Using the SOCRATES Profile Sheet, circle the client's Raw Score within each of the three columns. This provides information as to whether the client's scores are low, average, or high *relative to people already seeking treatment for alcohol problems*. The following descriptions are provided as general guidelines for interpretation of scores, but it is wise in an individual case also to examine individual item responses for additional information. The information should be adjusted as necessary when addressing drug problems.

Recognition	High scorers directly acknowledge that they are having problems related to their drinking, tending to express a desire for change and to perceive that harm will continue if they do not change.
	Low scorers deny that alcohol is causing them serious problems, reject diagnostic labels such as "problem drinker" and "alcoholic," and do not express a desire for change.
Ambivalence	High scorers say that they sometimes *wonder* if they are in control of their drinking, are drinking too much, are hurting other people, and/or are alcoholic. Thus a high score reflects ambivalence or uncertainty. A high score here reflects some openness to reflection, as might be particularly expected in the Contemplation stage of change.
	Low scorers say that they *do not wonder* whether they drink too much, are in control, are hurting others, or are alcoholic. Note that a person may score low on ambivalence either because they "know" their drinking is causing problems (high Recognition), or because they "know" that they do not have drinking problems (low Recognition). Thus a low Ambivalence score should be interpreted in relation to the Recognition score.
Taking Steps	High scorers report that they are already doing things to make a positive change in their drinking and may have experienced some success in this regard. Change is underway, and they may want help to persist or to prevent backsliding. A high score on this scale has been found to be predictive of successful change.

	Low scorers report that they are not currently doing things to change their drinking, and have not made such changes recently.
	Source: Miller & Tonigan, 1996. SOCRATES-8A and SOCRATES-8D are in the public domain and available online at no cost (https://casaa.unm.edu/inst/socratesv8.pdf).

8. University of Rhode Island Change Assessment (URICA) Scale

Instructions: Each statement below describes how a person might feel when starting therapy or approaching problems in his life. Please indicate the extent to which you tend to agree or disagree with each statement. In each case, make your choice in terms of how you feel right now, not what you have felt in the past or would like to feel. For all the statements that refer to your "problem," answer in terms of problems related to your drinking (or illicit drug use). The words "here" and "this place" refer to your treatment center.

There are five possible responses to each of the items in the questionnaire:

1 = Strongly Disagree
2 = Disagree
3 = Undecided
4 = Agree
5 = Strongly Agree

Circle the number that best describes how much you agree or disagree with each statement.

Statement	Strongly Disagree	Disagree	Undecided	Agree	Strongly Agree
1. As far as I'm concerned, I don't have any problems that need changing.	1	2	3	4	5
2. I think I might be ready for some self-improvement.	1	2	3	4	5
3. I am doing something about the problems that had been bothering me.	1	2	3	4	5
4. It might be worthwhile to work on my problem.	1	2	3	4	5
5. I'm not the problem one. It doesn't make much sense for me to consider changing.	1	2	3	4	5
6. It worries me that I might slip back on a problem I have already changed, so I am looking for help.	1	2	3	4	5
7. I am finally doing some work on my problem.	1	2	3	4	5
8. I've been thinking that I might want to change something about myself.	1	2	3	4	5
9. I have been successful in working on my problem, but I'm not sure I can keep up the effort on my own.	1	2	3	4	5
10. At times my problem is difficult, but I'm working on it.	1	2	3	4	5
11. Trying to change is pretty much a waste of time for me because the problem doesn't have to do with me.	1	2	3	4	5
12. I'm hoping that I will be able to understand myself better.	1	2	3	4	5
13. I guess I have faults, but there's nothing that I really need to change.	1	2	3	4	5
14. I am really working hard to change.	1	2	3	4	5
15. I have a problem, and I really think I should work on it.	1	2	3	4	5

Statement	Strongly Disagree	Disagree	Undecided	Agree	Strongly Agree
16. I'm not following through with what I had already changed as well as I had hoped, and I want to prevent a relapse of the problem.	1	2	3	4	5
17. Even though I'm not always successful in changing, I am at least working on my problem.	1	2	3	4	5
18. I thought once I had resolved the problem I would be free of it, but sometimes I still find myself struggling with it.	1	2	3	4	5
19. I wish I had more ideas on how to solve my problem.	1	2	3	4	5
20. I have started working on my problem, but I would like help.	1	2	3	4	5
21. Maybe this place will be able to help me.	1	2	3	4	5
22. I may need a boost right now to help me maintain the changes I've already made.	1	2	3	4	5
23. I may be part of the problem, but I don't really think I am.	1	2	3	4	5
24. I hope that someone will have some good advice for me.	1	2	3	4	5
25. Anyone can talk about changing; I'm actually doing something about it.	1	2	3	4	5
26. All this talk about psychology is boring. Why can't people just forget about their problems?	1	2	3	4	5
27. I'm here to prevent myself from having a relapse of my problem.	1	2	3	4	5
28. It is frustrating, but I feel I might be having a recurrence of a problem I thought I had resolved.	1	2	3	4	5
29. I have worries, but so does the next guy. Why spend time thinking about them?	1	2	3	4	5
30. I am actively working on my problem.	1	2	3	4	5
31. I would rather cope with my faults than try to change them.	1	2	3	4	5
32. After all I had done to try to change my problem, every now and again it comes back to haunt me.	1	2	3	4	5

Scoring

Precontemplation items	1, 5, 11, 13, 23, 26, 29, 31
Contemplation items	2, 4, 8, 12, 15, 19, 21, 24
Action items	3, 7, 10, 14, 17, 20, 25, 30
Maintenance items	6, 9, 16, 18, 22, 27, 28, 32

High scores on a SOC subscale indicate that the respondent is likely in that SOC. However, the SOC subscales are designed to be a continuous measure, therefore, the stages are not discrete and respondents can score high on more than one of the four stages.

Source: McConnaghy, Prochaska, & Velcier, 1983. Reprinted from material in the public domain. Available online at no cost (https://web.uri.edu/cprc/psychotherapy-urica).

9. Alcohol and Drug Consequences Questionnaire (ADCQ)

Instructions: There can be good and bad consequences to any change. These consequences may not be the same for everyone. In thinking about your decision to change your alcohol or drug use, we would like to know what consequences are important to you. This is not a test: There are no right or wrong answers. We simply want to know what you think.

My primary problem drug is (write in name of primary drug, e.g., alcohol, cocaine)

_____

All questions below refer to my primary drug use.

When I consider stopping or cutting down my primary drug use, the following reasons are important to me. "IF I STOP OR CUT DOWN . . . ."

Circle the number which applies to you.

Item	Not Important	Slightly Important	Moderately Important	Very Important	Extremely Important	Not Applicable
1. I will feel better physically.	1	2	3	4	5	0
2. I will have difficulty relaxing.	1	2	3	4	5	0
3. I will change a lifestyle I enjoy.	1	2	3	4	5	0
4. I will have fewer problems with my family.	1	2	3	4	5	0
5. I will feel frustrated and anxious.	1	2	3	4	5	0
6. I will have more money to do other things with.	1	2	3	4	5	0
7. I will be more active and alert.	1	2	3	4	5	0
8. I will get depressed.	1	2	3	4	5	0
9. I will have fewer problems with friends.	1	2	3	4	5	0
10. I will feel better about myself.	1	2	3	4	5	0
11. I will regain some self-respect.	1	2	3	4	5	0
12. I will accomplish more of the things I want to get done.	1	2	3	4	5	0
13. I will have a better relationship with my family.	1	2	3	4	5	0
14. I will have difficulty coping with my problems.	1	2	3	4	5	0
15. I will feel withdrawal or craving.	1	2	3	4	5	0
16. I will have too much time on my hands.	1	2	3	4	5	0
17. I will have difficulty not drinking or using drugs.	1	2	3	4	5	0
18. My health will improve.	1	2	3	4	5	0
19. I will live longer.	1	2	3	4	5	0
20. I will be more in control of life.	1	2	3	4	5	0
21. I will feel bored.	1	2	3	4	5	0
22. I will be irritable.	1	2	3	4	5	0
23. I will be more financially stable.	1	2	3	4	5	0
24. I will miss the taste.	1	2	3	4	5	0

Item	Not Important	Slightly Important	Moderately Important	Very Important	Extremely Important	Not Applicable
25. I will have a better relationship with my friends.						
26. I will feel stressed out.	1	2	3	4	5	0
27. I will save more money.	1	2	3	4	5	0
28. I will miss the feeling of being high.	1	2	3	4	5	0

Scoring: Scale scores are derived by summing benefits and cost items, dividing by the maximum possible subscale score, and multiplying by 100.

Benefits Score: Total the scores on items 1, 4, 6, 7, 9, 10, 11, 12, 13, 18, 19, 20, 23, 25, and 27. Divide the total score by the maximum score of 75 (15 items X 5). Multiple by 100. Score: _____

Costs Score: Total the scores on items 2, 3, 5, 8, 14, 15, 16, 17, 21, 22, 24, 26, and 28. Divide the total score by the maximum score of 65 (13 items X 5). Multiple by 100. Score: _____

Source: Cunningham, Sobell, Gavin, Sobell, & Breslin, 1997. Adapted with permission.

10. Alcohol Decisional Balance Scale

Client ID#: _____ Date: _____/_____/_____ Assessment Point: _____

Instructions: The following statements may play a part in making a decision about using alcohol. We would like to know how important each statement is to you at the present time in relation to making a decision about your using alcohol. Please rate the level of importance to each statement on the following 5 points:

1 = Not important at all
2 = Slightly important
3 = Moderately important
4 = Very important
5 = Extremely important

Please read each statement and circle the number on the right to indicate how you rate its level of importance as it relates to your making a decision about whether to drink at the present time.

How important is this to me?	Not at All	Slightly	Moderately	Very	Extremely
1. My drinking causes problems with others.	1	2	3	4	5
2. I like myself better when I am drinking.	1	2	3	4	5
3. Because I continue to drink some people think I lack the character to quit.	1	2	3	4	5
4. Drinking helps me deal with problems.	1	2	3	4	5
5. Having to lie to others about my drinking bothers me.	1	2	3	4	5
6. Some people try to avoid me when I drink.	1	2	3	4	5
7. Drinking helps me to have fun and socialize.	1	2	3	4	5
8. Drinking interferes with my functioning at home or/and at work.	1	2	3	4	5
9. Drinking makes me more of a fun person.	1	2	3	4	5
10. Some people close to me are disappointed in me because of my drinking.	1	2	3	4	5
11. Drinking helps me to loosen up and express myself.	1	2	3	4	5
12. I seem to get myself into trouble when drinking.	1	2	3	4	5
13. I could accidentally hurt someone because of my drinking.	1	2	3	4	5
14. Not drinking at a social gathering would make me feel too different.	1	2	3	4	5
15. I am losing the trust and respect of my coworkers and/or spouse because of my drinking.	1	2	3	4	5
16. My drinking helps give me energy and keeps me going.	1	2	3	4	5
17. I am more sure of myself when I am drinking.	1	2	3	4	5
18. I am setting a bad example for others with my drinking.	1	2	3	4	5
19. Without alcohol, my life would be dull and boring.	1	2	3	4	5

How important is this to me?	Not at All	Slightly	Moderately	Very	Extremely
20. People seem to like me better when I am drinking.	1	2	3	4	5

Scoring:

Pros of Drinking	Cons of Drinking
2, 4, 7, 9, 11, 14, 16, 17, 19, 20	1, 3, 5, 6, 8, 10, 12, 13, 15, 18

To get the average number of Pros endorsed, add up the total number of points from the items and divide by 10. Pros of drinking alcohol (2+4+7+9+11+14+16+17+19+20) / (10 possible items for drinking) = Sum of items

To get the average number of Cons endorsed, add up the total number of points from the items and divide by 10. Cons of drinking alcohol (1+3+5+6+8+10+12+13+15+18) / (10 possible items for not drinking) = Sum of items

To calculate the difference score, subtract the Cons from the Pros. If the number is positive, the individual is endorsing more Pros than Cons for drinking alcohol or using drugs. If the number is negative, the individual is endorsing more Cons then Pros for drinking alcohol.

11. Drug Use Decisional Balance Scale

Client ID#: _____ Date: _____/_____/_____ Assessment Point: _____

Instructions: The following statements may play a part in making a decision about using drugs. We would like to know how important each statement is to you at the present time in relation to making a decision about your using drugs. Please rate the level of importance to each statement on the following 5 points:

1=Not important at all
2=Slightly important
3=Moderately important
4=Very important
5=Extremely important

Please read each statement and circle the number on the right to indicate how you rate its level of importance as it relates to your making a decision about whether to use drugs at the present time

How important is this to me?	Not at All	Slightly	Moderately	Very	Extremely
1. My drug use causes problems with others.	1	2	3	4	5
2. I like myself better when I am using drugs.	1	2	3	4	5
3. Because I continue to use drugs some people think I lack the character to quit.	1	2	3	4	5
4. Using drugs helps me deal with problems.	1	2	3	4	5
5. Having to lie to others about my drug use bothers me.	1	2	3	4	5
6. Some people try to avoid me when I use drugs.	1	2	3	4	5
7. Drug use helps me to have fun and socialize.	1	2	3	4	5
8. Drug use interferes with my functioning at home or/and at work.	1	2	3	4	5
9. Drug use makes me more of a fun person.	1	2	3	4	5
10. Some people close to me are disappointed in me because of my drug use.	1	2	3	4	5
11. Drug use helps me to loosen up and express myself.	1	2	3	4	5
12. I seem to get myself into trouble when I use drugs.	1	2	3	4	5
13. I could accidentally hurt someone because of my drug use.	1	2	3	4	5
14. Not using drugs at a social gathering would make me feel too different.	1	2	3	4	5
15. I am losing the trust and respect of my coworkers and/or spouse because of my drug use.	1	2	3	4	5
16. My drug use helps give me energy and keeps me going.	1	2	3	4	5
17. I am more sure of myself when I am using drugs.	1	2	3	4	5
18. I am setting a bad example for others with my drug use.	1	2	3	4	5
19. Without drugs, my life would be dull and boring.	1	2	3	4	5
20. People seem to like me better when I use drugs.	1	2	3	4	5

Scoring:

Pros of Using Drugs	Cons of Using Drugs
2, 4, 7, 9, 11, 14, 16, 17, 19, 20	1, 3, 5, 6, 8, 10, 12, 13, 15, 18

To get the average number of Pros endorsed, add up the total number of points from the items and divide by 10. Pros of drug use (2+4+7+9+11+14+16+17+19+20) / (10 possible items for using drugs)= Sum of items

To get the average number of Cons endorsed, add up the total number of points from the items and divide by 10. Cons of drug use (1+3+5+6+8+10+12+13+15+18) / (10 possible items for not using drugs) = Sum of items

To calculate the difference score, subtract the Cons from the Pros. If the number is positive, the individual is endorsing more Pros than Cons for using drugs. If the number is negative, the individual is endorsing more Cons then Pros for using drugs.

Source: Prochaska et al., 1994. Reprinted from material in the public domain. Available online at no cost (https://habitslab.umbc.edu/files/2014/07/Drug-Decisional-Balance-scale20item.pdf).

12. Brief Situational Confidence Questionnaire (BSCQ)

Name: _____   Date:_____

Instructions: Listed below are eight types of situations in which some people experience an alcohol or drug problem. Imagine yourself as you are right now in each of the following types of situations. Indicate on the scale provided how confident you are right now that you will be able to resist drinking heavily or resist the urge to use your primary drug in each situation by placing an "X" along the line, from 0% "Not at all confident" to 100% "Totally confident."

Right now I would be able to resist the urge to drink heavily or use my primary drug in situations involving...

1. UNPLEASANT EMOTIONS (e.g., if I were depressed about things in general; if everything were going badly for me).

I feel... |————————————————————|
              0%   100%
              Not at all confident   Totally confident

2. PHYSICAL DISCOMFORT (e.g., if I were to have trouble sleeping; if I felt jumpy and physically tense).

I feel... |————————————————————|
              0%   100%
              Not at all confident   Totally confident

3. PLEASANT EMOTIONS (e.g., if something good happened and I felt like celebrating; if everything were going well).

I feel... |————————————————————|
              0%   100%
              Not at all confident   Totally confident

Right now I would be able to resist the urge to drink heavily or use my primary drug in situations involving...
4. TESTING CONTROL OVER MY USE OF ALCOHOL OR DRUGS (e.g., if I were to start to believe that alcohol or drugs were no longer a problem for me; if I felt confident that I could handle drugs or several drinks).

I feel... |————————————————————|
              0%   100%
              Not at all confident   Totally confident

5. URGES AND TEMPTATIONS (e.g., if I suddenly had an urge to drink or use drugs; if I were in a situation where I had often used drugs or drank heavily).

I feel... |————————————————————|
              0%   100%
              Not at all confident   Totally confident

6. CONFLICT WITH OTHERS (e.g., if I had an argument with a friend; if I were not getting along well with others at work).

I feel... |————————————————————|
              0%   100%
              Not at all confident   Totally confident

7. SOCIAL PRESSURE TO USE (e.g., if someone were to pressure me to "be a good sport" and drink or use drugs with him; if I were invited to someone's home and he offered me a drink or drugs).

I feel... |————————————————————|
              0%   100%

Not at all confident   Totally confident

8. PLEASANT TIMES WITH OTHERS (e.g., if I wanted to celebrate with a friend; if I were enjoying myself at a party and wanted to feel even better).

I feel... |————————————————————————————————|
               0%   100%
               Not at all confident   Totally confident

Scoring: Each of the 8 scales produces a score from 0% to 100 %. Identify 1 to 3 situations where the client has the lowest confidence rating for further discussion.

Instructions for presenting findings to clients are available online (www.nova.edu/gsc/forms/BSCQ%20Instructions.pdf).

A blank self-confidence profile chart is available online (www.nova.edu/gsc/forms/BSCQ%20blank.pdf).

> *Source: Bresslin, Sobell, & Sobell, 2000. Adapted from material in the public domain.*

13. Alcohol Abstinence Self-Efficacy Scale (AASES)

Name: _____   Date: __ __ / __ __ / __ __ __ __

Instructions: Listed below are a number of situations that lead some people to use alcohol. We would like to know how confident you are that you would not drink alcohol in each situation.

Circle the number that best describes your feelings of confidence not to drink alcohol in each situation during the past week according to the following scale:

1 = Not at all confident
2 = Not very confident
3 = Moderately confident
4 = Very confident
5 = Extremely confident

Situation	Confident not to drink alcohol				
	Not at all	Not very	Moderately	Very	Extremely
1) When I am in agony because of stopping or withdrawing from alcohol use.	1	2	3	4	5
2) When I have a headache.	1	2	3	4	5
3) When I am feeling depressed.	1	2	3	4	5
4) When I am on vacation and want to relax.	1	2	3	4	5
5) When I am concerned about someone.	1	2	3	4	5
6) When I am worried.	1	2	3	4	5
7) When I have the urge to try just one drink to see what happens.	1	2	3	4	5
8) When I am being offered a drink in a social situation.	1	2	3	4	5
9) When I dream about taking a drink.	1	2	3	4	5
10) When I want to test my will power over drinking.	1	2	3	4	5

11) When I am feeling a physical need or craving for alcohol.	1	2	3	4	5
12) When I am physically tired.	1	2	3	4	5
13) When I am experiencing some physical pain or injury.	1	2	3	4	5
14) When I feel like blowing up because of frustration.	1	2	3	4	5
15) When I see others drinking at a bar or a party.	1	2	3	4	5
16) When I sense everything is going wrong for me.	1	2	3	4	5
17) When people I used to drink with encourage me to drink.	1	2	3	4	5
18) When I am feeling angry inside.	1	2	3	4	5
19) When I experience an urge or impulse to take a drink that catches me unprepared.	1	2	3	4	5
20) When I am excited or celebrating with others.	1	2	3	4	5

Scoring:

Subscale	Item Number
Negative Affect	1,3,9
Social/Positive	10,11,12
Physical and Other Concerns	2,7,8
Cravings and Urges	4,5,6

To obtain a mean overall Abstinence Self-Efficacy or Temptation score, sum scores from all items and divide by 12.

To obtain mean scores for individual subscales, sum item scores for each subscale and divide by the number of items (3).

Source: DiClemente, Carbonari, Montgomery, & Hughes, 1994. Adapted from material in the public domain.

AASES available online at no cost (*https://habitslab.umbc.edu/files/2014/07/Alcohol-Abstinence-Self-efficacy-Scale-20item.pdf*).

Drug Abstinence Self-Efficacy Scale (adapted version of AASES) available online at no cost (*https://habitslab.umbc.edu/files/2014/07/Drug-Abstinence-Self-efficacy-scale.pdf*).

14. Motivational Interviewing Knowledge Test

Instructions: Choose the best answer for each of the following questions. Each question has only one correct answer.

---

1. Which of the following is NOT consistent with the MI approach to counseling?
a) rolling with resistance
b) avoiding argumentation
c) confronting denial
d) supporting self-efficacy

2. Within the MI framework, advice may be given by a therapist to a client
a) at any time
b) when the client requests it
c) after the therapist receives permission to give it
d) never
e) both a and b
f) both b and c

3. According to Miller and Rollnick (1991), when a therapist argues that a client's behavior needs to change, the client often responds by
a) accepting the need for change
b) arguing against change
c) asking for advice
d) moving to the next stage in the process of change
e) all of the above

4. Two strategies which are usually effective for avoiding the confrontation-denial trap are
a) giving advice and reflective listening
b) reflective listening and eliciting self-motivational statements
c) skills training and warning
d) aversive conditioning and supporting self-efficacy

5. The MI approach is
a) completely non-directive
b) highly authoritarian
c) directive but client-centered
d) primarily educational
e) all of the above

6. To develop discrepancy, therapists using the MI approach
a) inform clients about the harmful effects of their behavior
b) direct clients to stop the problem behavior
c) warn clients about the future consequences of their behavior
d) point out differences between the client's own stated goals and current behavior
e) none of the above

7. According to Miller & Rollnick (1991), resistance is best seen as
a) a trait of difficult clients
b) a healthy assertion of independence
c) a function of a mismatch between the client's stage of change and the therapist's strategies
d) an indicator of poor prognosis which, if persistent, indicates that the client should be dropped from counseling
e) none of the above

8. Within the MI framework, ambivalence about change on the part of the client is seen as

---

a) normal and useful

b) a major roadblock to change

c) pathological

d) irrelevant

9. Which of the following therapist behaviors is NOT a roadblock to a client's self-expression

a) interpreting or analyzing

b) warning

c) reflecting

d) reassuring, sympathizing, or consoling

10. Within the MI framework, individual client assessment is seen as

a) a stumbling block to change

b) an unnecessary distraction since the only effective treatment is already known

c) a vital part of determining a client's needs

d) a dehumanizing and authoritarian exercise

11. Which of the following is NOT an MI-consistent strategy for handling resistance?

a) simple reflection

b) amplified reflection

c) argument

d) reframe

e) emphasizing personal control

Please read this exchange between counselor and client and answer the questions that follow:

> 1-C: I know I messed up. I ruined my family, my wife hates me, I got fired from my job, and now I just feel so hopeless. I'm sad all the time, and it's like I can't do anything about it.
>
> 2-T: Where did you work?
>
> 3-C: Joe's Auto. I just felt lost there all day, like I didn't want to be there.
>
> 4-T: Did your boss know you were drinking?
>
> 5-C: Yeah, when he fired me, he told me he could smell the alcohol. God, he must really think I'm a loser.
>
> 6-T: What you are is an addict.
>
> 7-C: I'm not addicted, OK. I just need a few beers after work to calm down.
>
> 8-T: No, you are an addict. You have to admit you are powerless over it before you can better.

12. Therapist statement #2 represents

a) a failure to express empathy

b) a failure to develop discrepancy

c) a failure to explore ambivalence

d) all of the above

e) none of the above

13. Therapist statements #2 and #4 indicate which MI trap?

a) labeling trap

b) Q-A trap

c) expert trap

d) premature focus trap

e) blaming trap

14. Therapist statement #6 reflects which MI trap?

a) labeling trap

b) Q-A trap

c) expert trap

d) premature focus trap

e) blaming trap

15. Therapist statement #8 represents
a) a confrontation of denial
b) an accurate reflection
c) a failure to roll with resistance
d) both a and b
e) both a and c

For the following exchange between client and therapist, answer the questions below:

> 1-T: What would you like to discuss today?
> 2-C: Look, the judge said I gotta come here, but I don't think I need to be here, so don't expect me to cooperate with you.
> 3-T: You feel that things are fine.
> 4-C: I'm not saying that everything is perfect, but I'm not a dope fiend.
> 5-T: Do you feel that others see you that way?
> 6-C: Yeah! People at work are always on my case about it, saying I'm gonna die someday from it. They just need to mind their business.
> 7-T: Sounds like they're concerned.
> 8-C: Yeah, well, I guess.

16. Therapist statement #3 is a demonstration of
a) the MI trap of labeling
b) the MI trap of premature focus
c) the MI principle of rolling with resistance
d) the MI principle of expressing empathy
e) both c and d

17. This therapist is using which opening strategy?
a) listen reflectively
b) affirm
c) summarize
d) all of the above

18. A therapist who responds to a client's reluctance to accept the label of alcoholic by saying, "I've been in this business for 15 years and I know an alcoholic when I see one" has fallen into
a) the reflection trap
b) the authenticity mode
c) the expert trap
d) the motivational interviewing mode

19. The importance and confidence rulers are
a) a means of assessing client readiness
b) an intervention that is inconsistent with MI
c) used only with clients who are in the action stage of change
d) a way of rolling with resistance

20. According to Miller and Rollnick (2002), a therapist should respond to client change talk in all of the following ways, except by
a) elaborating on the change talk with an open question
b) reflecting the client's change talk
c) asking the client to commit to a treatment plan
d) summarizing the client's language

21. The purpose of querying extreme consequences of maintaining behavior is
a) to elicit the cons of behavior change (counter change talk)
b) to warn the client about negative consequences of their behavior
c) to elicit the pros of behavior change (self-motivating statements)

d) to scare the client straight

22. What would be the best therapist response to elicit change talk in the following situation?

> T: "How confident are you on a scale of 0 to 10 that you can make this change?"
> C: "About a 4."

a) So, you're about a 4.
b) Why are you a 4 and not a 0?
c) You've got some confidence, but not a lot.
d) Why are you not a 10?

Motivational Interviewing Knowledge Test Answer Key

---

1. c) confronting denial

2. f) both b and c

3. b) arguing against change

4. b) reflective listening and eliciting self-motivational statements

5. c) directive but client-centered

6. d) point out differences between the client's own stated goals and current behavior

7. c) a function of a mismatch between the client's stage of change and the therapist's strategies

8. a) normal and useful

9. c) reflecting

10. c) a vital part of determining a client's needs

11. c) argument

12. d) all of the above

13. b) Q-A trap

14. a) labeling trap

15. e) both a and c

16. e) both c and d

17. a) listen reflectively

18. c) the expert trap

19. a) a means of assessing client readiness

20. c) asking the client to commit to a treatment plan

21. c) to elicit the pros of behavior change (self-motivating statements)

22. b) Why are you a 4 and not a 0?

Source: Moyers, Martin, & Christopher, 2005. Reprinted from material in the public domain. Available online at no cost (https://casaa.unm.edu/download/ELICIT/MI%20Knowledge%20Test.pdf).

Appendix C—Resources

Motivational Interviewing and Motivational Enhancement Therapy

Motivational Interviewing Network of Trainers (MINT) (www.motivationalinterviewing.org). This website includes links to publications, motivational interviewing (MI) assessment and coding resources, and training resources and events.

Motivational Enhancement Therapy Manual (https://casaa.unm.edu/download/met.pdf). This manual describes the history of motivational enhancement therapy (MET) and its use in Project MATCH. It provides an overview of MET, its relationship to the stages of change, the structure of MET sessions, and a thorough review of the assessment and personalized feedback process used in MET.

Institute for Research, Education & Training in Addictions Motivational Interviewing Toolkit (https://ireta.org/resources/motivational-interviewing-toolkit). This website provides educational materials about MI and links to no-cost MI resources.

Stages of Change

Health and Addictive Behaviors: Investigating Transtheoretical Solutions Lab at the University of Maryland, Baltimore County (https://habitslab.umbc.edu). This website provides an overview of the Transtheoretical Model of behavior change, printable assessments and scoring information, related publications, and learning tools.

Training and Supervision

Motivational Interviewing Assessment: Supervisory Tools for Enhancing Proficiency Manual (www.motivationalinterviewing.org/sites/default/files/mia-step.pdf). This collection of tools is for mentoring counselors in MI skills used in the engagement and assessment stage of counseling people with substance use disorders (SUDs). It includes teaching tools, counselor self-assessment skill summaries, MI rating guides and forms, transcripts and ratings of sample MI interviews, and trainer instructions.

Center on Alcoholism, Substance Abuse, and Addictions (https://casaa.unm.edu). This multidisciplinary research center at the University of New Mexico provides links to alcohol and drug assessment tools, MI coding tools and therapist manuals, and audio files and uncoded transcripts of counselor role plays that can be used for training.

Motivational Interviewing Resources (https://motivationalinterviewing.org/motivational-interviewing-resources). This MINT webpage provides links to downloadable coding manuals for assessing counselor fidelity to the MI spirit and practice skills including the *Manual for the Motivational Interviewing Skill Code (MISC)* (https://casaa.unm.edu/download/misc.pdf), the *MISC 2.5* (https://casaa.unm.edu/download/misc25.pdf), the *Motivational Interviewing Treatment Integrity Coding Manual 4.2.1* (https://motivationalinterviewing.org/sites/default/files/miti4_2.pdf), and the *Assessment of Motivational Interviewing Groups—Observer Scale (AMIGOS–v 1.2)* (https://motivationalinterviewing.org/sites/default/files/amigos_rating_form_v1.2.pdf)

Substance Abuse and Mental Health Services Administration

Screening, Brief Intervention, and Referral to Treatment (SBIRT) (www.samhsa.gov/sbirt). This website has information on dissemination and implementation of SBIRT and additional resources.

Substance Abuse and Mental Health Services Administration-Health Resources and Services Administration Center for Integrated Health Solutions (www.integration.samhsa.gov). The Center for Integrated Health Solutions promotes development of integrated primary and behavioral health services to better address the needs of people with mental disorders and SUDs, whether they are seen in specialty behavioral health or primary care settings. This website provides information and resources on screening tools (www.integration.samhsa.gov/clinical-practice/screening-tools), motivational interviewing (www.integration.samhsa.gov/clinical-practice/motivational-interviewing), and tobacco cessation (www.integration.samhsa.gov/health-wellness/wellness-strategies/tobacco-cessation-2).

Treatment Improvement Protocol (TIP) 63: *Medications for Opioid Use Disorder* (https://store.samhsa.gov/product/TIP-63-Medications-for-Opioid-Use-Disorder-Full-Document-Including-Executive-Summary-and-Parts-1-5-/SMA18-5063FULLDOC). This TIP reviews the use of the three Food and Drug Administration-approved medications used to treat opioid use disorder—methadone, naltrexone, and buprenorphine—and other strategies and services to support recovery.

TIP 60: *Using Technology-Based Therapeutic Tools in Behavioral Health Services* (https://store.samhsa.gov/product/TIP-60-Using-Technology-Based-Therapeutic-Tools-in-Behavioral-Health-Services/SMA15-4924). This TIP provides information on implementing technology-assisted care. It discusses the importance of technology in reducing access to treatment and highlights the importance of using technology-based assessments and interventions in behavioral health services.

TIP 59: *Improving Cultural Competence* (https://store.samhsa.gov/product/TIP-59-Improving-Cultural-Competence/SMA15-4849). This TIP helps providers and administrators understand the role of culture in the delivery of mental health and substance use services. It describes cultural competence and discusses racial, ethnic, and cultural considerations.

TIP 57: *Trauma-Informed Care in Behavioral Health Services* (https://store.samhsa.gov/product/TIP-57-Trauma-Informed-Care-in-Behavioral-Health-Services/SMA14-4816). This TIP helps behavioral health professionals understand the impact of trauma on clients. It discusses patient assessment and treatment planning strategies. These strategies support recovery and building a trauma-informed care workforce.

TIP 52: *Clinical Supervision and Professional Development of the Substance Abuse Counselor* (https://store.samhsa.gov/product/TIP-52-Clinical-Supervision-and-Professional-Development-of-the-Substance-Abuse-Counselor/SMA14-4435.html). This TIP presents guidelines for clinical supervision in SUD treatment. It covers supervision methods and models, cultural competence, ethical and legal issues, performance monitoring, and an implementation guide for program administrators.

TIP 42: *Substance Abuse Treatment for Persons With Co-Occurring Disorders* (https://store.samhsa.gov/product/TIP-42-Substance-Abuse-Treatment-for-Persons-With-Co-Occurring-Disorders/SMA13-3992). This TIP gives SUD providers information on co-occurring mental and substance use disorders. It discusses terminology, assessment, and treatment strategies and models.

TIP 39: *Substance Abuse Treatment and Family Therapy* (https://store.samhsa.gov/product/TIP-39-Substance-Abuse-Treatment-and-Family-Therapy/SMA15-4219). This TIP describes the integration of family counseling approaches into SUD treatment. It also discusses cultural competency, considerations for specific populations, policy and program issues, and guidelines for assessing violence.